# THE STIGMA MATRIX

**GLOBALIZATION** IN EVERYDAY LIFE

SERIES EDITORS
Rhacel Salazar Parreñas
Hung Cam Thai

EDITORIAL BOARD
Héctor Carrillo
Jennifer Cole
Kimberly Kay Hoang
Sanyu A. Mojola
Saskia Sassen

# The Stigma Matrix

*Gender, Globalization, and the Agency of Pakistan's Frontline Women*

**FAUZIA HUSAIN**

STANFORD UNIVERSITY PRESS
*Stanford, California*

Stanford University Press
Stanford, California

© 2024 by Fauzia Husain. All rights reserved.

No part of this book may be reproduced or transmitted in any form
or by any means, electronic or mechanical, including photocopying
and recording, or in any information storage or retrieval system,
without the prior written permission of Stanford University Press.

Printed in the United States of America on acid-free, archival-quality paper

Library of Congress Cataloging-in-Publication Data

Names: Husain, Fauzia (Professor), author.
Title: The stigma matrix : gender, globalization, and the agency of
    Pakistan's frontline women / Fauzia Husain.
Other titles: Globalization in everyday life.
Description: Stanford, California : Stanford University Press, 2024. |
    Series: Globalization in everyday life | Includes bibliographical
    references and index.
Identifiers: LCCN 2023017900 (print) | LCCN 2023017901 (ebook) |
    ISBN 9781503632370 (hardcover) | ISBN 9781503636057 (paperback) |
    ISBN 9781503636064 (epub)
Subjects: LCSH: Women employees—Pakistan—Social conditions. |
    Women—Employment—Pakistan. | Stigma (Social psychology)—Pakistan. |
    Purdah—Pakistan. | Globalization—Social aspects—Pakistan.
Classification: LCC HD6190.5 .H873 2024 (print) | LCC HD6190.5 (ebook) |
    DDC 331.4095491—dc23/eng/20230901
LC record available at https://lccn.loc.gov/2023017900
LC ebook record available at https://lccn.loc.gov/2023017901

Cover design and illustration: Lindy Kasler
Typeset by Newgen in Minion Pro 10/14.4

*To Faryal Husain, Bibi Jan Tajik, and Nadia Naqi.
Mother, grandmother, best friend. Thank you for everything.*

*Contents*

|   | Acknowledgments | ix |
|---|---|---|
|   | INTRODUCTION | 1 |
| 1 | THE GLOBAL CONSTITUENTS OF SEXUALIZED STIGMAS IN PAKISTAN | 26 |
| 2 | THE MESO LEVEL OF THE STIGMA MATRIX: THE CONTEXTS OF STIGMA IN FRONTLINE WORK | 61 |
| 3 | VEILED DELICACY: AGENTIC RESPONSES TO STIGMA IN THE PAKISTANI POLICE FORCE | 83 |
| 4 | SACRED CONDUITS: STIGMA AND THE AGENCY OF HEALTH WORKERS | 117 |
| 5 | MAVENS OF MOBILITY: HOW AIRLINE WOMEN NAVIGATE STIGMA | 157 |

6  SPECTACULAR AGENCY: STUNNING DRAMAS    196
   OF RECRUITMENT

CONCLUSION
MOVING FORWARD WITH THE STIGMA    228
MATRIX

*Appendix*       249
*Notes*          267
*Bibliography*   269
*Index*          279

## *Acknowledgments*

This is one of my favorite sections to read in a book, but is a difficult one to write. So many people have helped in so many ways, that I worry about being able to list them all and about thanking them as deeply as they deserve. This book is the product of several years of effort, effort that was undertaken in at least three different countries and across several personal and professional relational contexts. Where to start with the giving of gratitude? I will start with the person who trained me, Allison Pugh, my advisor, from whom I learned not just the nuts and bolts of academic work but also what a caring, compassionate, and feminist academic looks like. As a writer, teacher, and advisor, you are my role model, and for providing that peerless template, I am truly grateful to you.

Thank you to my dissertation committee, Isaac Reed, Andrea Press, and Rachel Wahl, for providing such thoughtful guidance at the University of Virginia and beyond. In addition to my brilliant committee, I am also grateful to the sociology department and to the faculty at UVa. In particular I'd like to thank Sarah Corse, Elizabeth Gorman, and Josipa Roksa for their useful advice and generous support.

Thank you to my fellow graduate students, advisees, and friends Hexuan Zhang, Anna Cameron, Brooke Dinsmore, and Pilar Plater. And thank you to Jaime Hartless, Sarah Mosseri, and Gabriella Smith, my primary academic family.

At the University of Toronto, thank you to my postdoc supervisor Sarah Kaplan for her generous support and wise advice. And thank you to Andras Tilcsik, Sonia Kang, and Dionne Pohler for timely and useful advice about numerous academic issues. Thank you also to the wonderful folks who contribute so much to GATE and to the GLab: Sarah Kaplan, Andras Tilcsik, Sonia Kang, Dionne Pohler, Daphne Baldassari, Joyce He, Kira Lussier, Sharmila Adhya, Hyeun Lee, Vanessa Conzon, and Alyson Colson.

At Queen's University, I would like to thank Martin Hand for his generosity and valuable advice. And thank you to my amazing colleagues Thomas Abrams, Golshan Golraiz, Annette Burfoot, and Norma Mollers for the fruitful conversations and warm collegiality.

Outside the academy, I'm grateful to my grandmother, Bibijan Tajik, who dreamed very big dreams for me when I was a child. My mother, Faryal Husain, who raised and educated me, almost singlehanded. My brother Adnan, sister-in-law Mishal, niece and nephew Sonia and Ibrahim, who fed, sheltered, and comforted me when I first moved to Canada and started writing this book. My cousins, Samer Burney and Dennis Hall, and their children, Zara, Kazim, and Amir, for being my home away from home in Washington, D.C., during my MA and PhD. My father, Mujahid Husain, who passed away years before I started my academic career but who helped me develop resilience.

In Karachi, I'd like to thank Nadia Naqi, who was an invaluable source of support throughout my fieldwork. For introducing me to gatekeepers and informants, listening to my ideas and analysis, and helping me get past impossible hurdles managing access, transport, security, and other issues—this work is richer because of your tireless contribution. Thank you for being my friend!

Thank you to my uncle and aunt, Asif Tajik and Hina Tajik, and my friends, Adnan Madani, Bina Khan, and Aysha Adil, who make Karachi home for me, even when I've been away for years. Thank you also to friends who make the United States feel like home whenever I visit; Natalia Mahmud, Sahar Said, Hanna Siddiqui, Jaime Hartless, Sarah Mosseri, and Gabriella Smith.

For their valuable work on this book, I would like to thank Marcela Cristina Maxfield, senior editor, and the team at Stanford University Press—Gigi Mark, David Zielonka and Sarah Rodriguez. Thank you to copyeditor Martin Schneider for his capable and attentive work. Thank you also to Charlie Clark at Newgen.

Finally, I don't have the words to thank the women and men who provided me with such an intimate glimpse into their professional and personal lives. I am unable to name these amazingly generous people here for privacy reasons. This work owes everything to the extraordinary generosity, hospitality, and kindness I received from my participants during my field work in Pakistan.

# THE STIGMA MATRIX

# INTRODUCTION

ON A FRIDAY AFTERNOON IN April 2020, Inspector Sharafat Khan was attacked by a mob of worshippers. She had only recently become one of two women to command a mainstream (i.e., co-ed) station house in Karachi. She was trying to implement COVID-19 restrictions in the district under her command. The worshippers pelted her with stones. Videos of the attack soon went viral. In them, Khan, uniformed, can be seen cornered by a crowd of men, her nose bleeding as she screams to her police force to take action against the mob. In interviews with the media, members of the mob later justified their attack. They said it was warranted on account of her disrespectful behavior.

Khan was not the first woman agent of the state to suffer such an assault upon her dignity. Just eighteen months earlier, in October 2018, Assistant Superintendent of Police Sohai Ali Talpur successfully thwarted a terrorist attack on a Chinese embassy in Karachi. The case received considerable publicity in the media, as TV channels and newspapers carried stunning images of the operation. In them, Talpur, in uniform, can be seen leading a force of armed men. The men are all wearing bulletproof vests. Talpur, fortified with only a revolver, is pictured leading the charge. These striking images of Talpur and her team gained traction on international media outlets as varied as CNN, Reuters, and the *Hindustan Times*. Certain Chinese nationals were so taken by Talpur's bravery that they sent her proposals of marriage. But the international praise for Talpur's bravery was tempered, at the local level, by doubts and censure. In cynical tweets, cartoons, and news reports, local critics asserted that Talpur's involvement was nothing more than a publicity stunt, that she had used her rank to push herself into the limelight and that in truth, the credit belonged to her male subordinates (see Zahra 2018).

A few miles east of the embassy where Talpur thwarted a terrorist attack, another woman agent of the state also braved threats of violence in the line of duty. Shiza Hayat, a lady health worker, goes door to door administering the polio vaccine to children in her neighborhood. In the course of her duties, she said, she was intimidated by armed men. "For four days after the polio drive ended," she said, "I noticed these men sitting outside my gate. They had guns and they looked very threatening. I was too scared to go out. If I needed to buy something, I would sneak out the back door." This intimidation had come on the heels of a warning from her neighbors: "They told me very forcefully to give up polio work," she said. "They think that lady health workers are lewd women because we provide the community with information and tools for contraception. . . . And they particularly dislike the vaccine work we do; they think the polio vaccine is part of an American conspiracy to sterilize Muslim children."

The dignity assaults that Khan, Talpur, and Hayat endured are not unique. In fourteen months of field research in Karachi, Pakistan I witnessed, in site after site, frontline women workers, who, courageously face tremendous hardship and danger in the course of their work, reduced to tears by the insults, jokes, and threats lobbed at them by the public as well as by bosses, subordinates, clients, and even members of their own families. I watched public health workers who have braved terrorist threats to complete their polio vaccination work sob over the poor treatment they received at the hands of their bosses. I saw state-employed airline attendants, stoic in the face of plane safety problems, weep as they talked about family members who no longer spoke to them on account of their "disreputable jobs." And I heard policewomen compare their workplaces to sewers that contaminate women's dignity and their reputations.

While global gender mainstreaming initiatives have created opportunities for women like Khan, Talpur, Hayat, and other frontline women workers to take up new public roles on behalf of the Pakistani state, these measures have also brought these women into confrontation with cultural beliefs that call their competence, commitment, and their very social identity into question. The public nature of their jobs pit frontline women against local logics of gendered distancing, or what I call "purdah norms." Purdah, literally "curtain," describes a South Asian practice of women's seclusion (see Papanek 1973). While it sometimes involves the physical segregation of women from men, for instance, through the erection of screens in public spaces that women can retire behind, at other times doing purdah means enacting norms of gendered distancing, such as veiling, lowering the gaze, and circumscribing interactions with non-kin men (see Husain 2020; Masood 2018). Purdah norms delineate certain spaces, temporalities, and roles as "dirty" for women (George 2000; Patel 2010; Grünenfelder 2013a, b; Rai et al. 2007; Mumtaz and Shaheed 1987). Those who violate the gendered boundaries of space and time by working in male-dominated occupations, like policing, for instance, or by taking on night shifts, are seen as immoral women, unworthy of respect or obedience (Grünenfelder 2013).

This book is concerned with the lives of these so-called dirty women. It follows the trials and tribulations of women like Khan, Talpur, Hayat and other frontline women workers employed by the Pakistani state to serve Pakistani citizens in the arenas of policing, health work, and aviation. Many of these women are the first in their family to venture out of their homes for work. Many have embraced their public-facing jobs in a desperate bid to support their families and serve their communities. But their jobs require them to weather persistent assaults on their dignity.

Although they can be fleeting—the women describe them as background noise—the dignity assaults endured by frontline women deserve our closer scrutiny. The bruising episodes frontline women encounter don't just wound their bodies, their emotions, their reputations, and their dignity, they also mark frontline women as outsiders, who on account of their gender are ill suited for their public roles and offices. Whether brutal or subtle, the gestures of violence, disobedience, insolence, and mockery that frontline women ceaselessly face are like stigmata, leaving physical, emotional, and reputational scars on their victims. The marks they make don't just undermine specific security operations, like the physical distancing measures Khan was implementing in order to help the state stem the spread of COVID-19, but also disrupt the public standing of the women they target. And more broadly, such marks shape public beliefs about women's ability to occupy positions of authority in the machinery of the state.

The pelted stones, the questioning memes, and the intimidation draw attention to the women's presence and mark them as being out of place, as if they do not deserve to wield the authority or hold the offices they occupy, as if they do not belong in the spaces they patrol in service to the state. Such stigmata, therefore, operate as a mechanism of gendered exclusion, a device that limits women's capacity to perform their duties for the state and, consequently, their ability to integrate fully into the state that they serve at considerable personal sacrifice.

As Khan's encounter with the mob and Hayat's intimidation by her neighbors shows, the dignity assaults frontline women confront are not spontaneous localized events but are rather the dynamic products of gender norms and security processes that are global in nature. Khan was attacked by a mob while implementing measures connected with a *global* pandemic. The mob's anger must therefore be understood in the context of broader public sentiments around COVID-19 policies at the time. The imposition of restrictions around COVID-19 quickly prompted a slew of conspiracy theories in Pakistan. News reports about the virus were taken to be false, and the prescribed health measures were read as part of a foreign conspiracy aimed at causing harm to Muslims. Doctors, insisted members of the public, were trying to make money from hospitalizations, while the government was angling for aid money from the west. Some even argued that news of the virus was an excuse to insert a chip into the brains of Muslims, so that antagonistic foreign nations could access the thoughts of their victims. Similar conspiracy theories frame the violence against health workers like Hayat who administer the polio vaccine at the behest of not just the Pakistani state but also its global allies. Because of the vaccine's transnational backing, these women are seen as agents of a western conspiracy to render Muslim boys infertile and speed up the sexual maturation of Muslim girls.

The stigmatizing affronts that frontline women face, therefore, are not simple. They are not local nor spontaneous nor unstructured but rather are deeply rooted in global processes, both recent and of longer standing. To tease apart this complex of global processes, this book introduces a new multiscalar framework—the stigma matrix—outlining a new theoretical approach that can help us understand how contemporary global policies build on colonial histories and local inequalities to shape women's experiences of stigma as well as their responses to it. By encouraging us to step back and look beyond the micro-level interpersonal contexts where stigma is inflicted, the stigma matrix framework provides a more comprehensive, more global understanding of stigma. It allows us to apprehend how stigmas, such as the ones Khan, Talpur, and Hayat endured, feed upon a long history of racialized gender inequality and how they continue to draw sustenance from various levels of social life—from macro-level socioeconomic policies through meso-level organizational arrangements to micro-level interactions and experiences.

Adopting a multiscalar approach to stigma allows us also to understand what it is that stigma accomplishes, how it works as a tool for hegemonic domination. This framework draws inspiration from Patricia Hill Collins's theorizing (Collins 2000) and builds on the work of sociologist Imogen Tyler (2020); these theoretical antecedents are discussed in more detail in chapter 1. Below I describe the particular shape that the stigma matrix takes in the context of Pakistan's frontline women.

## THE STIGMA MATRIX AND PAKISTAN'S FRONTLINE WOMEN

In the case of Pakistan's frontline women, the stigma matrix is composed on the bedrock of colonial history. As I show in chapter 1, purdah norms and the panic around women's appearance in public space are rooted in the colonial encounter, a traumatic history that continues to shape local perceptions of transnational engagement with Pakistan and frame contemporary processes of globalization. Contemporary cynicism about the intentions of global actors and agencies and ongoing fears about the risk that global processes might pose to women's sexual modesty and to the social norms surrounding gender can be traced back to the colonial era. And it is on this historic ground of cynicism and suspicion that contemporary global forces converge to create new tensions and pressures for Pakistani women.

Neoliberalism works to pull working-class women into public roles within the Pakistani state, for instance by making aid money conditional upon the state's implementation of gender mainstreaming policies. The global process of securitization exerts another pull by necessitating women's induction into security roles, like policing and polio eradication, where they help the state to expand its capacity by addressing and serving veiled women citizens. And the global process of Islamization, rooted in the Islamic revival of the 1970s (see Salvatore and LeVine 2005), pressures women who adopt these public roles to also serve as emblems of the nation's religiosity by demonstrating compliance with the norms of purdah and adopting public gestures of pious propriety.

While the interplay of these global forces may sound abstract, their synthesis has had a very concrete impact on women's lives. All three contemporary global forces—neoliberalism, securitization, and Islamization—directly impact the hierarchies that women must confront in their day-to-day lives. All three forces shape both the issues of class and the arrangements around gender for working-class families. Neoliberalism leaves such families scrambling to preserve their class positions in a brutal and increasingly privatized job market. Securitization creates new hurdles for working-class actors seeking mobility through the stable but shrinking government employment sector, for instance, by making such jobs conditional upon the completion of costly security checks. Islamization reinforces gender hierarchies by subjecting women to the authority of men in their families and at work.

In short, as it is composed of cross-cutting global forces, which interact with local norms and hierarchies, the stigma matrix operates like a megastructure that reshapes and reinvigorates local gender and class inequalities, which were already infused with stigma during the colonial period. Figure 1 provides a map for understanding how the stigma matrix is composed through the complex interaction of multiple global forces with local beliefs and hierarchies.

By focusing on the multiple levels of stigma's composition, we are better able to grasp what stigma does, how it impugns women's dignity in service

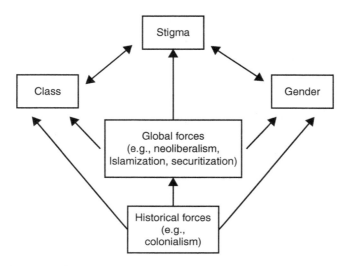

**FIGURE 1.** The stigma matrix

to hegemonic projects of domination. The stigmas associated with purdah violation, for instance, work to limit women's occupation of public space. By formally or informally reinforcing the norms of purdah, Pakistani state elites are able to forge alliances with religio-political parties and also to cobble together a heterogeneous citizenry under the unifying banner of religious nationality. In the chapters that follow, I describe the functions that gender-based stigmas served in nineteenth century colonial India (an empire that included the land now occupied by Pakistan), and I show how such stigmas continue to help preserve women's marginality in service to various political projects, and I document the pain that such stigmas produce for the women who must confront them.

The framework described in this book not only provides useful insights into the pressures Pakistani frontline women face, and the resources they use to navigate them, it can also help us understand the connection between stigma and inequality in other contexts. In the concluding chapter I discuss how the stigma matrix framework can be used to better understand gaslighting in intimate partnerships as well as diversity initiatives that aim to redress inequality in the workplace. When marginalized actors, like women, are formally recruited via diversity drives into contexts of work that previously excluded them, such as the police force, *The Stigma Matrix* shows, they still have to contend with cultural forms of exclusion that continue to haunt their workplaces and the broader arenas that they occupy.

To be sure, frontline work is not entirely without its compensations. Their public facing jobs provide Pakistani women with money and purpose, with the capacity to provide for children, to care for aging parents, and to serve their communities. Shiza Hayat's health job helped save her family from starvation after a spinal injury left her husband, a taxi driver, unable to work. Shahbano Taj, a policewoman I spoke with, told me she had taken on police work in order to support her divorced mother and younger siblings after her father abandoned them. Mehr Ali, a single mother of two, said her airline work had kept her stove burning at home and her children in school.

For each of these women, their work brought more than just personal benefit. Shiza Hayat said that she was motivated in her polio eradication work not only by the salary she received but also by her belief that she was "protecting the world's children from a crippling disease." Shahbano Taj told me proudly that her job enabled her to demonstrate to her village that "women too are somebody, they too can work and earn and take on positions of authority." And Mehr Ali said that her work allowed her to provide comfort and aid to aged or unaccompanied women travelers, especially those who had never flown before, "by speaking in Urdu and through small gestures of caring, we are able to give them a feeling of connection," she said. "We give them a feeling of belonging, a personal, Pakistani kind of intimacy that they wouldn't find on any other airline."

Despite their valiant and heartfelt service, women frontline workers say they are belittled and treated with scorn. Shahbano Taj said that women cops are seen by their male bosses as "nothing, less than nothing." Shiza Hayat said that the stigma of her job had affected not only her own, but also her daughters' relationships. "My younger daughter, Sarah, someone came and said to her in-laws' that Sarah's mother is nothing but a street walker," she told me tearfully. And Mehr Ali said that her marriage broke up because of her job, "my husband couldn't stop with his constant suspicion, that she is flying out of the city overnight, God knows what she gets up to."

How do women navigate the conflicts created by their stigmatizing jobs? What kinds of resources do they bring to bear in negotiating the backlash they face for their occupation of stigmatized roles on the frontlines of service for the Pakistani state? And how do their efforts fare?

This book answers these questions in order to better understand how stigma, a mechanism of gendered exclusion constituted through the conjunction of global forces with local hierarchies, is configured and contested. Such contestations are described by scholars as destigmatization, "the process by which low-status groups gain recognition and worth in society" (Lamont 2018). Since destigmatization is a crucial route to equality and social inclusion, its study has been earmarked as deserving of special attention. In her 2017 presidential address at the annual meeting of the American Sociological Association, Michelle Lamont argued that in the context of multiple claims for recognition by destigmatization movements, like #MeToo and #BlackLivesMatter, it has become urgent for sociologists to gain a better understanding of how to extend cultural membership to those who have been denied it via cultural mechanisms like stigma (Lamont 2018). The incorporation of marginalized actors into arenas of power, such as the state, after all, depends not just on their admission to these spaces but also on their access to dignity within them.

By focusing on Pakistani frontline women's efforts at navigating stigma, this book offers a fresh perspective on both, the obstacles and the opportunities that equity-seeking groups encounter as they undertake the long trek toward recognition and belonging. It does so by focusing on the experiences and routine practices of women like Khan, Hayat, and Ali, frontline workers who serve the Pakistani state and its transnational allies and who are subjected to various kinds of humiliation for their service. It asks, how do women frontline workers, like Khan, navigate the stigma produced at the intersection of local and global imperatives of gender and security? How do they contest this mechanism of exclusion and what can we learn from their efforts?

### A QUESTION OF WOMEN'S AGENCY

These questions are essentially questions about women's agency, a concept sociologists use to describe an individual's capacity for taking action in a given situation. What kinds of agency are impeded by the stigma matrix, and what kinds of agency can overcome it? To answer this question, I use empirical data collected over fourteen months of fieldwork to develop a new multidimensional account of women's agency. My conception of agency borrows from feminist theory as well as pragmatic sociological theory and is the primary contribution of this book. Agency, I show in the pages that follow, is multifaceted, involving at least two distinct forms of capacity: (1) a capacity for making or disrupting meaning that I call *symbolic capacity* and (2) a capacity for recruiting others to the meanings or projects we wish to advance, what I call *relational capacity*. Drawing on my observations of women's efforts to navigate stigma, I argue that agency involves not just mobilizing signs to make new meanings and tell new stories about ourselves, our work, and our identities but also the capacity to attract allies who will believe and support the meanings we make or unmake. While the symbolic wing of agency works to unsettle or reinforce the structures of meaning that make up stigma, agency's relational wing works to foster connection and forge relationships that can support an actor's effort to destabilize the meanings and hierarchies that anchor stigma.

In short, agency, this book argues, involves not just doing but also connecting, not just aesthetic display-work but also relational effort. I describe this multidimensional conception of agency as well as its academic antecedents in more detail in chapter 3.

Parsing out the different dimensions of agency not only helps us see the multiple ways that marginalized actors navigate stigma; it also allows us to apprehend agency's global character. Like stigma, agency also draws on multiple contexts of meaning, from the micro and immediate contexts women occupy to the macro and global contexts they serve. This global dimension of symbolic agency is demonstrated in chapter 5. And finally, as I show in chapter 6, agents work to recruit not only those within their immediate orbit but also distant allies, local as well as global. Thus, like stigma, agency too includes a global dimension, and this global character of agency becomes clear when we tease apart agency's multiple facets. By outlining agency's connection with broader contexts of meaning and relating, this book expands feminist thinking about Muslim women and the contexts that inform their agency.

## THE CONTEXTS OF WOMEN'S WORK

Feminist scholars have suggested that agency is embedded (see Korteweg 2008). By this they mean that agency is dependent on the specific settings in which it takes form. Inspector Khan, for instance, has access to a very different set of resources for tackling stigma than does Ali, an airline attendant. Khan, as the head of a co-ed police station, has access to weapons, potent symbols of force. But Ali is provided with no such tool, her arsenal is made up of makeup and designer purses, and she considers these as efficacious tools for navigating stigma. "When you present yourself well," she argues, "when you put your best foot forward, then some people are deterred from harassing you, they feel intimidated by your dressing, and they get the impression that I am not someone who will put up with rude behavior." But unlike Ali, Hayat, a health worker, attributes more efficacy to the tool she deploys in her effort to navigate stigma—her veil. Guns, she says, can fan the flames of resentment. "We do not like it when they send armed police with us on our polio work," she claims, "the police slow us down, and they also create more tensions. . . . When I am working in a red zone [a high-risk area], these are zones where the people are from a different ethnic group, they don't speak much Urdu, and they are very suspicious of the government. Then I prefer to go into that community alone, with just my veil for protection. I put on my veil, and I say, 'I am your Muslim sister.' I use the veil to underscore our common, religious identity, and then they are very brotherly and protective toward me. They respond very warmly to that 'brother-brother' language, and it is all because of my veil." As these women's accounts show, each context of frontline work provides women with a distinct set of local and global symbols they find useful for contesting stigma.

Each site of work also provides women with different relational resources. The police force is a male-dominated organization where women (less than 2 percent of the force) are also concentrated at the lowest ranks. Lady health workers, on the other hand, work in an exclusively female force, and their clients are primarily women and children. Unlike the police, health workers do not have station houses from which to operate. Their work, which was initially focused exclusively on lowering maternal mortality rates, occurs either on the doorstep of citizens' homes, where they supply the polio vaccine to children or in the private corners of the homes of veiled, low-income women, where LHWs offer condoms and iron supplements to their clients free of charge. Airline attendants' work takes place primarily while airborne. Their jobs take them to cosmopolitan locations like New York or Beijing. Although airline attendants work in an occupation that is seen as feminine, their workforce contains a roughly equal mix of men and women.

In each site, therefore, frontline women must navigate different kinds of gender and class hierarchies. Policewomen must operate in a male-dominated and male-coded work environment, where they also occupy a low status, in part due to their concentration at the lowest ranks. Health workers operate in a female-dominated workplace, but their bosses, the doctors and government servants they report to, are mostly men from more privileged backgrounds than the LHWs. And airline attendants work in a context where the numbers of men and women are relatively balanced and where their male colleagues come from similar class backgrounds as the women.

Each context of work is also differently configured by global processes. Policewomen only interface with global organizations and actors when they are in senior positions, known locally as the officer class. Those located on lower rungs within the organization (most women are concentrated here) are referred to derogatively as "rankers" and only meet with global actors directly if they are assigned to provide security to them. Nevertheless, cops are involved in projects with global connections, for instance providing security to polio workers and manning anti-terrorism operations.

Health workers, in contrast, interface with a slew of transnational organizations and actors as a routine part of their job. They participate in training programs with various global agencies, and they carry out health tasks at the behest of transnational initiatives and agendas. Some of the agencies they work with include the Aman Foundation (Bill Gates's foundation in Pakistan), the World Health Organization, and USAID.

Finally, airline attendants interact with global actors and spaces in a more direct and intimate way. Their jobs take them to various overseas locations, where they receive stipends and spending allowances in U.S.

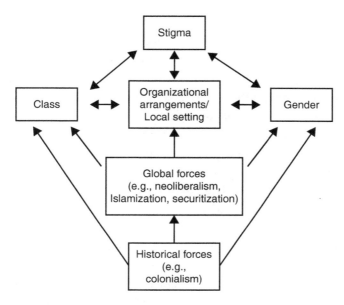

**FIGURE 2.** The stigma matrix II

dollars. Together, the exposure to foreign contexts and the funds they receive as part of their travel allowance transform airline attendants' perspectives of themselves and their class position. Thus, each organizational setting provides women with different class/gender hierarchies to navigate and a distinct set of relationships with the various processes of globalization. Figure 2 shows how a consideration of context figures in our map of the stigma matrix.

By focusing on how the different configurations of global processes and gender within each work context frame women's experiences of the stigma matrix and their strategies for navigating it, this book offers new insights into the obstacles faced by frontline women in the Global South and the resources at their disposal for managing these obstacles. Just as stigma is neither simple nor spontaneous, women's efforts to navigate it are neither uncomplicated nor one-dimensional. Yet, despite the differences, women across these three work landscapes draw on similar symbols and strategies, and their efforts run into similar obstacles. These similarities help to bring the contours of the stigma matrix into sharper relief.

## THE CENTRALITY OF PURDAH

One set of symbols that women marshalled across all three sites was connected with the notion of purdah. Some women keenly took up signs of fidelity to purdah norms (e.g., by veiling, refusing night shifts, bringing chaperones to work); others jettisoned the norms of purdah and tried instead to convey brutality or cosmopolitanism through their personal aesthetics and interactions. But in all three sites, women grappled with the gendered norms surrounding women's appearance in public space. Given the centrality of purdah for all three groups of women, it appears as an important motif in this book. I describe the various ways purdah norms were taken up or discarded in each site, and I outline the relational consequences of these agentic choices.

Although the diverse invocations of purdah did at times provide frontline women with a sliver of honor in their stigmatized occupations, they also wound up reinforcing women's marginality in their fields of work. When women mobilized the gendered signs of purdah fidelity, such as veils, whiteness creams, and motherhood, in order to convey a modest, middle-class grace, they wound up reinforcing gendered ideas about women's inability to occupy and enact public roles. Their motherhood, menstruation, and delicacy in the matter of toilets became explanations for their marginality within their fields of work. Thus, Superintendent Kazmi, the male boss in charge of one of the elite police training centers I observed in Karachi, cited gendered delicacy as an explanation for women's lower status in the police force. "You can send men anywhere, anytime," he told me. "Women have to be provided privacy, they have to be provided a bathroom, they have to feed their child, they have to go home and cook, so obviously, the role they play in the police force is different from that of men."

When women rejected the gendered signs associated with purdah, however, for instance, by mobilizing the idioms of jihad in ways that are usually associated with masculinity, their efforts got snagged by a different set of hierarchies, those centered on class. Class, sometimes dependent on educational qualifications and at other times on signs of gendered decency, worked to hamstring women's efforts to overcome stigma just as stringently as did gender norms. In the case of the police, for instance, women who jettisoned the gendered norms of purdah were stymied in their destigmatization efforts by purdah's relation with class. Their desertion of purdah norms was read by their colleagues as evidence of their low-class background, and the women were therefore seen as undeserving of respect or cooperation.

In short, for frontline women the stigma matrix was a double-edged sword. When frontline women used purdah's idioms to redefine the classed meanings of their social situations, their efforts were tripped up by gender structures. When they used the same idioms to redefine the gendered meanings that undermined their reputations, their efforts were lacerated by the structures of class. The multi-scalar macro-to-micro framework of the stigma matrix helps us to understand the multifaceted character of stigma, which relies on multiple structures to ensure women's ongoing marginality in state-based fields of frontline work.

### SPECTACULAR AGENCY

Women's efforts are not always doomed to fail. While their agency is often hamstrung by class or gender structures in the course of routine interactions with colleagues, clients, and family members—actors with whom they regularly interface—this book also outlines a different kind of strategy women sometimes use, primarily in public settings, that offers a more palpable success. To deal with the gendered stigmas they face in the course of their frontline work, women sometimes try to generate publicity for their inequality. They deploy short, sharp bursts of affectively charged displays in order to generate wider attention to their plight. By doing so, they seek to publicize abuse, punish abusers, and critique the status of women in society. I refer to this stunning publicity-seeking display work as *spectacular agency*. Spectacular agency uses spectacle as a tool for managing stigma and exclusion within the public sphere. Like a flashbulb, this kind of agency generates extraordinary but short-lived attention for the women's plight and generates a quick but temporary social connection women can use to vault over the class and gender structures that usually impede their meaning-making efforts.

By showcasing the different kinds of agency women employ in their effort to navigate stigma, this book reveals both the impediments and the resources at marginalized women's disposal. Women's successful integration into previously male-dominated work contexts, this book argues, rests neither on the ingenuity of their display work nor on their capacity to marshal allies—both those forms of individual agency, I show, produce results that are either tenuous or costly. Alone, the different facets of individual agency are unable to vault over the multiple impediments posed by the stigma matrix. Women's escape from stigma will ultimately rest on a broad-based effort from multiple sources working in concert to dismantle the stigma matrix. Such a disassembly will require (1) the production and circulation of new symbols and scripts women can draw on in their destigmatization performances; (2) the restructuring of social relations women draw on for support (e.g., increasing the number of women in the police force); and (3) a reconfiguration of the sources of value at work, such that grassroots effort and community knowledge count at least as much as the degrees, credentials, and English-speaking skills of actors from or proximate to the Global North (e.g., in the health care sector).

By describing the stigma matrix and women's efforts to grapple with it, this book takes the first step toward dismantling this important mechanism of inequality. It does so by describing how the matrix is composed, what kinds of feelings and inequalities it produces, what kinds of strategies women use to navigate it, and how it evades women's efforts to tackle its effects. By tracing the various contours of the matrix, this book asks how we might take it apart.

### WHY STUDY PAKISTAN? THE UNIQUE VANTAGE OF FRONTLINE WOMEN

In order to find ways of dismantling the stigma matrix, we need to understand the intimate connection between stigma and global processes, like neoliberalism. Stigmas, like the ones highlighted in this book, are often far too easily dismissed as the localistic outcomes of a particular culture. Muslim cultures, in particular, are far too often seen as providing an easy explanation for women's inequality. In order to get past these easy explanations, which problematically assume that cultures, especially Muslim ones, are static, monolithic, and impervious to global processes, we need to critically examine the experiences of women like Khan, Talpur, and Hayat—actors who serve as gendered conduits to connect local and global agencies with purdah-practicing women subjects in the Global South, subjects who would otherwise remain beyond the reach of global imperatives around security and the economy.

Pakistan's frontline women serve as channels for globalization in three ways. First, they encase global programs and policies in a kind of protective cover that works to both obscure the movement of these policies and also to shield them against public outrage. Lady health workers, for instance, carry vaccines and contraceptives into the homes of purdah-practicing women, and they carry data about these women's sexual health and intimate practices back out to the agencies that superintend LHW work. This transport is sometimes carried out in clandestine ways. Humera, for instance, said that her clients sometimes do not want their husbands and their in-laws to know that they are receiving contraceptives from their lady health workers. In such cases, Humera told me, "I will give them an injection, and I say to the family sitting around, that this is just a vitamin B injection." Similarly, Farzana, another LHW, said that women's families are sometimes reluctant to share private and personal information with government agents. "They ask, 'What is it to you, how many children we have, when we got an injection, what we eat, how we wash?'" In these cases, also, LHWs find ways to get around male members of the family and cajole their women clients into divulging personal data.

Similar cover is provided by policewomen, who act as chaperones for women complainants, witnesses, informants, and suspects during interviews and in the course of security operations. When the police need to conduct a raid on a civilian home, I was told by several officers, they bring women police along with them. "We are sent into the house first," said Rana, a constable. "That way, if there are women in the house, then no one can complain that the police has offended their modesty."

Second, frontline women serve as conduits for global processes by providing extension to the state and its global partners. They carry local and global agendas into arenas that national and transnational agencies would not otherwise be able to penetrate. Bill Gates's Aman Foundation, for instance, relies on lady health workers to carry various family planning tools and policies into the homes of purdah-practicing women. And policewomen conduct body searches of veiled women citizens in the course of routine security operations, physically engage with women when managing protests, and help to interrogate women citizens in the course of investigations. Their gender is seen as a valuable resource in these operations. "When they encounter a woman," a male officer told me, "people, especially women citizens, can sometimes feel more easy, they will divulge things to her that they hesitate to share with a man, so we do find it useful to work with women during interrogations or to manage informants."

Third, frontline women fulfill a signal purpose for national and transnational agencies. The state and its global partners routinely circulate images and descriptions of women agents in both publicity materials, such as brochures and websites, and news reports. When Assistant Superintendent of Police Sohai Ali Talpur successfully thwarted a terrorist attack on a Chinese embassy in Karachi in 2018, media stories about her bravery helped generate goodwill for Pakistan in China. Such images also help project a progressive image of Pakistan as a country committed to gender progress and one that involves women in crucial global missions (Rai et al. 2007). In 2015, for instance, Pakistani policewomen working to complete an elite commando training course received favorable coverage from transnational media outlets like *The New York Post* (e.g., Perez 2014). Newspapers and television channels carried dazzling images of these veiled Pakistani policewomen, who were pictured training to shoot military-style weapons in a stated effort to combat terrorism. The American media outlet NBC included a story about these women with headlines that read, "Lady Killers: Meet the Women Fighting the Taliban in Pakistan." In other publicity documents, frontline women are depicted as selfless heroes who deserve the attention of transnational donors and funding agencies. Women associated with polio eradication, for instance, are routinely represented in a heroic guise as fearless volunteers who risk their lives for the world's children (e.g., Martin 2014; Gates 2022).

In short, Pakistan's frontline women serve as conduits to transport, protect, extend, and signal the success of local and global agendas and initiatives. They shield women Pakistani citizens from the abrasive masculinity of the state and its global allies. They extend the reach of both local and global policy initiatives. They symbolize the caring egalitarianism of the state and its allies. And they shield local and global security agendas against charges of brutalizing or offending the dignity of purdah-practicing women during the course of security and other global operations.

But to provide cover and extension to the state and its global allies and to the women these entities needs to address, frontline women must surrender their own cover. In order to carry national and transnational initiatives into arenas protected by the norms of gendered privacy, they must give up their own privacy. This loss they feel keenly, mourn deeply, and struggle valiantly to compensate. Their struggles on the seam where globalization meets its subjects in the Global South provide us with an incomparable glimpse into the threads that tie local and global imperatives and subjects. This book identifies one structure that emerges out of that seam and names it the stigma matrix, an apparatus that cranks the levers of class and gender in order to produce stigma, a useful tool for hegemony.

### METHODOLOGICAL APPROACH

Engaging in a study of globalization as a sociologist is an incredibly fraught enterprise. Both the field of globalization studies and the discipline of sociology have been critiqued for their persistent Eurocentric and colonialist biases. The field of globalization studies, as Connell has charged, has long centered the global core (Connell 2007). Scholars theorizing about global trends have tended for some time to write as if their findings about social life in Europe and North America also describe changes occurring elsewhere. When they do write about the periphery, globalization scholars engage exclusively with literatures, conversations, and ideas of interest to the core. Their work, aimed at expanding social thought in the Global North, therefore does not engage with the ideas, concerns, or ways of knowing that abound in the locations they are writing about.

Meanwhile, sociology, as Julian Go has asserted, suffers from a number of fundamental issues—problems that have lingered from the very foundation of the discipline (Go 2016). These include (1) a proclivity for orientalism, which is a term describing a set of long-running stereotypes, especially about Muslims, that were used in the nineteenth century to justify the imperial subjugation of these peoples, and that have also been used in the twenty-first century to rationalize policies like the War on Terror;

(see Abu-Lughod 2002); (2) a habit of analytical bifurcation, which means failing to detect the interconnections between empire and colony when crafting theories of modernity; and (3) a failure to recognize the agency of colonized people, who are seen as passive recipients of modernization through processes like colonization and globalization (see also Bhambra 2013).

To get past some of these colonialist and Eurocentric biases in sociology and globalization studies, I drew inspiration from the prescriptions of postcolonial scholars to develop a strategy that informed my collection, analyses, and discussion of data. Specifically, my methodological approach followed three principles: (1) *Seeking interconnection.* Throughout the course of data collection and analysis, I worked to remain alert to the ways that north and south are interconnected, even at the micro level of stigma production. By being attentive to the ways that Pakistan has been entangled, both today and in the past, with global processes that connect it in various ways with countries like the United States and the United Kingdom, I aimed to avoid the analytical bifurcation that Go sees as a serious limitation in sociological research (see also Bhambra 2013).

(2) *Seeking affinities and resemblances.* Since the broad macro processes shaping Pakistani interactions are, at least in part, shaped by globalization, it follows that local trends may also bear some resemblance to processes of inequality and marginalization observed in other contexts. I worked during data collection and analysis to seek out these resemblances and to understand my findings not as unique characteristics of an exotic, static, and isolated setting but as local versions of broader global tendencies and mechanisms of inequality.

(3) *Attention to agency.* While Julian Go has expressed concern that sociologists fail to recognize the agency of previously colonized peoples, recent feminist work has highlighted a different kind of worry. In recent books and articles, scholars have warned that the relentless search for Muslim women's agency by sociologists and anthropologists working in the post–Saba Mahmood context may have produced a new dilemma. The recent literature on Muslim women's agency has become overly preoccupied with the local contexts that embed women's agency (see Sehlikoglu 2018). This ever-sharpening focus on the particularistic constituents of Muslim

women's agency, scholars worry, may inadvertently revive an imperialist bifurcation in social theory. When it is too closely focused on the localized contexts, agency scholarship can wind up creating the impression that Muslim women display an agency that is unique and distinctive from that displayed by women in other settings, such as the Global North. While western women display a liberal form of agency, Muslim women enact an agency that is pious, compliant, and conforming. Such a perspective reinvigorates problematic Islam/west binaries by suggesting that Muslim contexts are essentially different from western ones.

To sidestep this issue, I adopted a multidimensional approach to women's agency, focusing not only on the meaning-making effort women engage in but also on the relational effort they undertake. This multidimensional approach allowed me to understand Muslim women's agency as both localized and global, drawing on layers of structure and meaning that range from the micro level of interaction to the broader, macro, and global level of meaning and relating. In their efforts to negotiate stigma, my participants invoked not only local symbols and relationships, like chadors or kinship language, but also global ideas and discourses like postfeminism (a distorted neoliberal form of feminism that equates women's emancipation with consumerism). By drawing on these symbols and ideas, women sometimes sought to recruit actors within their immediate interpersonal orbits, like clients or bosses, and at other times they tried in spectacular fashion to recruit more distant allies, like journalists or social media users.

In sum, I worked to get past the metrocentrism, cultural relativism, imperial bifurcation, and orientalism of both sociology and globalization studies by adopting a three-pronged approach to data collection, analysis, and discussion. I traced the interconnections between local and global arenas, sought the similarities between these apparently disparate social locations, and attempted to remain sensitive to the ways that both local as well as global contexts serve as resources for women's agency.

## THE DATA

This book is based on fourteen months of ethnographic fieldwork with women frontline workers in Pakistan's largest city, Karachi, which is also my hometown. It focuses on three groups of women—policewomen, "lady health workers," and "air hostesses"—all public servants who help the state and its global allies get past societal norms of gendered distancing and, in so doing, wind up compromising their own respectability. These particular service jobs were selected for study not only because of their connection to stigma, purdah, and globalization but also because they represent three different configurations of gender and work. Policing is a male-coded, male-dominated work setting, air hostessing is a female-coded, mixed-gender work setting, and primary health care is a female-coded, female-dominated work setting. All three occupations are government or semi-government jobs that have not usually required a college education on the part of applicants and have therefore appeared as attractive opportunities for working-class women seeking economic mobility through the stable state job. To understand the cultural price women must pay for this mobility, I drew on both primary and secondary sources of data.

Primary data sources included 120 in-depth, formal interviews with the women (40 in each group). These interviews were recorded on tape and transcribed for analysis. The interviews were conducted primarily in Urdu, of which I am a native speaker. Analysis of interviews was undertaken using NVivo qualitative data analysis computer software. I also talked formally and informally with various actors associated with the women, such as policemen, doctors, trainers, journalists, family members, neighbors, activists, and the women's colleagues.

In addition to interviews, primary data consisted of detailed observations of the women's homes and workplaces as well as of their interactions with each other and with supervisors, subordinates, and family members. Interviews and observations took place in a range of sites relevant for frontline work, from a women's police station, where runaway girls and abused women seek shelter, to the High Court in Karachi, where policewomen chaperone women detainees. I witnessed health workers getting thrown out of a government hospital where they were trying to hold a meeting. I followed them as they trekked door to door administering the polio vaccine, and I watched as citizens slammed doors in their faces. I observed airline women trembling fearfully at the edge of a swimming pool at a Pakistan International Airlines safety training session and chatted with them in the restrooms, to which they quietly retreated when they wanted to smoke a cigarette. When I report conversations that I had in the course of these observations, I use a single set of quote marks to indicate that the speech was recorded not on tape but in my notes taken after the interaction.

For secondary data, I relied on a number of official and unofficial texts, including training manuals, official websites, news coverage, and social media commentaries on the women's activities. Combing through this secondary material provided me with access to the broader discourses, signs, and cultural schemas that are the target of women's destigmatization efforts and that help to shape them. Or to put it more succinctly, secondary data helped me understand the "landscapes of meaning" (Reed 2011) against which, like a jewel held up to the light, the women's efforts and discussions become legible. More details about access and data collection are provided in the methods appendix.

## OVERVIEW OF THE BOOK

The chapters that follow take us deep into the lives of policewomen, airline attendants, and health workers—working-class women whose joys and sorrows provide us with a glimpse into the workings of the stigma matrix. The book helps us understand the disappointment of Sania, a 25-year-old police constable who was bitter that her college education couldn't help her escape the daily indignities of police work. And the exhaustion of Mumtaz, a 45-year-old health worker who said that her work had transformed her into a rickshaw—ungainly but efficacious. And the loneliness of flight attendant Mahnaz, who made up excuses to get out of going to family events because she can no longer face the taunts and jeers of relatives who impugn her job.

The rest of the book is divided into seven chapters, each laying out different aspects of the stigma matrix and of the agency women enact to negotiate it. In chapter 1, I delve into the global histories and contemporary processes, including colonialism, neoliberalism, securitization, and Islamization, that together help to compose the macro level of the stigma matrix in Pakistan. This chapter also discusses women's experiences and their explanations for the stigma they face as frontline workers.

Chapter 2 focuses on the meso level of the stigma matrix and helps readers become acquainted with each of the field sites—policing, community health work, and aviation—investigated in this book. Each of these sites is positioned differently in relation to global forces and each, therefore, configures the stigma around purdah violation in different ways. The stigma matrix, therefore, manifests differently in each site. This chapter provides an overview of these differences, preparing the reader for a more in-depth look at each setting.

Chapters 3–5 provide an in-depth account of the strategies women deploy to navigate stigma in each setting. Chapter 3 provides readers with a detailed discussion of agency as it is conceptualized and developed in this book and then focuses on policewomen and their efforts to enact a form of agency I call *veiled delicacy*, a set of performances that addresses stigma by working to unsettle the classed meanings of police jobs. Chapter 4 describes the efforts of lady health workers to enact *martial motherhood*, a moral performance that attempts to sanitize their problematized identities but cannot overcome class barriers, which reinforce women's marginality within state health arenas. To manage the stigma surrounding their work, airline attendants draw on the cultural and material resources provided by their transnational travel to enact a postfeminist cosmopolitan performance. Their efforts showcase the complex constituents of agency, which draws not only on localized signs and symbols but also on global resources and discourses. These cosmopolitan performances and their consequences are described in chapter 5.

While chapters 3–5 examine women's failures in getting past some of the structural impediments posed by the stigma matrix, chapter 6 brings data from all three sites together to outline a potential source of success. Specifically, it describes how women in all three field sites access and deploy spectacular agency, using spectacle to make abuse visible, punish abusers, and critique the status of women in society. This chapter also outlines the global character of agency, which can seek to enlist not only local and proximate supporters but also distant and global ones. Finally, the conclusion ties the threads of the preceding chapters together and examines the theoretical significance of the book. It discusses what stigma does, what it produces, and what functions it serves. It analyzes the various benefits women secure for society by taking on their public roles. And it discusses ways that women can be supported in their efforts to cultivate inclusion within the state. Together, these seven chapters illuminate various aspects of the stigma matrix—how it is composed, what it produces, and the agency women deploy to navigate it.

By outlining the multiscalar composition of stigma, as well as the multifaceted character of agency, this book provides a new way for scholars to parse the various dimensions of an insidious mechanism of exclusion—the stigma matrix. And it helps readers to comprehend a more nuanced view of women's efforts and their agency. In the pages that follow, I take readers into the lives of women affected by a matrix of local and global, historic and contemporary stigma forces and, in doing so, invite readers to think about ways that we might work to dismantle this painful mechanism of exclusion and inequality.

# 1 | THE GLOBAL CONSTITUENTS OF SEXUALIZED STIGMAS IN PAKISTAN

'YOU'RE TOO SLACK,' PUBLIC PROSECUTOR Sheikh tells Sana. Inspector Sana is second in command at a women's *thana* (police station) located in Karachi. We have come together to the High Court, where Sana has just testified before the magistrate, and are now sitting in a tiny office jam-packed with desks, chairs, steel-cupboards, and men, all of them employed by the prosecutorial office, listening intently to Sheikh's "hilarious" monologue about Sana's incompetence. On most days, Sana looms larger than life at the women's station, where she, along with the boss, Huda, throws her weight around. Both women frequently bully their subordinates, telling them to fetch tea and press their uniforms. One time I heard Sana tell Ameera, a constable, to "polish my shoes," a demand that appeared to have seriously upset Ameera, who complained to me about it for days. Sana speaks very roughly to her subordinates, she calls them 'fatty' and tells them that 'tea served by your hand tastes like dirt.' I have witnessed her yell at civilians, telling a vagrant who was relaxing on the sidewalk outside the women's station to 'get lost, motherfucker.'

But she seems diminished today, as she sits in the dusty and dilapidated prosecutorial office. All around us, papers spill out of files, which are stacked up to the ceiling. The men sit loose-limbed behind their desks, while Sana and I are pressed in a corner, squeezed into low-slung chairs, looking up at the men. In the corridor outside, people mill around the stately, sandstone court building that was built during the British Raj. Women are few, many covered from head to toe in black robes and veils. The crowd is interspersed with a smattering of women lawyers looking smart in white tunics and trousers under black blazers, stylish symbols of their profession. Right outside the prosecutorial office, rough-looking unshaven men are sprawled on the floor, their wrists shackled to benches. They're smoking cigarettes and spitting betel juice while they await *hazari* (presentation before the judge). The air is thick with the stench of sweat, cigarette smoke, and urine.

Sheikh has been scolding and berating Sana for over ten minutes, his voice raised against the din of justice-seekers and Karachi's traffic. 'You've got to pull yourself up,' he tells her, 'Last week, your subordinate had the temerity to question you!' he says with apparent contempt. 'You should have shown her who is boss,' he insists, 'tighten the screws on these rankers, otherwise they will walk all over you.' His tirade is interspersed with comments on the beauty of Sana's various colleagues. 'Where is Ambreen, these days?' he asks. 'She's a beauty!' He names a prominent, high-ranking woman officer, praising her looks and claiming to have trained her in police work. 'You trained her?' Sana asks, looking doubtful. '*Hanh* [yes], when it came upon her, I was the one who helped her prep for the law exam,' he replies. This claim is unconvincing; I have met the woman in question, a high-ranking, well-spoken, widely traveled civil servant with a background in legal training, and I cannot envision these sessions ever taking place.

After fifteen minutes of this, Sheikh, who has thus far ignored me, asks Sana who I am. She replies proudly, 'This is my sister. She is a PhD scholar from the United States, she is researching us.'[1] 'Researching you?' Sheikh asks incredulously, looking around the room at his male colleagues. He turns to me: 'What could you possibly learn from her?' he laughs. 'She is a clown! And so is Huda!' All the men laugh. Sana blushes and bows her head. Tears fill her eyes, but she blinks them away.

This humiliating encounter between a male lawyer and a woman police inspector is a textbook example of stigma, as it is actualized in the interpersonal encounter. Although the word *stigma* originally referred to physical marks, like the tattoos, scars, and brands that were impressed on the skin of criminals, slaves, or traitors in order to alert others as to their status, it was reconceptualized by Erving Goffman, who in his 1963 book *Stigma: Notes on the Management of Spoiled Identity* developed a more interactive and relational account of stigma (Goffman 1991).

Stigma, according to Goffman, emerges when people violate our expectations about the kind of person it is reasonable to envisage in a particular setting. For instance, if our expectations lead us to imagine that a police inspector will be a man, then Sana, a slender woman dressed in frilly women's clothes and wearing flashy makeup, may come as a shock. When people like Sheikh enact their discomfort around this departure from the norm by making crude jokes, for instance, or asking hostile questions, they are stigmatizing norm-defiers like Sana. Through his jokes and references to women's beauty and their supposed need for help in passing exams, Sheikh was marking women cops as deviants unsuited to the role of policing. Stigma is produced in this encounter not only by the things Sheikh says but the context in which he says them, namely, a court office, an official and professional space inhabited by witnesses (the other lawyers), who with their laughter also contribute to the stigmatizing interface. Thus, stigma, as this encounter shows, is interpersonal and relational. It is actualized in face-to-face encounters, and it draws on and shapes a set of relationships, like those between cops and lawyers, men and women.

But stigma is not just the product of a single interactive encounter like the one described above. Although Goffman's theoretical commitments—he was interested primarily in social interaction—caused him to "mark off . . . neighboring facts," such as the political-economic structures and historical processes that reside above and behind the interaction, the encounter between Sana and Sheikh suggests that we need a more expansive perspective. To understand the encounter between Sana and the lawyer, we need to focus not only on the interaction between these two people (and their witnesses) but also on the background processes and ideas that make women seem mismatched to the role of policing in Pakistan. We need to understand not just the relationship between Sheikh, as a prosecutor and a man, and Sana, as a cop and a woman, but also the connection between neoliberalism, gender, and public space, which are the macro-level factors that frame this encounter.

And at the meso level, we need to understand how organizational structures frame Sheikh's interaction with Sana. For instance, we need to take into account the composition of the police force in Karachi, where a mere 2 percent of women serve in a force that is largely made up of men and where women are also concentrated at the lowest ranks. And we need to examine the ideas about men, women, status, honor, and work that are embedded within the police force's rules, programs, and artifacts and that circulate like tokens carrying gendered meaning among their workers. Sana, for instance, had arrived at the courthouse that day in a dilapidated police van belonging to the women's station. The van didn't always start. Moreover, Sana didn't know how to drive and had to ask the station house's security guard to drive her. To fuel the vehicle, Sana's boss and close friend, Huda, had to cajole her male colleagues at the bigger, male-dominated station house that abutted her own women's thana for money. 'Whenever I run out of money for fuel,' Huda told me, 'I go over to the male cops, and I say to them, "Brother, please give me some money for petrol." They always have money, and I never do.'

The comparative poverty of the women was reflected in the shabby condition of their workspace, the dilapidated state of their vehicle, and their lack of access to policing resources, like guns or bulletproof vests. Their poverty was shaped also by the history of women's incorporation in the police force in Pakistan as well as by the gendered logics that the police leadership employs when it distributes tasks and resources between men versus women (see chapter 3).

The need to look beyond the micro-level contexts of stigma is underscored by the recent work of sociologist Imogen Tyler. Focusing on the stigmatization of welfare recipients in the UK, she argues that by looking up and back when examining stigma, at the social hierarchies and the social histories that shape it, scholars can grasp what stigma accomplishes (Tyler 2020). Stigma is not just a set of marks people impose on each other in the course of interpersonal encounters, it is a purposeful instrument used by those in power to engineer inequalities. In the case of welfare recipients in the UK, for instance, stigma justifies the erosion of safety nets, as the dole is marked as shameful and its recipients underserving. Taking a cue from Tyler's work, this book takes a multiscalar approach to understanding the broader contexts of stigma. Stepping out and back from the micro-level interpersonal encounter, it traces the macro-level global processes that shape stigma and the meso-level organizational structures that mediate it.

This multiscalar approach, which is captured in the framework of the stigma matrix, also draws inspiration from the theorizing of social theorist Patricia Hill Collins, whose groundbreaking work has served as an invaluable resource for feminists trying to better understand inequality (Collins 2000).

Two insights from Collins's work are of particular relevance to the framework of the stigma matrix developed in this book: (1) that experiences of oppression and inequality are historically and socially specific. This insight suggests that to better understand stigma and destigmatization, we must reflect on the specific histories as well as the social contexts within which particular stigmas take shape. The second insight is (2) that systems of oppression are composed out of interrelated and intersecting domains of power (e.g., gender as well as class). Therefore, to understand Sana's humiliation at the hands of Sheikh, we must consider not just gender but also class. Sheikh's interactions with me, an elite woman educated in the West, for instance, took a very different tone. While he berated and mocked Sana, he treated me with deference. This included asking me for my impressions about his workplace, offering me tea, and offering to introduce me to the magistrate. This last offer appeared to terrify Sana, who tried to dissuade me from meeting the magistrate because "they are very powerful people."

Thus, oppression, we learn from Collins' work, is produced not just in the interpersonal domain, where stigma is conventionally examined by sociologists (e.g., the interaction between Sana and Sheikh), but also in the domain of structures (e.g., class and gender), practices and discourses (e.g., the norms and discourses around purdah). I draw on Collins's ideas to build on stigma theories, like Tyler's, which seek to improve Goffman's framework by historicizing and contextualizing stigma encounters and looking beyond them at the larger domains of power that shape them.

Since it draws inductively on research conducted in Pakistan, a postcolonial country located in the Global South, the stigma matrix framework developed in this book extends the work of both stigma scholars and those who study intersectionality. It does so by adding a global dimension to the notions of power and inequality developed in these prior theories. In Pakistan, a country that was shaped by a colonial history and by ongoing entanglements with transnational institutions (such as the International Monetary Fund) and with powerful countries in the Global North (such as the United States), global dimensions of power frequently come up in micro-level interactions (e.g., in conversations) and are visible at the meso level (see chapter 2) and at the macro level, which is the focus of this chapter. At the macro level, interactions like the one between Sana and Sheikh have been shaped by colonial histories and contemporary global entanglements. These include both policies and practices associated with British colonialism in the nineteenth century, and policies and prescriptions instituted by neoliberal processes in the twentieth and twenty-first centuries. The first hint of the connection between women's micro-level experiences and the macro-level processes that have shaped them can be found in frontline women's narratives about stigma. As they offer explanations for the stigmas they experience, women suggest the importance of space, race, gender, and culture. Similar themes emerge in historical and contemporary accounts of Pakistan's experience with global processes.

### STIGMA AND THE SEXUALIZATION OF SPACE

When I asked Bee, an airline attendant in her early twenties, about her experiences of stigma, she brought up sexual harassment. "Many of our passengers," she said, "come from backgrounds where women are restricted from coming out in public." "Such passengers," she explained, "are in any case prone to eye every woman who has come out of the home in an odd way. But when we put on the hostess uniform," she continued, "then we are looked at in a worse way altogether, and those who are air hostesses, they have a bad image." But the uniform and the public nature of their job didn't just give air hostesses a bad image according to Bee, these factors also made them vulnerable to sexual harassment. "But thankfully," she said, "in flight, we are provided with such extensive security that no one can, no one can even touch us. If he does, we will have him arrested." For Bee, the stigma surrounding her work is connected with the sexualized meanings of space. Since women are culturally confined from occupying public space, they are given "odd looks" when they do occupy it. And if they put on a uniform, which marks their membership within a service-based occupation connected with hospitality, they are seen not merely as odd and out of place but as something worse. By connecting this "something worse" with the protection air hostesses need in order to remain unmolested in their workplaces, Bee connects the airline women's visibility in public space with sexual danger and threat. By marking them as hospitality workers, their occupation of space in uniform marks airline attendants as sexually violable and exploitable.

Meena, a police constable, offered a much more comprehensive account of the connection between sexuality and the stigma associated with frontline workspaces. We were sitting in the courtyard of the women's police station during Meena's evening shift, and I was telling her about some of the things people had been telling me about reputation management at work. "They are misdirecting you," she said to me impatiently. "See, when a girl goes out to work, it doesn't matter how strict about sexual propriety she is, people make assumptions about her based on the circumstances of her job," she said. "They assume that her propriety is compromised because her work involves interaction with strangers." Leaning back in her chair, she considered all my field sites. "For instance," she said, "take health workers. They call them bad; they call us also bad also," she admitted, "but they call them bad because, you know what is in their mind?" she asked. "Health work is bad because of the nature of the job," she said. "They work closely with doctors, and they visit a lot of clients, they go to clients' houses, so people assume they must be having relations with people." She looked at me meaningfully and said, "I mean physical relations. People assume health workers must be keeping those improper relationships, and they must be stealing medicines and so on, so that is what people say about them." Meanwhile, when it comes to air hostesses, Meena said, they are seen in a negative light because "air hostesses go on different flights, they meet many different, different people. Now, you see, that is their work. They have to smile and speak to everyone. That is their duty. Whether they want to or not, they have to pose themselves that way, so it's not necessary that they are like that, flirtatious. It is possible that those girls are very strict in their personal lives, but it's their job, their need. They have to work like that, control their own reactions, their distaste for a passenger who is too forward. This is the requirement of their job. They've got to smile and smile and welcome everybody, whether it's a good person or a bad person, meaning even if he grabs your hand, you can't angrily swat him away. You have to face him in a particular mode, because you are fearful that you might lose your job." In Meena's view, health workers prompted suspicions about their character because of their need to visit clients' homes where people assumed they were involved in sexual impropriety. While airline attendants had a bad image because their jobs took them to all kinds of places, brought them into contact with all kinds of people, and prevented them from thwarting the sexual overtures of unsavory passengers.

And when it comes to the police, Meena said, "It's not just female but male police are also seen as bad." To illustrate she provided the example of her own family. "See, even my own family used to feel that the true story of the police is like what is depicted in dramas and films, like what you see in Indian movies or on television here," she said, remarking that in these media depictions, "The *thana* [station house] is a very dirty place.... Women police are depicted as the stooges of the men." She leaned in to me and whispered, "For example, right now, if a woman is brought to the lockup—this is a very shameful thing, but I am telling you because you are my sister and my friend, I am telling you so you can get an idea about what is in peoples' minds—a woman who is brought into custody, she asks us things like, 'There's no male here, is there?' 'You won't make us do the wrong thing [coerce them to have sex], will you?' 'You won't send the gents in to us, will you?' In their minds, the *thana* is a space of corruption, booze, dirty acts, dirty things." This cultural connotation of the station house as a place of sexualized corruption makes women prisoners fearful that if they fall into the hands of the police, even the hands of women police, they will be sexually exploited.

Like Bee, Meena also connects the stigma surrounding her work with the sexualized meanings of space. Women who need to engage in paid work, she argues, find their reputations compromised because of the sexualized meanings of their workplaces. Since the station house is sexualized and associated in the public's mind with corruption, policewomen are seen not as protectors of women or sanitizing elements who can help boost the police force's moral reputation but as sexual brokers who facilitate the corrupt appetites of policemen by providing their colleagues with access to the bodies of the women in their charge. Because of the itinerant and service nature of their work, airline women are assumed to be unable to withstand or avoid sexual overtures and harassment. And health workers, because of the peripatetic and intimate nature of their job, are assumed to be involved in sexual relationships with doctors and clients. In each of these instances, the individual character or sexual propriety of a woman worker is irrelevant. It is sufficient for a woman to have ventured into the various sexualized spaces connected with her public-facing frontline work for her reputation to be tarnished. Because they have ventured into public arenas of interaction, health workers are seen as sexual objects available for doctors to harass. Airline attendants are seen as vulnerable to sexualized approach and policewomen are seen as engaged in lewd commerce. To venture into public space, even for work, is to be seen as exploitable, violable, and lewd. Simply by entering these spaces, women are marked, sexually, as depraved, deviant, and vulgar.

Frontline workers are stigmatized for their need to regularly occupy sexualized public spaces, but ironically, it is this very stigma that creates their jobs in the first place. Frontline women are employed by the government precisely because public space is sexualized and productive of stigma for women who enter it. It is for this reason that women workers are hired to serve as a bridge between the state and its various clients and subjects. It is to circumvent the gendered norms and stigmas connected with public interactions that health workers were recruited to carry public health interventions to the women they surveil and serve. Policewomen act as chaperones, acting as a kind of veil to shield women apprehended by the state against the stigma of being in the custody of male police. Airline workers help the state to serve women passengers on board their aircraft, and health workers carry state health projects into their veiled clients' homes. The state requires women agents for its various agendas precisely because public space and the interactions that take place within public space are sexualized.

Yet, such spaces are sexualized, in part, through the speeches and actions of elites, including those connected with government. Such elites don't just reinforce the idea that women should remain safely at home; they demonize women who seek to resist the norms and ideas that problematize their participation in the public sphere.

On March 8, 2020, large groups of women assembled in various Pakistani cities to participate in the *Aurat March* (Woman's March), an annual event that has been held since 2018. The protestors held up placards in Urdu and English, demanding recognition for the various abuses Pakistani women have had to face in public and private arenas of life. Their efforts were marked by a strong backlash. In one highly publicized speech, Mengal, a cleric and a member of the Wafaqul Madaris curriculum committee and therefore one of the people charged with providing input on what *madrasa* students should be taught in Pakistan, suggested that since they had ventured out of their homes and into public spaces chanting slogans like "My body, my choice," women should be ready to be sexually assaulted. His comments were prompted, he told reporters, by his belief that a woman should not leave her home without "purdah" and indeed, should not leave her home at all unless there is an absolute "need" for her to do so, because when a woman leaves her home, "Satan stares at her and says I am accursed, and I will cast a slur on your face."

In another sermon, which circulated widely on social media, Mengal suggested that women who live in university hostels keep eggplants in their toilets, presumably in pursuit of sexual gratification. The laughter his remarks prompted suggests that the storage of an eggplant in the toilet was taken as a sign of the sexual deviance of such women. He is not alone in associating women's occupation of public spaces such as university hostels with sexual deviance and corruption. In another highly publicized video, prominent cleric Maulana Tariq Jameel claimed during a telethon that included, among other participants, Pakistan's then prime minister, Imran Khan, that the COVID-19 pandemic was in part the result of women's indecency. "Who has torn honor to pieces in my country?" he asked during his speech. "Who makes my country's daughters dance? Who is asking them to wear skimpier clothes? Whom should I hold accountable for this sin?"

he asked, suggesting that women's immodesty had drawn the wrath of God and punishments like the pandemic.

The former prime minister of Pakistan, Imran Khan, has also publicly drawn a connection between sexual violence and purdah. In an interview with the Pakistani news channel Geo, he claimed that purdah helped stem sexual assaults by dampening temptation, as not everyone is possessed with willpower. In a subsequent interview on the HBO program *Axios,* the prime minister suggested that rapes were on the rise in Pakistan because "if a woman is wearing very few clothes it will have an impact on the man unless they are robots. It's common sense" (see Sharma 2021; Swan 2021).

The remarks of these elites illuminate the connection between purdah, sexualized public space, and stigma. The corollary of purdah is the sexualized character of public space. To wander into this sexually charged terrain is not only to become stained but also to become a stain, a sign of society's degeneracy, its moral corruption, and therefore, its vulnerability to disaster.

While these speeches appear to anchor purdah and the sexualization of space with religion and tradition, the stigma surrounding women's occupation of public space, as I will show in this chapter, is not merely connected with religious ideologies. Space was sexualized and therefore became stigmatizing for women in part as a result of Pakistan's colonial history. By sexualizing space and stigmatizing the sexuality of indigenous women, British colonialists in India rigged relations of power to run through the matrices of race, class, and gender. The structures they erected to reify racial differences on the axis of gender continue to shape public space in ways that impact women's mobility, their motility, their dignity, and their authority in public arenas of interaction and engagement. Before I delve into that colonial history, however, it is important to understand how my women participants talk about purdah.

### WOMEN'S ACCOUNTS OF PURDAH

In their discussions about purdah, women in all three field sites distinguished idealized forms of purdah, which involve complete seclusion, from contemporary forms, which involve veiling and avoiding contact with men. Women's ideas about idealized forms of purdah, which I will refer to here as "seclusion purdah," varied by field site. Policewomen and health workers, who made considerably less money than airline attendants, described seclusion as a highly desirable but impossible luxury. "Who wouldn't like it?" Shireen, a police constable, asked. "I'd stay home, the food would be cooked, the house would be clean, I would be relaxed, no bus to catch, the children would be relaxed that our mother is home with us." But, she explained, "If I don't work, we wouldn't be able to pay our rent." Like Shireen, several policewomen spoke of seclusion wistfully, and many complained bitterly about the impossibility of adopting this practice. "To remove oneself from the dirty gaze," Bano said, "I'd be glad to do that, but then my children would starve." Like policewomen, health workers also spoke of seclusion as an ideal that was unavailable to them. "My husband's work is very uncertain," Laila said. "Some months they call him for work, and some months he is unable to work, as it is very hard, physical labor, so he gets injured. So in those times, my salary comes to the rescue."

When I asked them what purdah looked like in its idealized form, women would reach into their own past for descriptions. In its pure form, they claimed, purdah involved complete seclusion from the male gaze. But seclusion was a vanishing privilege connected with a "decent" family system that had come under fire because of the economy. These women claimed that their own fathers, who had worked as mechanics, drivers, or clerks, had kept the women of the household in respectable seclusion. "I was raised in complete seclusion," Mehr, an LHW, asserted. "I left my father's house only to go to school, otherwise I would not even go near the front door," she said with evident pride. "But after my marriage, all such luxuries were lost to me," Mehr continued with apparent sorrow. "My husband is unable to meet the expenses of our household, and so I had to give up that seclusion and get a job, otherwise my children would not have been able to go to school."

Policewomen, similarly, spoke wistfully of the desire to adopt a more ideal form of purdah that involves seclusion. Their attempts to grasp at this ideal sometimes involved puzzling strategies. "I wish to be transferred to a men's station," Maria said to me, referring to the unisex stations that being thoroughly dominated by men, operate as de facto men's stations. Maria was posted at a women's station, and I was surprised that she would wish to leave this gender-segregated situation for a male-dominated one. "How would that help you do better purdah?" I asked her. "At the men's one, they don't expect you to come in to work every day. If there is a need for your duty, they will phone you. Otherwise, they tell you to stay home, as they do not have facilities for women to sit at the station." "But" I asked, "when you are called, you would have to go, and work alongside men, doesn't that make it more difficult to do purdah?" "No," Maria responded. "I would be home most of the time. All my housework would get done, my children would have my attention, and I would only go to work sometimes, so I would be able to manage that, going sometimes, so that would be better." Maria's explanation made me realize that what women were lamenting was not just a loss of seclusion but a loss of freedom over time and attention. Having to work meant giving up time that could have been devoted to domestic chores and childcare. Having to work meant having to catch a bus, report to a boss, struggle in the rat race. Such a necessity, women argued, was demeaning. Women of the past, grandmothers, great-grandmothers, had not been so demeaned. These ancestors were treated as if they were precious.

Parveen drew on her family history to describe the connection between seclusion and the preciousness of women. "My grandmother never left her father's home except on the occasion of her marriage," she said, "and even during that single journey from paternal home to marital home, my grandmother was shielded from the gaze by a palanquin, carried by male members of the family. She was carried in a palanquin to her husband's house, like a queen. No one saw her face." When she related these aspects of her grandmother's style of purdah, health worker Parveen said, "Imagine! Her feet never even touched the ground outside of the threshold of her house." For Parveen, who kept massaging her knees as we spoke and who complained that her health work had produced corns and calluses on her feet, seclusion purdah was an idyllic institution that had protected women not only from the pollution of the male gaze but also from the physical drudgery of work. But sadly, this system was part of a glorious, lost past.

The fantastic yearning descriptions that policewomen and LHWs produced are instructive. For these women purdah, in its ideal form, was connected with a glorious but retreating past. In this time of idealized values, now unattainable, women were provided with privacy and protection, their seclusion was a sign not only of the family's financial sufficiency but also of the preciousness of women. The women who had enjoyed purdah, in this glorious past, were too dear, too delicate, and too beloved to be sent out into the rough world. That they can no longer enjoy this freedom from work is thus a matter of grief for the women who are forced by circumstances to suffer the rigors of wage work.

When clerics and elites abjure contemporary women to embrace seclusion purdah's modalities, they too invoke an idealized past, one that is sanitized of its classed realities. For the clerics and for the women they address, seclusion is not just an ideal but a fantasy. Their fanciful accounts mirror those produced by imperial writers' descriptions of purdah. In the colonial period, purdah, like *sati* (the immolation of widows) operated as a stereotype that falsely universalized racial difference. Although purdah was practiced by Muslims and some non-Muslims during colonial times, it was even then a privilege enjoyed primarily by elite women (see Rajan 1993; Nair 1990). Indeed, historians suggest that purdah in British India functioned less as a means of confining women and more as a way to restrict men from entering women's spaces.

Despite its circumscribed use, purdah operated as a central signifier of racial difference (and indigenous inferiority) for white writers in the eighteenth and nineteenth centuries. Since the zenana (similar to a harem, refers to a part of the house reserved for women) was closed off to white men, this segregated space acquired an erotic charge, becoming an arena that represented both the licentiousness of indigenous men and the repression of indigenous women. Rudyard Kipling's 1888 short story "Beyond the Pale" provides one instance of this view. In it, purdah appears as a universal institution practiced by all Indian women, regardless of religion or class. The practice is so rigidly enforced, in Kipling's story, that his native character, a Hindu widow, is punished for her violation of its codes with amputation.

Unlike British men, British women were allowed access to the quarters of purdah-practicing women. These white women visited and described native women's living conditions in travel writings and memoirs. In their descriptions, the harem appears as a space of stifling indolence and oppression that inspires feelings of disgust and pity. The inhabitants of these spaces, indigenous women, are described as having been degraded to an animal state—eating, drinking, and lolling about. Purdah-practicing women are described as greedy, idle, mindless, dull, soulless, brutish, and peevish. Their humanity has been eroded because of their lack of occupation and social engagement. The confinement of indigenous women within the zenana or harem is described as a form of slavery.

To be sure, these representations of Muslim harems were shaped by the social characteristics of the nineteenth-century travelers who wrote them. Largely middle- or upper-class, these British women upheld a bourgeois view of the family, of labor relations, and of women's occupations (Foster 1921). Their writing worked to shore up orientalist narratives about colonized society as a space of oppressive, timeless tradition, a space that was therefore needful of imperial intervention. These orientalist discourses did not just represent indigenous gender arrangements in universalistic, simplistic, and negative ways; they also glossed over the ways that British women, at home and in the colonies, were also segregated and restricted by norms of interaction as well as norms around spatial arrangements. In Britain, for instance, white women were constrained by convention to rely on chaperones when venturing out to attend parties or social engagements. But British cultural constructions glossed over the gendered mechanics of segregation at home, instead constructing a binary of native/white difference.

The writing of colonial-era British men and women helped produce a stereotypical image of purdah as an institution of complete seclusion, a space of women's confinement and relegation to a life of opulence, indolence, idleness, and luxury. The stereotype not only erased the variations and the fluidity of purdah practices but also reaffirmed the essential difference between colonizer and colonized.

The similarities between British colonial constructions of purdah and the ideals that LHWs and policewomen evoke in their talk of seclusion, luxury, and "freedom from work" are striking. For contemporary Pakistani clerics and working-class women, the practice of purdah is, as it was for colonial-era rulers, writers, and travelers, a space of luxurious retreat and a marker of racial and cultural difference. Whereas for colonial writers, purdah denoted the cultural inferiority of indigenous peoples, their propensity to idleness, and their oppression of women, for contemporary working-class Pakistani women, like the policewomen and health workers I interviewed, purdah denotes the cultural superiority of distinctly local values that honor women by protecting them, not just from the unruly male gaze but also from the harsh practicalities, brutal indignities, and vicious vicissitudes of the public arena.

It is interesting too, that unlike cops and health workers, airline women did not describe purdah as a luxury. Airline women drew salaries that were nearly double what policewomen made and three times higher than the salaries of LHWs. Moreover, airline women were frequent travelers, visiting countries in the Middle East, Europe, and North America. Enjoying a mobility that is usually the privilege of elites, these women described seclusion not as a privilege connected with a romanticized past but as an outdated practice connected with a narrow and impractical view of the world. "Wearing a veil is fine," Shehzeen commented. "We also sometimes wear a scarf, but we wear it very neatly, very elegantly. Our focus is that one should look stylish and well put together." Similarly, Maya argued that idealized notions of purdah, which attempted to preserve women from public exposure, were impractical. "Look, the world has changed," she said. "It is simply not possible now to remain confined, and people who practice strict purdah, we see passengers like that, they put on these huge wraps or burkahs, they can't see where they are going, they look messy, they are tripping on their veils. That is no way to live in this world."

Airline women took exception not only to the aesthetics of seclusion practices, such as large, baggy veils, but also to what such practices suggested about social attitudes. "People who want to lock women up at home," Leena argued, "they are holding on to a mindset that is out of step with the rest of the world. Even in the Middle East, for example, Arab women are going everywhere. They are doing all kinds of things. This idea that women have to stay home, it's a Pakistani cultural thing, not a religious requirement, but these people make it about religion." Shehnaz, who was listening to this conversation, agreed. "Purdah is in your gaze," she suggested. "Mind your own business, that's purdah. Don't poke your nose in someone else's business, that's purdah," she said, invoking the secondary meaning of purdah, which is "curtain," to suggest that purdah involved privacy, not seclusion and confinement.

Like Shehnaz, Reema also described purdah as a form of privacy. Rather than a space of confinement, purdah, Reema argued, was about sparing women from surveillance. "Our people, they are too interested in what everyone else is doing. If a woman is sitting somewhere, they have a hundred questions: Why is she out of her house? Why is she not wearing a veil? Why is she this, why is she that?" she complained. "But when you go out [of the country]," Reema said, "you realize that people in other countries don't pay so much attention to other people's business. You can sit where you like, drink coffee on a sidewalk in Times Square. No one will look at you. No one will wonder what you are up to. It is very relaxing." Like Reema, several airline women claimed that venturing into public space in Pakistan could feel stressful. Unlike foreign countries, where one could relax and enjoy a cup of coffee on a café sidewalk, the women argued that in Pakistan, gender norms around purdah made public space feel uncomfortable. When they went out, they said, they felt like all eyes were on them, which made them feel constrained. For these women, the norms of purdah were connected with an unacceptable local habit of gendered surveillance. Cultural beliefs about purdah made airline women the subject of interest and speculation when they inhabited public arenas. For them, being able to occupy public space in peace and without the intrusion of a suspicious public gaze was a fantasy that could only be fulfilled by traveling abroad.

The stigma that has come to haunt women's occupation of public space has been inscribed into that space by more than just imperial travelogues and short stories. The orientalist literary ideas about purdah were reinforced by a complex set of material, cultural, and social-scientific practices that operated together to stigmatize indigenous peoples, specifically in relation to their sexual practices. In the next section, I will discuss how public space in colonial India was inscribed with racialized stigmas around sexuality.

### COLONIALISM, SEXUALITY, AND STIGMA

Colonial space was not just organized through stereotypes, such as those related with purdah; it was also spatially organized to accentuate racial difference (King 1976; Dalrymple 1994; Mills 1996). Cities under colonial rule in India were spatially segregated. Whites lived and worked in Civil Lines, pristine, elegant neighborhoods that were constructed at a remove from native areas. This spatial segregation was justified at the time as a health measure, but it also worked to maintain and accentuate the difference between the rulers and the ruled. In contrast with the sprawling and overcrowded native settlements that housed Indians, Civil Lines neighborhoods were organized with mathematical precision on a grid plan and boasted wide, straight avenues that featured spacious residences built on classical lines and were set on spacious and neatly landscaped grounds.

In addition to racial segregation, spatial divisions also gendered differences. By placing Civil Lines at a distance from native settlements, the British government in India not only separated white rulers from the brown people they ruled, they also segregated and protected white women from native men, who were seen as lascivious (Ballhatchet 1980). This protective segregation was organized not only in the cities, where colonial administrators worked, but also in the resorts where they retreated for the summer. Built high up in the hills and away from native areas, resorts like the one in Simla provided protection and leisure opportunities for British women and children.[2] Indians were forbidden from entering the clubs where the British socialized and were also forbidden from using the main thoroughfare in these vacation settlements.

Besides erecting enclaves in physical space, whites also secured distinction from natives by relying on cultural texts and artifacts that represented white settlements in contrast with native areas. Colonial discourses constructed white settlements as civilized spaces that contrasted sharply with native areas, which were represented as mysterious, barbaric, dangerous, and potentially contaminating spaces. In novels and short stories, like *A Passage to India,* the well-known novel by E. M. Forster, the spaces inhabited primarily by natives, figured as sexualized and threatening arenas. In *A Passage to India,* it was sufficient for a white woman to have merely entered indigenous space for there to be an assumption that something of a sexual nature had transpired (1924).

By producing and reinforcing stereotypes about vulnerable white woman needing protection from lascivious Indian men, colonial era texts accomplished an important purpose, one that has been discussed by historian Jenny Sharpe. The British zeal for protecting white women, Sharpe tells us, originated with the 1857 Indian Uprising, referred to by British rulers as "the Mutiny." British rulers quickly described the Mutiny as a barbaric attack on innocent white women, who were rumored to have been raped, tortured, and mutilated by rebels. By constructing the uprising as a sexualized threat rather than a political problem, Sharpe argues, the British rulers leveraged the "savaged remains" of British women's bodies in service to a productive fantasy, where descriptions of "native savagery" elided any discussion of the "barbarism of colonialism." By emphasizing the need to protect British women via the construction of enclaves in the wake of the uprising, British rulers continued to displace attention from politics, instead maintaining the idea of threat to reaffirm stereotypes that supported justifications of the need for colonial rule (Sharpe 1993; see also Donaldson 1992; Rajan 1993). Ideas about white women's vulnerability to rape and their need for protection worked to further sexualize space in British India.

Tropes about lascivious Indian men and vulnerable white women obscured a brutal reality—the danger that white men posed to Indian women. Although this threat may not have been the subject of writing by authors like Forster, it nevertheless appears to have shaped native ideas about space. Indeed, as Sara Mills remarks, purdah practices were in part structured by native fears of attack or rape by British soldiers (Mills 2003). To illustrate, she provides the following account from a 16-year-old British soldier, Harry Bowen, who was stationed in Kanpur:

> There was one time I remember that an Indian woman strayed into the lines where we were barracked, and she got into very serious trouble. I don't know whether she'd come in by mistake or whether she was looking for business, but things must've got out of hand and she was passed from bed to bed and finished up as a dead body on the incinerator in the morning. . . . There'd been about twenty-four to thirty fellows involved, probably a lot more than that. She couldn't take it. It killed her. Of course, the police came, and they questioned a lot of people, but they couldn't pin it on any one person, so the whole thing petered out. (Gill 1995)

As this account suggests, it was sufficient for a native woman to simply wander into the wrong place to be raped and wind up dead, with no consequences for the offenders.

Even if an indigenous woman did survive an assault, she had little recourse to the law, which enshrined a number of biases and stereotypes about Indian women's sexuality. In an article examining the laws surrounding sexual assault in British India, for instance, Kolsky examines the misogynistic and racist biases that undermined native women's options for redress (Kolsky 2010). In manuals, statutes, verbal instructions, and verdicts, she shows, colonial rulers repeatedly upheld the view that native women could not be trusted and that their claims of rape therefore had to be verified through an examination of their class and caste backgrounds, their sexual history, and their personal history. In one judgment, for instance, the court made betel-stained teeth a reason for doubting a woman's sexual propriety and therefore her claims of sexual assault.

Thus, space was sexualized not only by the physical segregation of whites and natives, the confinement and protection of white women, the racialized stereotypes about the savagery of native men, the untrustworthy character of native women but also the threat that white men posed for indigenous women. Although this threat was obscured by the cultural constructions that represented brown rather than white men as threatening and white rather than brown women as vulnerable, the historical record suggests that it was often brown women who were victimized by white men.

## COLONIALISM AND SEXUAL THREAT

For British men, imperialism was, as scholars have noted, a sexually charged enterprise. Colonialism was an erotic project on two levels. On the symbolic level it involved the conquest and penetration of lands culturally constructed as dark, mysterious, virgin territories, and on the practical level, colonialism provided white men with opportunities for various kinds of carnal pleasures, not all of them consensual (Ballhatchet 1980; Dalrymple 2003; Ghosh 2006; Stoler 1989). Although much has been written about the sexual exploitation of colonized women, children, and men by British men, details of this sexual history are rarely discussed in Pakistani histories of the colonial period. The connection between purdah, sexual stigmas, and colonialism is therefore rarely remarked upon in this context. This history is nevertheless instructive and worth recounting here.

Histories of colonial sexuality reveal sex as a crucial motor of colonial rule. In a series of texts focused on this history, for instance, historian Ronald Hyam argues that imperialism was driven not only by the imperatives of "Christianity and commerce" but also those of "copulation and concubinage" (Hyam 1986). The willingness of Victorian Englishmen to go overseas at the behest of empire, he suggests, "depended quite crucially on the easy availability of a range of sexual consolations" in these conquered lands. The "sexual relationships" imperial agents enjoyed in the colonies, he argues, helped to "solder together the invisible bonds of empire."

Although Hyam's work, which has been described as an instance of British imperial apologist historiography, has been critiqued for its sexual orientalism and its defense of male supremacy, it nevertheless tells us a great deal about the significance of sexual oppression to empire (see Berger 1988). To illustrate the importance of what he calls "the sexual imperative" as a motor of empire, Hyam provides various instances of British men's "scandalous" activity in the colonies. "Sir David Ochterlony (the Resident of Delhi, 1803–25) took 13 Indian mistresses," he tells us, while "Col. James Skinner (founder of the crack regiment 'Skinner's Horse') was said to have had a harem of 14 wives." Hyam's account also contains direct quotes from the men who enjoyed various "sexual adventures" in the colonies. Captain Edward Sellon apparently wrote of his time in India thus:

> I now commenced a regular course of fucking with native women. They understand in perfection all the arts and wiles of love, are capable of gratifying any tastes, and in face and figure they are unsurpassed by any women in the world.

Although Hyam terms most of these sexual encounters "relationships" and describes the natives as "erotic collaborators," his own account suggests that the encounters involved a great deal of oppression and violence. "The deep-seated hostility of the Afghan people towards the British," he tells us, "may well have been due to their resentment of the undisciplined lust with which British soldiers fell upon the women of Kabul in 1841." Still, Hyam is somewhat sanguine in his description of British men's sexual activity in the colonies, suggesting, for instance, that the indigenous peoples involved were mostly prostitutes. He seems not to consider who these "prostitutes" were. Instead, he suggests that prostitution was, in the orient, "an old and honourably established business" and that Asian prostitutes were "amusingly playful hostesses," unlike their "nasty, dirty and coarse" British counterparts, who were "drawn from deprived backgrounds." In India and

Japan, he asserts, "prostitution was an honourable estate, and not furtively conducted. Asian prostitutes were likely to be higher up the social scale, educated and with a proper training for their art." These prostitutes, he suggests, "earned comparatively good money," did not usually appear to be "younger than 15," and were not "generally ill-treated."

Hyam's assumptions and illustrations take on a different complexion in light of Durba Mitra's findings in her recent book *Indian Sex Life* (Mitra 2020). In this compelling history, Mitra draws on archival material to demonstrate that from the perspective of British colonialists in India, *all* Indian women were potential prostitutes. In 1872, she tells us, the British colonial state initiated an extensive information-gathering survey about Indian women. This effort was prompted by the passage of new laws (the 1860 Indian Penal Code) prohibiting the buying and selling of girls for prostitution. In a questionnaire distributed widely among their various staff and administrators, the colonial state asked the following question: Who is the Indian prostitute? In their responses, colonial administrators claimed that "all Indian women were potential prostitutes."

Their presumptions about Indian women were founded on a host of factors: they assumed that Indian women were sexually deviant, possessed partly due to the static nature of their culture and traditions, with insatiable sexual appetites. Local institutions and familial arrangements, they thought, were at once too oppressive and insufficiently regulatory and so were unable to restrain women's sexuality.

As a result of the rulers' stereotypes and assumptions, all a native woman had to do to be suspected of prostitution was to be poor or working-class (e.g., nannies and factory workers), be Muslim (Muslims were suspected of contracting sham marriages in order to disguise their sexual commerce) or low-caste Hindu, be single after age 15, be a widow, be in a polygynous marriage, or have a husband who worked at sea. In short, anyone who wasn't in a monogamous, upper-caste, or upper-class marriage was suspected of being a prostitute.

The cultural stereotypes and assumptions that colonial administrators injected into their responses to the survey about Indian prostitutes eventually found their way into the policies and regulations they crafted in an effort to manage the sexuality of Indian women. This long process, from the exploration of Indian women's sexuality in the initial survey, to the development of sexual typologies and sociological theories about their sexuality in later stages, to the creation of surveillance mechanisms and medico-legal procedures for the regulation of Indian women's sexuality, Mitra shows, worked to stigmatize Indian women's sexuality. Throughout this long social scientific and legal process, British colonialists constructed Indian women as sexually deviant and made their deviance into an index that reflected society's backwardness and lack of evolution.

The sexual stigmas seeded by colonialism continue to flourish in the discourses produced by Pakistani clerics and elites today. Thus, women's sexual deviance, as exemplified by activities such as dancing, is mobilized as an explanation for the punishing plague of COVID-19. Women who live in hostels, away from their family's monitoring and surveillance, are assumed to be involved in acts of sexual depravity with vegetables. Women who insist on chanting slogans like "My body, my choice" are said to be inviting sexual assault. Purdah, as Prime Minister Imran Khan suggested in a June 2021 interview, is taken as a bulwark against sexual assault. In his suggestion that purdah is a ward against rape, Khan appeared to reaffirm problematic colonial binaries. Pakistani men are not like western men, he seems to imply in his interview on HBO. "We don't have discos here, we don't have nightclubs," he said. "It is a completely different society, [and] way of life here. So, if you raise temptation in society to a point—all these young guys have nowhere to go—it has a consequence in the society." His suggestion that purdah is necessary because Pakistan is a "different society," one where men are unable to tame their savage lusts, is tragic. Tragic since the historic record suggests that the necessity of purdah was amplified in the nineteenth century as a defense against the sexual aggression of white men, not brown ones.

### NEOLIBERALISM, SEXUALITY, AND STIGMA

Colonialism has not been the only global force to nourish the stigmas surrounding Pakistani women's sexuality and their relationship with public space. Working-class women's experiences of stigma have also been shaped by the global forces that have molded Pakistan's economic and gender policies since the creation of the country in 1947. While a complete and detailed history of purdah and the various transformations of its various modalities and meanings are beyond the scope of this book, I want to focus now on to two specific global processes, Islamization and neoliberalism, that scholars see as particularly consequential for understanding gender relations in Pakistan and that are especially important for understanding the unique dialectical pressures that shape frontline women's workplace experiences.

Although, they may seem discrete, neoliberalism and Islamization are intertwined forces (see also Savci 2021). Their interconnection in Pakistan's case is anchored to the state's concerns with legitimacy. When I speak of neoliberalism, I am referring to a set of economic prescriptions, crafted in the late 70s by the International Monetary Fund, the World Bank, and the U.S. Department of the Treasury and promoted by these institutions as ideal measures for the reform of crisis-riddled developing countries. Sometimes referred to as the Washington Consensus, these reforms involve a set of deregulatory polices, such as privatization, that aim to diminish the state's role in economics of accumulation. By ceding its ownership of assets, for instance in power generation, the neoliberal state takes on a regulatory rather than a redistributory role. The process of neoliberal reform has an impact not only on capital, which moves into private hands, but also on the welfare and service functions of the state. Under neoliberalism, public utilities and support initiatives such as public hospitals are privatized, so that relief roles are no longer fulfilled by the state but are taken over by private institutions and charities. The neoliberal state abandons its welfare functions in order to create economic efficiencies, which are supposed to ensure the development of a stable, consumption-based economy.

But in giving up its welfare and redistributive functions, scholars suggest, the state loses a crucial source of its authority. It can no longer rely on provisions of public service or redemptive functions to assure its legitimacy and must now seek other ways of winning over consent for its rule from the public. In many countries, the state makes up for the loss of its redemptive functions by focusing more emphatically on security. In these security states, "the defense of the territory—the 'safe home'—becomes the passkey to all doors which one feels must be locked" (Bauman 1998). In other words, as it is no longer able to make service a justification for its right to rule, the neoliberal state derives its legitimacy through the promise of securing the bodies, the values, the properties, the social relations, and the interests of its citizens. This shift in the logics of rule involves the neoliberal regime in a new kind of biopolitics, one based on security.

In Pakistan, the legitimacy crisis precipitated by neoliberalism was resolved not only through a focus on security but also through recourse to religious nationalism. Two historic events tied neoliberalism and its associated process of securitization to Islamization in Pakistan in the late 1970s, the dictatorship of General Zia-ul-Haq and the Soviet-Afghan War.

In 1977, General Muhammad Zia-ul-Haq, Pakistan's chief of army staff, overthrew the democratic government of Zulfikar Ali Bhutto in a military coup and took over the reins of government. The general's rule lasted eleven years, ending only with his death in a plane crash in 1988. Since he took over from a democratically elected government, the general needed political allies as well as symbolic resources to cement and justify his regime. The *ulama* or religiously oriented political parties provided him with both. These clerics had not only been opposed to the rule of the previous prime minister, who was ousted by Zia-ul-Haq, but also subscribed to a set of ideologies replete with symbols and ideals that the general could use to explain and justify the need for his takeover. Religion provided a useful framework for this justificatory enterprise because the state had relied on it already, in the years following the country's birth in 1947, to unify a diverse population under the banner of religion.

Zia drew on religious rhetoric to craft legitimacy for his martial law regime. He framed the prior government, which he had overthrown, as un-Islamic and adopted the posture of a pious reformer who would not only put Pakistan back on a moral track with his Islamization program but would also save and protect his Muslim country from various external threats. Two kinds of external threats were used to craft the Zia-ul-Haq regime's security-based legitimizing narratives. The first involved Pakistan's neighbor and longtime foil, India. The second involved the 1980s Afghan-Soviet War.

The Afghan-Soviet War not only allowed the general to center religious imagery and ideals, such as the veil and jihad (holy war) as important signifiers of Muslim identity but also opened the doors to US bilateral aid,[3] which had petered off in prior years for two reasons. First, American aid declined during the Bhutto regime because of Bhutto's clandestine pursuit of nuclear technology. Second, after Zia-ul-Haq swept away democracy in his military coup in July 1977, Pakistan became a pariah state. In April 1979, the Carter administration in the United States, imposing the Symington Amendment on Pakistan, cut off most forms of economic and military aid. Global political conditions changed dramatically later that year, however. In 1979, the Iranian Revolution deposed the Shah of Iran, depriving the United States of one of its trusted allies in the region. Then the Soviets invaded Afghanistan. Together, these two events transformed Pakistan's strategic significance in the region, as Pakistan came to be viewed as a frontline ally against communism. By December 1979, all sanctions against Pakistan had been lifted and Pakistan became the recipient of a generous aid package. By 1985, it was the fourth-largest recipient of U.S. bilateral military assistance. By 1987, the approval of a $4.02 billion military and economic aid package made Pakistan the second-largest recipient of American aid.

Some of this aid money took the form of loans, administered by the World Bank and IMF, and came with the structural adjustment policies associated with neoliberalism, such as privatization, deregulation, reduction in social spending, and the removal of subsidies and price controls. By the end of the 1980s, the public-sector share of total industrial investment had fallen from 73 to 18 percent (Brown 2016). Privatization policies entailed the loss of public-sector jobs, while deregulation policies raised the price of food and fuel for consumers.

The job losses and the inflation brought about as a result of these neoliberal policies were consequential for gender arrangements within urban families. Large cross-sections of men in urban employment–oriented areas began to find it impossible to meet their family's economic needs. Even though male leadership in the family is anchored to men's breadwinner role, such men were forced to seek supplementary sources of income or to accept the financial contribution of their wives (Mumtaz and Shaheed 1987).

The familial impacts of neoliberal economic reform were reflected in many of my interviews. As working-class women, many of my informants said, they were the first women in their family to venture out of the home for work. As daughters of taxi drivers, clerks, factory workers, and low-ranking policemen, they had grown up in homes where the men were engaged in wage work and the women cared for the home. These male breadwinner–based gender arrangements were seen as reflecting a good, *khata-peeta* (well-resourced), decent, and normative family background. Being unable to maintain this normative lifestyle free from the financial necessity that forces women to give up the safety and privacy of home, to surrender their focus on the well-being of their children, and to submit to the vicissitudes of work was a source of humiliation and grief for many of my participants.

But Zia-ul-Haq's neoliberal and Islamization policies did not just shape the economic imperatives and gender arrangements in working-class homes. Together, these two projects also worked to amplify the sexualization of public space and the stigmatization of women's sexuality. As Masood Ashraf Raja has remarked, Zia-ul-Haq's Islamization policies were largely performative, enacted through ritual, appearance, performance, and law (Raja 2011). Besides the circulation and celebration of symbols like martyrdom and jihad, the project focused primarily on women, their bodies, their position in space and in the family. Official and unofficial policies made the figure of the urban middle-class woman a vehicle for the demonstration of Islamization and a symbol of the project's success. This is why Amina Jamal has described Zia-ul-Haq's Islamization project as "a gendered discourse of citizenship," one that turned normative ideas about the appropriate place, conduct, and propriety of women into key symbols of the state's success in accomplishing a religious character (Jamal 2013).

The regime popularized the notion of *"chador aur char divaar"* (veil and four walls) as the ideal and only acceptable modality of social existence for a virtuous woman to adopt. By circulating the slogan of the veil and four walls, the government suggested that women should ideally remain within the secure and sacred confines of home (the *char divar,* or four walls); when they do venture out due to a pressing need, they must do so within the confines of the *chador* or a large wrap used as a veil. Through this slogan, which is still in circulation in the Pakistani public sphere today, Zia-ul-Haq's Islamization project reanimated some of the gendered stigmas and sexual stereotypes from the colonial period.

By suggesting that women belong either within the home or within the folds of a chador, the state gendered space in two ways. First, it made the home a gendered zone, connected with women, privacy, sexual protection and decency. Second, with the notion of the chador, a more mobile kind of confinement than the home, the state made the public sphere also a gendered and sexualized zone, one that women should not access, unless their bodies were sheathed and obscured within the folds of a veil. By mobilizing two signs of confinement, the image of the chador and char divar, connected women with the domestic, the private, and the hidden arenas of life and, in doing so, sexualized their bodies and stigmatized their occupation of other spaces or forms of embodiment.

The trope of the veil and four walls does not just activate gendered logics around space, connecting private space with the feminine, the private, and the intimate; it also activates several other binaries connected with globalization. These additional binary logics, which the trope of "chador and char divari" activates, mirror some of the tropes and dichotomies utilized by the British colonial state prior to partition in 1947. The rhetoric of the veil and four walls not only positions women within the private sphere, it also makes their inhabitation of this arena, and their embodiment of public/private gendered binaries, a sign of society's adherence to traditional as opposed to westernized (and therefore morally corrupt) values. "Westernization" symbolized by women's presence in the public sphere is taken to signify the erosion of "tradition," which is conflated with Islam and coded as "authentic" culture. Authentic tradition stands in timeless contrast with corrupt and foreign, modern, and "western" values and gender arrangements.

Thus, the gendered logics that pit public against private zones are connected also with logics that set modernity in dichotomous opposition against tradition, Islam against the west, and local against foreign values and culture. Imperial-era logics and dichotomies therefore inflected the gendered logics Zia-ul-Haq mobilized in his Islamization project. These binary logics don't just define the normative locus of women's movement and the limits of their comportment; they also sexualize women's bodies and stigmatize the presence of these bodies in public space.

Zia-ul-Haq's Islamization project activated stigmatizing gendered logics and stereotypes through a host of formal and informal stigma mechanisms. Formally, a set of discriminatory laws, such as the Hudood Ordinance, were passed, purportedly in an effort to Islamize society by bringing regulations around sex and alcohol consumption in line with religious law.

The ordinance criminalized extramarital sex, defined as including both adultery and fornication. It also removed the crime of rape from the Pakistan Penal Code and sought to redefine it in religious terms. Rape would now come under the Zina Ordinance, which criminalized *zina* (illicit intercourse) and would now be described as *zina-bil-jabr* (illicit intercourse with force).

In reality, these laws borrowed elements from colonial law. For instance, the statutory definition of *zina-bil-jabr* structures crime around the concept of consent. In implementing these laws, the Pakistani courts rely on forms of evidence and assumptions that are foreign to Islamic traditions. For instance, the same factors that were central determinants for the outcome of colonial-era rape cases—fresh complaint, the victim's moral character, the victim's virginity, and physical evidence of force and resistance, continued to feature in zina case law, even though these factors have no application in Islamic law (see Kolsky 2010; Chadbourne 1999; Burney 1999).

By redefining rape and criminalizing extramarital sex, the Hudood Ordinance made women vulnerable to the misuse of these laws by ex-husbands and other family members. Women who got married without their family's approval, for instance, could find themselves accused by family members of engaging in illegal extramarital sex. Those who were sexually assaulted and unable to prove the attack could find themselves charged for engaging in illicit sex.

These laws also provided the police with the opportunity to harass men and women who had gone out together in public space. The police would routinely stop such couples and demand to see their *nikahnama* (marriage certificate). Those who could not produce one would either have to pay a bribe or get taken to the police station for questioning.

In addition to these formal laws, the state also enacted a number of informal gendered policies in pursuit of Islamization, which further sexualized women's bodies and stigmatized their occupation of public spaces. Women government employees were ordered to wear traditional national dress (i.e., shalwar kameez) and to veil. Women bureaucrats were banned from foreign service, and women were barred from being hired at banks, which were all controlled by the state (Mumtaz and Shaheed 1987; Rouse 1994; Weiss 1992). Women's sports teams were disallowed from traveling abroad or from competing before a mixed-gender audience. Girls were instructed to wear chadors to school, even though many of these institutions were sex-segregated. Women broadcasters employed by the state television channel (the only channel operating at the time) who refused to veil were fired. Advertisers were forbidden from casting women in commercials for products that were not directly related to women's activities (Mumtaz and Shaheed 1987).

The informal gender policies were taken up not only by the state but also by ordinary citizens. In an address to the nation, General Zia-ul-Haq urged citizens to work not only on reforming themselves but also on reforming their neighbors. As a consequence, Mumtaz and Shaheed note, an unprecedented atmosphere of community vigilantism came into existence. People appeared to feel that they now had a license to pass judgment on the morality of people in public space. Women's dress and their presence in public space became key arenas of vigilante attention. Teachers refused to teach women students who were not dressed in chadors. Some professors refused to lecture when women were seated in the front row of the lecture hall; others refused to have women in the classroom at all. People appeared to object not only to women who came out bareheaded (i.e., unveiled) in public, they began also to object when women spoke out, pursued a career or drove a car (Mumtaz and Shaheed 1987; Jafar 2005). Women venturing out in public space, at universities, in parks, or in shopping centers, were confronted by strangers instructing them to "fix your *dupatta* [veil]."

Much has been written about the dialectal ways these gendered formal and informal policies shaped the experiences and opportunities of middle-class urban women. Less has been written about the ways that these policies shaped the experiences of working-class women such as my participants. For middle-class women, the trope of the veil and four walls created both opportunities and constraints. It increased their visibility in the public sphere at the same time that it set limits on their appearance in these zones. The visibility of middle-class women was enhanced by Zia-ul-Haq–era gender logics in two ways. First, his policies invited strenuous resistance from middle-class and elite women who poured into the public sphere to protest his reforms (Toor 2014). Second, the general and his allies responded to this protest by relying for support on women members of the Jamaat-i-Islami, a religious political party that supported Zia-ul-Haq. By appearing in public in support of Zia-ul-Haq's Islamization project, these veiled women of the Jamaat signaled the acceptability of certain kinds of public appearance—veiled and in support of a worthy cause (Shaheed and Mumtaz 1990; Jamal 2013).

The mobility of middle-class women was amplified also by the state's acceptance of neoliberal policies. The aid money the state has relied on since Zia-ul-Haq's period is administered by institutions like the IMF and World Bank,[4] which not only make deregulation a condition for the receipt of aid but also include gender mainstreaming requirements to their reform packages (Jamal 2013). Such gender mainstreaming policies have been beneficial for some classes of women, such as elite women, who have filled the quotas and women's seats created by these policies in sectors like the legislature and the government administration.

The policies associated with these loans have also benefited elite and middle-class women in another way. The deregulation policies required by neoliberal loans have led to an expansion of the private sector and the creation of new and better job opportunities for elite and middle-class women. Elite and middle-class women have become teachers in private schools and doctors in private hospitals and have taken up positions in the privatized banking sector, the telecom sector, and private media enterprises, to name but a few. These private-sector work contexts are relatively safe for women. They adhere to corporate policies that are somewhat effective in protecting women from harassment.

In addition to jobs, middle-class and elite women have also benefited from privatization through their access to car financing from private banks. Cars can keep elite and middle-class women somewhat safe from harassment. When they drive, women do not have to walk to bus stops or wait on sidewalks for buses or other public transport. They also do not have to navigate the crowds on Karachi's busy thoroughfares, where they may be forced to confront those who view women's presence in public space as offensive. Cars also provide women with the ability to move at speed across vast expanses of space in relative privacy and safety. Such luxuries are not available to working-class women, like my participants, who are compelled to walk or take the bus in order to get to work. For many of these women, even a rickshaw is often too expensive.

The slogan of the chador and char divari advanced by Zia-ul-Haq's regime, therefore, did not just shape women's experiences in urban, public spaces, but it also universalized a set of ideals that is simply not achievable by all women. In rural areas, for instance, poor women cannot afford to remain sequestered in their homes. They are forced by their poverty and lack of resources to walk long distances for water and fuel and to work for hours in the fields, where neither four walls nor ceilings are available to ensure their privacy.

The chador and char divari ideal is also often not achievable for women from working-class families. Many of the men these women used to rely on for financial support have found their financial capacities severely eroded due to the neoliberal economic policies that the Islamizing state brought into being. Some of these men used to work in public-sector jobs, which have been transformed through neoliberal policies of privatization. Unlike government jobs, private-sector work provides neither job security nor the protection of unions. Even if they manage to hold on to their jobs after their employment contexts have become privatized, private-sector workers rarely enjoy the pensions, the health care plans, or the other benefits that state jobs offer. Worse, privatization did not just move jobs from the public to the private sector; in many cases, it eradicated jobs altogether.

As working-class men lost their access to secure and stable work, the women who relied on their incomes were compelled to find work in their stead. Thus, working-class women were forced to enter the workforce even as women's work and their occupation of public space were consistently and officially stigmatized. Some such women opted to work out of their homes (e.g., taking up stitching, running beauty services or tutoring neighborhood children); others sought work in gender-segregated contexts (e.g., teaching at all-girls schools, working in gender segregated garment factories) and in workplaces that were located near women's homes. But some working-class women, like my participants, were induced by financial difficulties to work in settings that did not provide such gendered conveniences. They took on work that required them to travel greater distances from home and that limited their capacity to avoid interacting with men. Many of them were unable to enjoy either the protection of cars or the opportunity to work in clean, well-organized office spaces that limit women's interaction with the public and protect them from having to field unwanted advances and encroachments upon their dignity. For these women, going out to work meant walking on public roads and traveling in public buses. For my participants, it also meant interacting with a public that often views women's presence in public spaces with hostility. And according to these women, the chador offered scant protection against the stigmas associated with women's presence in public space.

When they wait at bus stops, working-class women's veils do not protect them from the propositions of men. Even in their veils, lady health workers experience various kinds of sexual harassment in the course of their polio vaccination work. "Sometimes we ring the bell, and some man comes out, he makes kissing sounds, and he says, 'What's that you're serving? I'll take it, beautiful!'" Farzana says. Similarly, policewomen say that their veils provide only a limited kind of protection. "When I went to the main office yesterday, I was fully covered, I was wearing a *burkah*," Rashida, a police officer, told me in tears. "There was a man there, in uniform, and he was calling out to me, 'Baby, come here baby.' I don't know what he wanted, but I was feeling scared. He kept saying, 'Come on, baby,' and then my husband [also a police officer] suddenly appeared on the scene and he flew into a rage, he shouted at the man, 'That is my wife, you bastard!' I'm still not sure what exactly was happening, but my husband was very angry."

Working-class women who do not wear chadors or veils are subjected to much more severe forms of harassment. Airline attendants, who are not able to wear chadors while at work (they are required to wear elegant uniforms and makeup) are seen as sexually compromised women. "When people come to know that I am an air hostess," Bee said, "they don't want me to marry into their family, they say, 'Marry an air hostess? No!'" Whether they adopt a *chador* or not, working class women who have been compelled by financial constraints to venture out of the *char divar* are frequently confronted by stigmatizing encounters, including sexual harassment from strangers and colleagues, as well as rejection by the families of prospective grooms.

## THEORETICAL IMPLICATIONS

Working-class frontline contexts of work are embedded in a context rife with sexual tensions arising from Pakistan's neoliberal and Islamizing projects and the residues of gendered stigma left over from its colonial past. All of these global processes have imbued public space, where frontline work takes place, with various raced, classed, and gendered meanings that are particularly consequential for working-class women. Together, colonialism and neoliberalism have combined with the imperatives of security and religious identity to code public space as sexually threatening for women. The notion of sexual threat not only shapes dilemmas around women's individual sexual identities and reputations but also molds the contours of the community's broader social identity and collective dignity. Women's sexuality operated as an index during colonial times, when writers and philosophers suggested that the status of women was a gauge that reflected a particular society's developmental status. Native women's supposed propensity for prostitution, therefore, was seen in the colonial period, as an indicator of native backwardness and the low evolutionary status of indigenous communities. Women's sexual deviance, as exemplified by their supposed sexual excesses and lack of control, helped to justify colonial rule. The colonial state worked to discipline and control women's sexuality through the imposition of laws and policies, like those surrounding the registration and medical examination of prostitutes (Mitra 2020).

During the Zia-ul-Haq period, the regulation and protection of women's sexuality came to signify religious nationality. Unlike morally corrupt westernized women, decent Pakistani women abided by the conventions of the *chador aur char divar*. The imposition of these conventions produced paradoxical consequences for elite and middle-class women, providing them with more opportunities for participation in public life. For working-class women, however, these processes structured a dignity dilemma. Neoliberal policies pushed working-class women into the workforce at the same time that securitization and Islamization interacted with prior colonial cultural stereotypes to stigmatize their occupation of these new public roles.

In this chapter I have described how the stigma matrix has formed at the macro level through the interplay of persisting global forces. Global processes like colonialism, neoliberalism, securitization, and Islamization have helped form the larger contours of the matrix over a long period. In the eighteenth and nineteenth centuries, colonialism helped produce racialized stereotypes that worked not only to justify colonial rule but also to reify gendered institutions, like purdah, and infuse public space with sexual stigmas. In the twentieth and twenty-first centuries, contemporary global processes reinforced some of these stigmas by generating new pressures for institutions like purdah and the family. In the next chapter, I describe how the matrix is organized at the meso level of organizations.

Once they are drawn by economic pressures into a public sphere infused with sexual stigmas, women must navigate the specific and varied arrangements of their workplaces, where global agendas and logics are encoded into organizational structures and resources. They must train to become proficient in globalized routines and practices, such as basic training in the police academy, community health practices in vaccination, and aircraft safety routines in the airline. They must carry out globalized missions, like polio eradication and counterterrorism, even as they cope with resource poverty and the negative public perceptions of their occupations. Finally, they must navigate the ways their workplaces are shaped by and in turn work to reshape the structures of gender and class, whether through the provision of generous salaries and allowances or through the requirement of dirty and exhausting physical labor. In the next chapter, I describe how each of the contexts of frontline work examined in this book frame the stigmas generated by globalization as well as women's responses to these stigmas.

## 2 | THE MESO LEVEL OF THE STIGMA MATRIX: THE CONTEXTS OF STIGMA IN FRONTLINE WORK

**IN KARACHI'S EAST DISTRICT, I** am sitting in lady health worker Farah's two-room home. The walls are unplastered brick; the floor is untiled cement. Farah rents the upstairs portion of a tiny house, which is in a lane too narrow for cars to pass through. To get to her home I had to hop over puddles of sewage and edge around the neighbor's goat, which, tethered to the doorpost, was butting passersby. As I walked up to Farah's doorstep, the goat coiled its tether around my knees, causing me to stumble. Farah, watching from the doorway, let out an embarrassed titter. Then she called out to her husband to come and guard my car, which I had parked down the block, just beyond Farah's too-narrow lane. 'This is not a safe neighborhood. He has nothing to do anyway,' she said of her husband. 'He got laid off from work last year and hasn't been able to find another job.'

Over a cup of tea that she has cooked on a hob, Farah describes the stigma she feels in connection with her work. 'This is a poor neighborhood,' she says. She and her husband grew up in better parts of the city. But even though he is trained as a pharmacist, her husband, Kamal, has not been able to find work, and the couple's resultant poverty has forced them to move to this less attractive location. 'This is a difficult community to serve,' she says. 'The people here are mostly illiterate and terribly poor.' A case of polio was recently detected here, a finding that caused the ire of the entire health department to come down on Farah's shoulders. Farah goes house-to-house teaching mostly illiterate women—including migrants from the Iran-Pakistan border and refugees from Afghanistan—about vaccination and birth control. She works for the provincial government, and her job is dangerous. 'Almost everyone in this neighborhood has a stockpile of arsenal secreted in his house,' she says, 'and they are very suspicious of the government.' Farah's clients subscribe to the view that the polio vaccination campaign represents a western plot to sterilize Muslim children and are therefore hostile to her vaccination efforts. People in Farah's own extended family look down on her work, which involves entering strangers' homes, where 'they think anything can happen.' Two LHWs in the Pakistani city of Gujarat were recently gang-raped at a Basic Heath Unit (a district-level primary health care facility), Farah tells me. Several LHWs across the country have been killed in terrorist attacks. But Farah's fury today is aimed primarily at her male bosses. 'The doctors!' she fumes. 'They think we are nothing, less than nothing. They can't bring themselves to even sit next to us,' she complains. 'If we are at a meeting with them, like at a training session or something, they say, "Are we supposed to sit with these two-*paisa* [penny] LHWs?"' she says, visibly angry. 'But do you know what one doctor said to my supervisor after the last meeting?' she asks. "He said, "Aaaaaaah, your women, are they all lame and saggy? Or do you have some ripe and fresh pieces also?" As if the supervisor were his pimp, and just because we have to come out of the home for work, we belong to him, like his *baap ka maal* [father's property]!'

Farah's speech illuminates how meso-level dimensions of the stigma matrix, i.e., the arrangements surrounding frontline work, shape women's perceptions and feelings around the stigma of their jobs. Farah's extended family looks down on her for entering strangers' homes, "where anything can happen." She connects this "anything" with the sexual assault of health workers in Gujrat, indicating that the "anything" is connected with sexual danger. She says that the doctors, her bosses, look down on health workers, seeing them as untouchable because of their lowly "two-paisa" financial status, yet, since these women have come out of the home to work, she thinks the doctors simultaneously consider them as sexual objects, available for their bosses' gratification. Her description of the stigmas she experiences because of her work links structures of class and gender with the sexual dangers that certain kinds of space (unsecured, lacking privacy) present for women. Her work is stigmatizing because she is poor, lives in a poor neighborhood, works with poor people, and does work that puts her in sexual danger not only from her clients but also from her bosses.[1] Her experiences, and those of other frontline women, are shaped by the ways that their work is organized at the intermediate level of institutional arrangements.

In this chapter, I examine the meso level of the stigma matrix. At this level, each of the field sites examined in this book is differently positioned in relation to global processes, and each therefore presents a unique configuration of globalization, gender, and stigma. In each site, globalization intersects with local hierarchies to produce a distinct "landscape of meaning" and feeling around women, work, and honor (Reed 2011). In each site, the elements of purdah, gender, and globalization give rise to different cultural expressions. In this chapter, I introduce readers to each of the field sites investigated in this book and provide an overview of the objective (i.e., material) and subjective (i.e., cultural) structures that organize them. Table 1 provides a snapshot of each of the sites that the participants in this book inhabit.

**TABLE 1.** The contexts of frontline women's work

| Occupation | Gender composition | Cultural coding of occupation by gender | Hierarchy | Image in larger culture |
|---|---|---|---|---|
| Police force | Male-dominated | Seen as masculine and brutal | Leadership is mostly men | The occupation is seen as corrupt, venal and brutal |
| Lady health workers | Exclusively women | Seen as feminine and maternal | LHWs report to doctors and bureaucrats (mostly men) and Aid agency officials (mixed) | The work is seen as not real work but as *khidmat-e-khalq* (service to humanity). |
| Airline attendants | Mixed | Seen as feminine and hospitable | Some important structures, like the union are male-dominated | PIA is seen as a symbol of nationality and more recently, a decayed institution |

### POLICEWOMEN AND THE AESTHETICS OF QUALITY AND CHARACTER

The Midcity women's *thana* (police station) is located on the second floor of Heerabad, a sprawling, dusty, de facto male police station that is something of a landmark in this affluent, sleepy, old part of Karachi city.[2] Heerabad station is located among large bungalows circled by high boundary walls, topped with thick, pink bougainvillea, and festooned with creepers that run all the way to the ground. I drove to Heerabad station a little after noon. I had been on the phone with Chanda, who managed the women's thana inside Heerabad, all morning. She had first instructed me to come at 10 a.m. But then she kept calling me and putting me off, saying that none of the "girls" had shown up yet and she didn't want to waste my time. Finally, at noon, she told me she herself was on the way, so I should set out now too.

I lived quite a distance away, so I made haste. I parked on the street outside Heerabad station and darted in as quickly as I could. The place seemed deserted. I ascended the front steps and walked into a wide, dusty entrance hall. On the right, a number of doors opened onto rooms. On the left, a wide staircase wound its way up. Chanda had told me on the phone that the women's thana was on the second floor. I didn't see anyone around, so I went up the stairs and soon got lost. The hall curved and looped back to the staircase. I went all around the looping second floor looking for the women's station but couldn't find it.

In Pakistan, the term "second floor" typically leaves out the ground floor and therefore is what Americans would call the third floor. Maybe Chanda had meant the third floor, I thought, so after I had gone all the way around the circular hallway twice, I decided to go up one more level and see if the women's station was on that higher floor. It was not there. Instead, I found myself in another looping hallway, bordered by a line of rooms occupied by an inordinate number of men. In one of the rooms, the men were lying on string beds. Most were bare-chested, but a few were wearing vests. A complex of clotheslines had been rigged up above them, draped with uniforms. I began to feel alarmed by the emphatic masculinity of this space. I rushed back around the stairs, thinking, No way, the women's station can't possibly have been set up in the midst of the male sleeping quarters. I went down the stairs one level and went around the hallway again. Still no sign of the women's thana. I called Chanda's phone. No answer. Finally, I went down to the ground floor and looked around for someone I could ask for directions. No one was around. I was standing there trying to figure out what to do when a burly-looking man with an unkempt beard and messy hair suddenly appeared, saying, 'Yes, madam. What do you want?' I told him I was looking for the women's station. He looked uncertain. 'No one is there right now,' he said. I explained that I had an appointment with Chanda. After some argument, he finally agreed to show me the way.

We went back up one level and arrived at a door located at the curve of the hallway and marked with an easily overlooked sign stating "Women's Station." The door was locked. I told the man I would wait outside it. The hallway outside the door was full of garbage. Discarded polythene bags and empty potato chip packages lay in a heap on the floor among scattered cigarette butts. A board on the wall said something about USAID. I took a photograph on my phone, but the man, my guide, asked me to delete it.

Chanda arrived a few minutes later. She said she had gotten stuck in traffic. She unlocked the door, and we entered. Chanda's desk occupied the center of the mid-sized room. In the corner, another desk had been set up for Chanda's staff, but nobody had turned up yet. 'This is a small station,' Chanda told me. 'Technically, we have a modest staff. Around nine people are assigned to work here,' she said, listing them: 'One inspector, two sub-inspectors, and three LPCs [lady police constables].' She looked around the room and shrugged her shoulders. 'But only three people come for duty these days. The rest are on medical leave,' she said. 'One is just *ghair haazir* [absent without explanation],' she added. 'There's one inspector, she comes and sits for an hour or two and then leaves.'

According to Chanda, 'It's difficult to get the ladies to come to work.' She said she can't really blame them. There's no washroom here for the ladies. No drinking water. Also, the location of the station puts people off. It's situated too far from the bus stop, so it's hard for the girls to make it here. They have to walk, and they don't like doing that, especially after dark. Because of all these disadvantages, Chanda said, 'If I need them to come into work, I have to offer them a ride. Sometimes I have to pay them a tip out of my own pocket. It's very humiliating for me.' I asked her if the station was able to help women citizens much and she said, 'There's not much we can do. We don't have much in the way of resources. We have no lockup for ladies, for instance. We have no investigative officers, that's the biggest problem. If we need to register an FIR [first information report], we have to take the complainant to another women's station.'

Once I turned on my recorder, Chanda became increasingly heated. "Much of what you see here," she said, gesturing to her desk and to the computer that stood on it, "is not from the government. This is all USAID. We are running thanks to their kindness. This *thana* is functional because of their *mehrbani* [beneficence]. They have done us a favor," she said bitterly, "so things are running." Her gratitude to USAID, Chanda said, had motivated her to speak with me. 'You have come from the U.S.,' she said, 'your research is important, I owe it to speak to you.' Again, she started enumerating the materials she had received from USAID. "A lot of the stuff they gave," she said, "it got stolen and redistributed here and there. Even my car, USAID donated that, and even that, they [her male colleagues] are always after me to give up the car that I got, so how am I supposed to come and go?" she asked. "On a donkey cart?" I said that I had seen similar appropriations occur in the public health sector. "Yes," she replied, "this mentality is everywhere. Women are nothing, they give us nothing, so I'd say, the biggest frustration for me is that we don't have a proper place where we can function."

Chanda's speech reminded me of a conversation I had had with Firoza, a high-ranking woman police officer I met in her home. Like Chanda, Firoza also expressed bitterness about the status of women in the police force. The women in her cohort, she said, had to go to court to secure the promotions their seniority entitled them to. "There was a lot of discrimination, the height of discrimination, that our names would never come on the promotion list. They just sidelined us, left us to rot in the corner." When Firoza and her colleagues asked why they weren't getting promoted, they were told to go seek justice in court. The court decided in the women's favor. "If the court had not done that," Firoza said, "it wouldn't have happened." I found this surprising and said so. I said, "It's just not what one would expect, journalists and all the senior policemen I have met have been crowing to me about the progressiveness of the police force. They've been saying, look at the women superintendents we have inducted. Look at Superintendent Sohai Talpur."

"They [the police leadership] promote one, and then they make a huge fanfare out if it." Firoza replied. "They go around saying, 'Look, we have a lady SP!'" But Firoza was cynical about their motives. "They just do it for funds," she said. "They like to show western agencies their gender progressiveness, they like to display us, women police, in order to get funds." "What kinds of funds?" I asked. "Like recently, with the Germans," Firoza said, "the higher-ups put on a number of seminars. I wish I'd pulled the photos out to show you. Maybe next time, remind me. I'll show you," she said, looking agitated. "There were these really big seminars, here in Karachi and then in Islamabad also. In the end they managed to get some money out of them to build a day care center. They made one in Islamabad." "Well, that sounds useful," I said. "It's just eyewash," Firoza replied. "Then, another time, someone, some visitor came from America, immediately they gathered all the ladies from all over the city, just so they could display us to him, and they warned us strictly, 'Don't you dare say anything in front of him about promotions!'" Thus, in Firoza's view, women police were deployed like tokens by senior officers, who would display the women to foreign visitors and global agencies in an effort to showcase the force's success with gender-mainstreaming and, by doing so, aquire funds for further "improvements."

Back at the Hirabad thana, Chanda and I were drinking tea when her subordinate, Constable Adiba, finally entered. She too complained about the lack of facilities for women. "I joined the police force," she said, "because I liked their uniforms. They were very good looking, I thought." I asked her where she had seen women in uniform and she said, "Actually, there was a TV drama, *Pas-e-Aaina* [*Behind the Mirror*]. It had Rubina Ashraf [a well-known Pakistani actress] in it. She played an inspector. I used to watch it when I was small, and it made me very interested in the police." "What did you like about it?" I asked. "It all looked good. Rubina looked so good in her uniform," she said. "She had a kind of *bharam* [swagger]. I liked that. I thought it [police work] would be like that. Power! But it wasn't." "No?" I asked. "Where do we have power?" she said sarcastically. "Rubina conducted raids. She made a difference. It looked good that a lady is viewed with so much respect. Wherever she went, she was treated with respect, and she helped people. We can't help anyone. We don't have any power like that. In fact, if you find a woman who is able to shut down bad spots, like drug spots or anything like that, you can change my name," she said.³

The reality of the police force, Adiba said, had "left many women broken-hearted." Women who join the force soon come to find out that "they won't get the fruit of their labor. They get no return on their hard work." Indeed, according to Adiba, those who toiled hard at work, did so because they had no way to get out of it: "They're the ones who have no source [influential person to call upon for a favor], so they can't get out of it, they can't go *ghair haazir* [absent without explanation] or have themselves transferred to a post that allows them to stay home." The only other set of people who managed to get out of the drudgery that people like herself were forced to endure, according to Adiba, were those who could rely on their appearance, "those who, what can you say, their dress etc. That too has an impact." "How do you mean?" I asked her. "When someone looks good," she said, "the officers take that as a sign of quality. They don't look deeper. They just say, 'She looks good, so she must be good, and they cut her slack as a consequence.'"

Chanda wasn't alone in suggesting that appearance was taken as a signal of quality. Mussarat, a constable employed at another women's station, also emphasized the importance of appearance. "If you look good," she said, "people treat you well. You also feel good, you feel fresh, you feel motivated, you feel like a human." I had first met Mussarat at a women's station, which was located a twenty-minute rickshaw ride away from Chanda's Midcity station. I later followed Mussarat to the police training academy, where she was sent for a promotion course. The training academy was located deep in the heart of an industrial zone. To get to it, Mussarat had to take two different buses. Her training at the academy included two long drill sessions, which took place in an open field under the harsh sun. Unlike the women trainees, the academy provided me with an air-conditioned room with attached bathroom for my research. Whenever she heard I had come to the academy for my interviews, Mussarat would find a way to get out of training and come hang out with me. She would come into the office looking sunburned and disheveled, perspiring and panting. She would say hello and head straight for the washroom with a small toiletries bag in her hand.

First, she would wash her face thoroughly with a Ponds face wash that she carried with her. Then, she would rub her face with a heavy coat of Fair and Lovely, a thick whitening cream that is sold in the Pakistani market; several policewomen told me that it also works as sunscreen. Then Mussarat would pull out a small tin of talcum powder from her toiletry bag and she would apply this on top of the Fair and Lovely. In a final step, she would spray a deodorant all over her uniform.

Mussarat's routine was quite popular with other women too. Shiza, a constable undergoing training at the academy, advised me also to follow this regimen. "The sun, Fauzia," she said to me, "if you come here for the next two weeks, right now you are fair, but your color also will become wheatish," she said, using the local word used to describe a brown complexion. "They just make you stand in the sun for hours," she went on. "What do they care that the sunlight is hitting you, burning you for an hour and a quarter. The boys also keep standing, and we keep standing too." Shiza didn't just worry about the damage that prolonged exposure to sunlight would have on her complexion. She was also distressed by the perspiration and the odor the heat brought about. "This uniform," she said. "We have to wear it all day, this hot cloth in this hot weather. I have to wear it from 5:30 or 6:00 in the morning, all the way until 5:00 or 6:00 in the evening. I only have two uniforms, so I wear the same one for two days running, and then every other day I change my uniform and I wash it, and the strangest feelings come, Fauzia, when you take off the dank uniform and bathe. But the water here is salty, and it is hard on my hair."

Reema, a constable who worked at the same station as Mussarat and who had started at the training academy at the same time also followed the facewash/sunscreen/talcum powder regimen. "When I first came here [to the training academy]," she told me. "I didn't use to put on any makeup." But then, she said, the training took a toll on her looks. "Then these patches began to show up on my face," she said, "*jalay, jalay* [burned black] all over my face." The scars were related to the rigors of training in a dusty field under the harsh sun. "And on top of that, I developed an eye infection. My lids weren't opening, my eyes were red. Everyone told me, 'Oh, Allah! You should rest,'" she told me. "I got so scared, I went to a skin specialist, 'Ya Allah! What has happened?' I have become very ugly." The skin specialist told her to wear sunblock and "wear a paste, like you have to make a thick layer of it, because the sunblock alone does no good here. Look at my face, how dark I have become," she said.

In Reema's view, the tanned appearance of her skin made her look "ugly." "So I was telling my mother," she said, "that people say that police officers are very ugly, but I think I know now how they will turn me completely into a *bhoot* [monster], it will be through drill at the academy."

Reema's concern about her complexion in part had class overtones. Since elite women are able to manage their exposure to the sun and often also possess the time and the resources necessary to maintain an untanned and unblemished appearance, fair skin in this postcolonial context is read as a signifier of class status. The connection between class and appearance was driven home to me by Shifa, a colleague of Reema's. "The look and the comportment tell you about a person's background," she said. To illustrate, she presented the example of her own cohort: "Our whole attitude is different," she said. "Unlike the old police" who did not need much education in order to get inducted into the force, Shifa said, "we look good because we are a bit different, our attitude is a bit different. Now, my batchmates, we are all people with MAs, MPhils, PhDs, even MBAs. So, our style of speaking, our attitude is good, naturally, because our family background is different. We don't shout, we don't use abusive language, we don't use impolite pronouns, we speak politely." Thus, looking good was not just about looking fair-skinned and "fresh" (or without perspiration) but also about speaking "nicely and with elegance." A person who had all these qualities was someone with good "ikhlaq" (conduct), someone you would want to associate with. As Shifa put it, "Obviously every woman would like that, you know, for another person to behave in a respectful manner—the tone they use, the conduct they display—such a person is someone you'd be willing to be friends with, you'd say, her family background is good. She is a good girl or good lady. Then she deserves a good behavior, good treatment in return because she is worthy of respect."

The aesthetics of good conduct and good family background involved not only fairness, freshness, and polite speech but also veiling. Like the makeup and the polite speech, veiling underlines women's modesty as well as their class background. Several women, including Chanda and Adiba, connected veiling with quality. 'There are some women here,' Chanda complained, 'who ruin things for everyone. They roam around unveiled, they chat, joke, and flirt with the men, and they spread negative ideas about the police station as a place of moral corruption.'

The concern with veiling complicated women's abilities to carry out their training and their jobs. For instance, Samina, a young trainee who preferred to be called Sam, complained that police work sometimes made it difficult to maintain dignity via classed delicacy. "The current batch is majority men," she said. "We are only five girls. And sometimes it happens that the other women won't show up. I am alone, or there is only one other girl." At such times, she said, "I make up an excuse and get out of the drill." "What kind of excuse do you make?" I asked her. "I just tell the instructor I have a ladies' problem and can't exercise; they get embarrassed and let me sit on the sideline. But I feel that if there's only men around, then why should I make a spectacle of myself, and after all, I am a lady, I'm from a good background, so why should I not remind them of that?"

Since women's stations were underresourced and their uniforms did not give them the capacity to help people, shut down crime spots, conduct raids, investigate crime, or register complaints, aesthetics regrettably became a paramount metric of quality and competence for women in the police. Having fair skin and hair that was not coarse, speaking politely, veiling, and refraining from exhausting exercise were all signs of a person's good background, her competence, and her character. If a person was not able to cultivate the right kind of appearance, a modest look, and an elegant style of speech, then, women said, such a person was undeserving of respect. In chapter 3, I describe how these efforts played out in the Pakistani police context.

## LADY HEALTH WORKERS: WARRIORS NOT VOLUNTEERS

In Shamsheer, the name I give to a working-class district located in the North of Karachi, I was riding in a taxi with Humera, a lady health worker who has been serving her community for more than a decade. 'Do you know Bill Gates?' she asked me suddenly. The taxi was rattling loudly, and I didn't quite hear her.

'Who?' I asked.

'Bill Gates. He makes computers,' she said. Surprised to hear Humera roll out the name of a tech mogul, I said, 'I know who he is. I mean, I don't know him personally.'

'He has billions of dollars,' she said, 'Aman Foundation is his.' I hadn't known this and told her so. 'There's a lot of money in this sector,' she said. 'It's a billion-dollar game, health, and it all plays out on our backs.'

'Right,' I said.

'Because, like, look at you,' she said. 'Can you roam around Shamsheer without me?' she asked.

'No, I couldn't,' I said. 'I am totally reliant on your generosity.'

'Right,' she said. 'I took you to see a health house, [a portion of an LHW's house set aside for community health services] I took you to meet clients and to visit health workers, I showed you the ins and outs of the work. Without me, how would you get access?'

'Right,' I said.

She leaned forward and added, 'Would you go and knock randomly on people's doors?'

'I wouldn't be able to do that,' I said.

'They would not open the door to you if you tried,' she said. 'They wouldn't be willing to talk to you, even though *you*,' pointing at me, 'actually speak Urdu and are from this city, but even then, you are educated, your mannerisms, your accent, your clothes are strange for them,' she said, alluding to my middle-class traits. 'They [working-class and poor women] would be frightened of you, they would be too nervous to speak, they would tell you nothing if you hadn't met them through me.' She pretended to cower in her seat, '"Yes, ma'am, no ma'am, it's all fine, ma'am,"' she said in a meek voice, acting out the way she felt clients would respond to me if I were to approach them on my own. 'Even that much they wouldn't say,' she said. 'If you tried speaking to them on your own,' she continued, 'you wouldn't know what tone to use or what words to use. You are like us, and you are Pakistani, but you still would seem alien to a woman who does not think of leaving her home or interacting with outsiders.'

'That is all true,' I acknowledged.

'So, you need me to act like a bridge for you,' Humera said. 'When I knock on the door, she [the client] opens it because I live in her community, and she knows me."

'Right,' I said.

'And even if she doesn't know me,' Humera said, 'I dress like her, I speak like her, she can open up to me.'

'Right,' I said.

'This is why I always say, LHWs are the backbone of the healthcare system in Pakistan,' she said. 'Just like the backbone travels down the body connecting the head with the tail, we are like a backbone.'

The taxi rattled on, jostling us in our seats. We were driving through a warren of alleys. Carts selling vegetables and fish made the rough lanes even narrower. Roughly constructed little houses framed the alley, their metal gates hanging open to reveal little children playing the doorway. 'Take a left here, brother,' Humera said to the taxi driver, and we turned into an alley.

'These foreigners, these Amans and these UNs,' she said, 'can't get anywhere without us.' She leaned forward and peered out of the taxi. 'Take a right and stop by the banana cart,' she told the driver. 'Even now, they are calling me,' she said pointing to her phone, 'asking me, "Can you organize a field-visit,"' she said. 'If they tried to come here on their own, they'd get lost in two minutes, they wouldn't know left from right, up from down. They couldn't survive without us, because we are the *grassroots*, you see,' she said, surprising me with her use of the English word.

As we waited in the taxi, Mehr, another LHW, came out of her house and got in with us. 'I was telling Fauzia about Aman,' Humera told her.

'Aman, yes,' Mehr said.

'How do you like working with them?' I asked her.

'It's fine,' she said. 'They reimburse us for travel and stuff,' she added. 'But they have their own *agenda*,' she said, using the English word.

'Everyone has their own *agenda*,' Humera said.

'But they are better than the UN ones, I think,' Mehr said.

'The UN ones will drink your blood,' Humera agreed.

'There's a lot of corruption with the UN,' Mehr said.

'You have heard the stories, in the meeting,' Humera said to me.

'We work like dogs, and we get a tiny amount of money,' Mehr said. 'Meanwhile, the big people [the bosses] all these *ohd-e-daar* [officeholders], they draw huge salaries, and they also skim the funds set aside for photocopies and things.'

'Right,' Humera agreed. 'They get lakhs and lakhs.' One lakh is equal to a hundred thousand rupees, which was roughly a thousand dollars at the time of my fieldwork.

'And many of them have never even seen the field. They just come to the edge of the field. They don't dare to come in. They don't want to get dirty.'

'But when it comes to us,' Mehr said, 'they will tell us to go eat bullets even. For instance, if there will be a terrorist threat, workers will be getting killed, the officeholders will still send us out. They will say, 'No matter the cost, we want polio finished.'''

'And then they treat us like dirt,' Humera added, 'like we are nothing, less than nothing.'

Unlike policewomen who only occasionally come into contact with actors and agencies from the Global North, lady health workers (LHWs) interact with global actors and agencies regularly and in sustained ways. Their work brings them into contact with the Global Polio Eradication Initiative (GPEI), the Aman Foundation (Bill Gates's foundation in Pakistan), and the United Nations. This contact is definitive for health workers; foreign agencies set their targets, outline the modalities and practices health workers should use (e.g., what kinds of birth control they should promote), and monitor their work. Although LHWs draw their salaries from the government of Pakistan, they are also given modest stipends for the additional work they do for the polio campaign or for the Aman Foundation. Yet the sustained contact and the modest renumeration they receive from these agencies only work to aggravate the humiliations LHWs say they are forced to endure at work.

Humera and Mehr's complaints about their poor treatment by global agencies were echoed by many of the women with whom I spoke. In interview after interview, health workers complained that they were treated poorly by local and global actors alike. They said that their work, skills, and sacrifices were erased from discussion and their labors denigrated and devalued. Again and again, they said, 'we are treated as if we are nothing, as if we are equal in value to a slipper or a shoe.'

In her 2015 article, Svea Closser, an anthropologist who studied the polio campaign in Pakistan, understands the devaluation of health workers' labor and the occlusion of their perspectives as an expression of the construction of the "moral economy" of the global health sector (Closser 2015). The "moral economy," a concept in wide use in anthropological writings, refers to what we may think of as a circuit made up of morally charged "coins" (concerns, sentiments, emotions, values, norms, and obligations) that are constructed and circulated in connection with various social issues (e.g., security, violence, immigration) and that work to channel peoples' perspectives and their action about certain issues in particular ways.

When it comes to polio, Closser argues, the moral economy of the eradication campaign is designed to encourage donors to focus on the at-risk child, an almost sacred symbol that reshapes the meaning of the vaccination drive and of the people who are involved in administering vaccines. In a semantic field dominated by the sacralized image of the at-risk child, vaccinators, like LHWs, come to be represented not as workers but as heroes— selfless and extremely moral volunteers who are inspirational models of commitment to children. When situated alongside the "omnipresent" figure of the innocent and powerless child in need of rescue, the labor of the health worker is simultaneously elevated and obscured, esteemed and devalued. The rewards of heroism are moral, not material. Indeed, the low pay makes the work even more heroic, even more inspirational. The workers' poverty, their hunger, their exhaustion, their low pay, their working conditions, their lack of benefits, and the hardships they face in the course of their labor are all obscured by a discourse that prioritizes only one mission—child survival via vaccination.

Health workers read the symbols circulating in the global moral economy a bit differently. From their perspective, the sacralized image of the child is polluted by ideas about race, class, and gender. Rehana, for instance, claimed in an interview with me that global agencies only get "hyper" (that is, take vigorous action), when polio arrives at their own doorstep and begins to threaten White children. I asked her why she thinks this, and she replied, "The [polio] drive became more frantic after polio was discovered in America. A Pakistani-born American child visited Swat valley," she explained. "He was taken there for vacation and while he was there, he contracted polio." It was because of this case, Rehana said, that "the westerners have gone mad and make us do even more polio drives." The increased frequency of vaccination drives, she complained, "is very irritating for clients, so they scream at us, and it's also rough on our own children, who get ignored because we are forced by the workload to be out of the house all the time." Thus, from the health workers' perspective, the symbol of the child is fractured. LHWs don't envisage a universal child; they envisage several categories of children, all vying for attention. From their perspective, the global image of childhood refers to white children, whose protection is the true objective of global agencies. In defense of this white child, LHWs are pushed out of the home to protect brown-skinned Pakistani children while sacrificing their own children, who are left to fend for themselves while their mothers are out distributing the vaccine.

The fractured nature of the child symbol is also evident in Surraiya's claims. Western agents "don't care about Pakistani children," she asserted in an interview with me. "They only care about the disease." The only people who genuinely care about Pakistani children, according to Surraiya, are lady health workers, "more than their parents, we care," she said. "Their parents are trying to evade us and to get out of vaccinating their child, while we health workers, we say, 'Listen, we have seen the effects of this crippling disease, and once you have seen it with your own eyes, once you have seen a child who can no longer walk, your eyes will fill with tears and you will say, "I can't let this happen to anyone else."'"

It's not just the figure of the child that LHWs question, they also take issue with the construction of their work as heroism. Heroes are not paid in money, after all. "Every time we asked for a pay increase," Mehr complained to me, "we were told that this is not a job, it is *khidmat-i-khalq*" (service to creation, i.e., voluntary work). This framing of the work, Mehr said, has allowed the bosses to justify the LHW's low wages. "And they [the bosses] would say that that is why the payment is small. It is small because it is just a *wazifa* [a stipend]." But this claim, Mehr felt, was hypocritical, "Tell me this, how come our salary is a wazifa," she asked, "but yet, they [actors associated with the UN and GPEI] draw large salaries, drive around in air-conditioned cars, and sit in air-conditioned offices? I'll tell you why," she went on, "Because they speak English and write reports in English. Because they have degrees and wear pantsuits." Thus, Mehr rejected the moral explanations that her supervisors advanced to justify her low pay. LHWs' low compensation is actually a result not of the nature of the work, whether it is voluntary or not, but of classed attributes, such as fluency in English.

Instead of heroes, LHWs say they should be seen as warriors. The sacrifices LHWs are forced to embrace make them resemble soldiers, who are not only paid in cash and benefits for their service but are also honored by a grateful nation. "When conditions become too risky," Mona told me with evident pride, "everyone leaves the field—except for us. The UN employees, even the local doctors, all are withdrawn from the field," she continued, "and then, it is the lady health worker who is sent out into the maw of danger. She goes out with nothing but a prayer on her lips. We are the soldiers who go out to do battle. Many of us have been martyred in this cause. Do soldiers get paid?" she asked me. "Have you seen how the army celebrates its martyrs?"

While the moral economy constructed by the polio campaign makes the protection of children its primary and highest virtue, health workers make bravery the bigger and more important good. The value of health work resides, according to them, in the women's intrepid willingness to go where others cannot, in their ability to deliver a protection that others cannot provide. Since LHWs possess grassroots knowledge as well as a capacity to connect with the publics that local and global health agents seek to address, they are indispensable warriors. They cannot easily be replaced by local and global elites, who nevertheless draw bigger salaries. The value of health work, LHWs argue, should be compensated not in relation to the credentials of workers or their fluency in English, neither of which facilitates the work. Rather, compensation should be based on the arduous effort and the considerable risk the work demands.

Since they evaluate their work on the basis of emotions (fear) and relations (their ability to connect with clients), LHWs also resist their devaluation by bosses and other interlocutors on the strength of the same sentiments and relationships. In chapter 4, I describe LHW efforts to recuperate dignity and mitigate stigma in the health offices that superintend their work.

## GLOBAL BUTTERFLIES: AIR HOSTESSES AS ICONS AND VECTORS OF GLOBALIZATION

"Did you ever watch that drama, *Titliyaan* [Butterflies]?" airline attendant Shehnila asked me. She was referring to an Urdu-language drama serial focused on the social problems encountered by Pakistani airline attendants, which aired on a local television channel in the early 2000s. "That's how the society views us," Shehnila laughed. "They think we are butterflies, they call us *harjai* [fickle, flighty], right? They think we flit from flower to flower sampling the pollen. They think we don't have our feet on the ground."

While health workers think of themselves as a force that forms the backbone of the health system, connecting the policies and prescriptions crafted by transnational agencies with local subjects in Pakistan, and policewomen see themselves as global tokens, presented to global actors by local elites in exchange for global forms of aid, airline attendants view themselves as global butterflies, drifting from global location to global location, consuming the nectar of cosmopolitan experience and carrying the pollen of global ideas and interactions back to their home society.

The allegory of the butterfly does not only allude to the mobility and supposed flightiness of air hostesses; it also captures the aesthetic dimension of their situation. Air hostesses are not simply vectors of globalization, who like immigrants both produce and experience the interconnection of societies (Shams 2020); they are also global icons who embody their respective nation's place within the global comity of nations. Air hostesses don't just serve and protect passengers who use their aircrafts; they also embody Pakistan's struggles to resolve questions around the correct balance between tradition and modernity, the appropriate mix of local and global ideas and values appropriate to a Pakistani gendered identity. Their appearance—the uniforms they wear; the hairstyles, makeup, and mannerisms they affect—is thus a matter of official and collective deliberation, and their behavior overseas a matter of national importance. Media outlets carry articles on both sets of issues, the design of their uniforms as well as the national character airline attendants represent when they carry Pakistan overseas.

A 2015 blogpost remarks, for instance, "No matter how advanced society becomes and how much technology takes over, there is a pleasant sense of comfort about keeping up with traditions and customs. Pakistan's very first national flag carrier airline, Pakistan International Airlines understands this beautifully" (Rajput 2015). The post then goes on to name the various designers who have been involved since PIA's inception in crafting the image of its staff. This list of luminaries includes Pierre Cardin, who designed PIA's livery in 1966; Sir Hardy Amies, royal dress maker to Queen Elizabeth II; as well as prominent Pakistani designers Nomi Ansari and

Sania Maskatiya. The article then announces a catwalk event featuring sixteen contemporary designers and a display of uniforms designed to "capture modernity yet retain an aura of tradition."

Media coverage of airline attendants' indiscretions also raise issues of transnational representation and national reputation. A Pakistani digital news platform, for instance, described the various indiscretions committed by airline attendants abroad (shoplifting, illegal immigration, smuggling) as sources of international disgrace. "For quite some time, the national flag carrier [has been] in the news for all the wrong reasons," wrote the digital news outlet ProPakistani about the behavior of air hostesses abroad. "Once dubbed a jewel in the Asian airlines' crown, the PIA is struggling for last many years [sic] over its financial woes" (ProPakistani 2018). Similar sentiments were expressed also by airline women that I spoke with. PIA, they told me with apparent grief, was in the grip of a lamentable entropy.

In the good old days of the 1960s and 1970s, airline attendants claimed, PIA was a font of national pride. It was the "favorite airline of Jackie Kennedy," Rizwana, a senior air hostess who now worked primarily on the ground, told me. "In the old PIA, they used to pick classy employees, hired purely on the basis of merit," Shehnaz, another senior air hostess, said. "Back then, intelligence agents would actually come over to our neighborhoods to inquire about our background before we were inducted into PIA." But over time, airline attendants said, PIA had been ruined by political interference in the recruitment process and financial mismanagement.

Airline attendants were not alone in discussing this narrative about the tragic decay of PIA. Outside the field site too, journalists, friends, and other interlocutors would make sounds of regret when they heard that I was conducting fieldwork with PIA air hostesses. "Tsk, tsk," said one journalist. "It's a pity, it was a very fine institution in the '60s. It's a national scandal now." Such remarks point to the meaning that PIA holds for many Pakistanis. For many years, Pakistan International Airlines, the country's flag carrier, served as a kind of thermometer, a gauge that helped people get a reading on the state of the state. Public discussions around PIA track Pakistan's self-image over time.

Although it was invested with a great deal of national pride in the 1960s, today the airline is viewed as a national disgrace. Plagued by charges of corruption and incompetence, PIA, a mobile symbol of the Pakistani nation, has come to stand in for the various shortcomings of the Pakistani state. In this, it is like the Pakistani cricket team, another portable symbol of the state and a repository of the nation's dignity. Like sports teams, flag carrier airlines circulate outside a country's borders and therefore embody the nation's status and its identity in transnational contexts. Indeed, it is because the maintenance of a flag carrier continues to have such enormous symbolic value for national governments that many countries continue to maintain airlines, despite the nearly insurmountable costs associated with doing so (Thurlow and Aiello 2007).

Flag carriers serve nationality by fulfilling both signal and ordering functions. Flight routes chart friend and foe, admissibility and exclusion, while airline rules and rituals, such as those connected with airline attendant recruitment, ticketing, and boarding, organize citizenship in terms of global mobility. Such rules establish, for instance, who can and cannot travel, with what papers and under what material conditions. Rules surrounding airline attendant recruitment, similarly, organize gendered ideas surrounding nationality by stipulating, for instance, the height, weight, and personality benchmarks necessary for gaining entry into these symbolically charged occupations. Airline branding—the design of the livery, tailfin, and logo—can help objectify and commodify nationality, often with stratifying effects. For instance, the "Singapore Girl" branding of Singapore International Airlines, perhaps the most recognizable symbol of gendered nationality, constructs and mobilizes certain gender stereotypes for internal as well as external consumption (Hudson 2013). In brief, flag carriers perform the nation by enacting stereotypes and norms around gender that shore up claims of distinctiveness and cultural authenticity as well as trendiness and modernity. The cultural ideas they enact convey crucial information for both citizens and outsiders about the constituent elements of a nation's identity.

As portable symbols, flag carrier airlines don't just circulate symbols of nationality but for many postcolonial developing countries like Pakistan, national airlines like PIA also signify the nation's forward movement in time, its capacity for catching up with the technological advances of first world modernity. The national airline not only provides citizens with subsidized access to global locations, but it also has the potential to cement the nation's status as a well-resourced and globally mobile state.

The symbolic imperatives surrounding PIA and PIA's air hostesses lend an affectively loaded charge to the broadly circulating narratives of PIA's corruption and decay. Stigmas surrounding PIA crew are shaped not only by ideas about gendered decency but also by ideas about Pakistan's national trajectory, its connection with tradition and modernity, and its place in the global arena. Airline attendants' destigmatization efforts therefore partake of similar dichotomies. Their efforts to cleanse their identity and recuperate their dignity rest on dichotomous notions about the ways that tradition opposes modernity in the organization of gender and gendered social relationships. Their attempts to repair their reputations hinge on their ability to access symbols of cosmopolitan consumption, which they deploy to assert their break from a "socially backward" past and their adherence to a gender-progressive contemporary modernity. Relying on symbols like sophisticated makeup products and designer purses, however, they evoke a postfeminist form of cosmopolitanism that is unable to unsettle the gendered hierarchies that dominate their places of work. In chapter 5, I describe how airline women's cosmopolitanism undermines their agency at work.

**THEORETICAL IMPLICATIONS**

In this chapter I have described the various ways that frontline women experience globalization in each of their fields of work. Policewomen only occasionally come into contact with global actors and agencies. In the context of these sparse contacts, policewomen see themselves as tokens in relation to globalization. They assume that their induction into the police force is primarily symbolic, that they are recruited as symbols of the police force's gender progressiveness and deployed as tokens in exchange for transnational funds and resources.

Health workers, by contrast, interact with global actors and agencies in sustained and consequential ways. They experience this contact as exploitative. In their view, global agencies have their own agendas, which don't always intersect with the needs and requirements of the workers who implement them or the clients they serve. Rather than seeing LHWs as volunteers who selflessly sacrifice their lives at the altar of the child, LHWs insist, the state and its global allies should view them as warriors, deserving of recompense in the form of salary and honor.

Finally, airline attendants describe themselves, with some cynicism, as global butterflies. This self-description captures both the practical and the symbolic aspects of their connection with globalization. Like butterflies, airline attendants are mobile carriers or vectors of globalization. But in the local imagination, butterflies can be seen as frivolous, flighty, and fickle creatures. Airline attendants are denigrated by many Pakistanis for their striking appearance, but at the same time, the airline they serve is also invested with the hopes, aspirations, and disappointments of a nation still trying to resolve issues around its global status and its relationship with tradition vis-à-vis modernity. These postcolonial preoccupations with status, modernity, and tradition are intimately connected with ideas about gender and women's bodies, and they are reflected also in the women's destigmatization strategies.

Since each field site mediates globalization in distinct ways, each provides different resources for women's destigmatization efforts. Seeing themselves as tokens, policewomen invest a great deal of importance to appearance, and their efforts at destigmatization revolve around aesthetic issues. Health workers view themselves as warriors, a self-understanding that contrasts with the ideals and values circulated within the moral economy constructed by the Global Polio Eradication Initiative. According to health workers, the value of their work resides in the soldier-like sacrifices they make. In contrast with their global interlocutors, they interpret this suffering not through the notion of selfless volunteers but describe it via notions of jihad and martyrdom, idioms that provide actors with honor as well as the right to wages.

Finally, airline attendants describe themselves in relation to globalization as butterflies. In laying claim to this image, however, they reject local stereotypes about the supposed fickleness and shallowness associated with these decorative insects and instead emphasize the freedom and the nectars that butterflies obtain through their powers of flight. In each case women's perceptions about their place in the global arena is reflected in the strategies they use to contest their stigmatization at work. Together these field sites illustrate how local and global symbols and norms come together to shape both the stigmas and the destigmatization efforts of working-class women in the Global South.

## 3 | VEILED DELICACY: AGENTIC RESPONSES TO STIGMA IN THE PAKISTANI POLICE FORCE

AFTER COMPLETING ONLY SEVEN MONTHS in their vaunted posts, Huda and Sana, the maverick bosses of a women's police station in Karachi, Pakistan, were summarily dismissed from their authoritative positions and relegated to desk jobs. Their removal belied the widely held belief in the local field of policing that women's marginal status in the force could be explained by their need to adhere to local gender norms. 'Women require privacy,' my interlocutors suggested, 'they need protection' and 'so, they cannot do the kind of policing men do.' In particular, women's fidelity to the norms of *purdah* (gendered distancing) my participants claimed, inhibited their capacity for competence. If they were able to sidestep some of these norms, 'as Western women do,' my interlocutors suggested, Pakistani women would also rise to positions of authority in policing.

Yet Huda and Sana, who bucked many of the gender norms that supposedly held other women back (e.g., veiling, avoiding interaction with men, focusing on housework) wound up losing their positions rather than rising to higher positions of authority. Their resistance against the "restrictive" structures that supposedly limited women's capacities resulted not in the transformation of those structures, nor in an improvement of the women's positions but rather in their expulsion from authority.

Not only did the case of their dismissal fly in the face of local explanations for women's marginality in police work, but it also raised a set of recurring academic questions about Muslim women and their agency. Is resistance possible in Muslim contexts? Or are Muslim women confined to enact what sociologists refer to as "compliant agency"? (Burke 2012). Or is there perhaps a more nuanced way to understand Muslim women's agency and their exclusion from power, one that goes beyond the resistance/compliance binaries that still haunt scholarly notions of their agency?

### UNFOLLOWABLE WOMEN

Although it may appear paradoxical, Huda and Sana's dismissal did not surprise the women who worked with and under them. The woman who told me about their relegation, a station head at another women's station, called them "foolish women." These other women's perspectives, which diverged from those of the senior men I spoke with, helped me begin to understand how stigma shapes agency in this context.

Huda and Sana were ejected from their positions despite enacting a form of agency that men in the police force had suggested was vital for upward mobility in the field. This agency involved jettisoning some of the gendered norms and mores that supposedly held other women back, specifically, norms associated with purdah and displays of decency. But by jettisoning these mores and violating purdah norms, the two women courted a gendered stigma that their women subordinates were at pains to manage. Huda and Sana's purdah-defiant agency (e.g., belching, spitting, forging friendships with men) therefore was at odds with the forms of agency their female colleagues and subordinates favored. Most of the women at the women's police station I observed were moved by fears of stigma to enact a purdah-compliant form of agency (veiling, speaking politely, avoiding interaction with men) that contrasted dramatically with Huda and Sana's defiant choices.

The clash between the women's agentic choices—Huda and Sana's versus those of their subordinates—illuminates the multifaceted character of agency. Agency, as this case shows, is not only about enacting compliance or resistance in relation to certain norms (in this case norms connected with modesty and purdah); rather, agency is also about securing relational ends, in this case the cooperation of subordinates at the women's police station. Performative dimensions of agency (i.e., whether one enacts purdah compliance or resistance) activate or undermine social bonds, such as the ones between bosses and subordinates. Huda and Sana's agentic choices compromised their relationship with their subordinates, who were disgusted by the two women's purdah eschewal and therefore withheld their support in the context of an important case of theft that the women's station was tasked with resolving. Without the loyalty of their associates, Huda and Sana's operational efficiency at work was compromised, causing them to botch the case and ultimately lose their positions at the women's station. Their dismissal, as I show in this chapter, was tied up with their inability to win over the allegiance of their associates, who in response to the stigma associated with their workplace preferred different forms of symbolic and relational agency than the ones Huda and Sana chose. By recounting the case of Huda and Sana's removal from office, this chapter illustrates precisely how women's agency flounders in the currents of the stigma matrix.

In what follows, I first discuss two important scholarly perspectives on agency in order to help readers understand the theoretical stakes of this chapter's argument. The case of Huda and Sana's removal is significant not only because it helps us to understand how stigma disrupts and distorts women's agentic capacities but also because the case sheds light on some of the limitations in feminist ideas about Muslim women's agency. In the theoretical framework section, I highlight these limitations and explain how they can be addressed through theoretical consideration of my empirical case. Next, I describe in detail the policing context, which shaped the stigma and embedded the agency of the women I observed. As I mention in the introduction to this book, feminist perspectives understand agency to be embedded, which means that agency draws on and in turn helps to shape the context within which it is enacted. Thus, it is important to understand how arrangements at the meso-level (organizational level) shaped interactions and relationships at the micro-level of interaction and agency. I follow up this contextual information with empirical detail and describe how policewomen enacted agency in response to their gendered and stigmatized organizational context. Finally, I recount how these agentic choices played out in a field of interpersonal relationships and what feminists can learn from these dynamics.

### THEORETICAL FRAMEWORK

After decades of theorizing, two approaches have come to dominate both the scholarly discussion on Muslim women and the wider public debates about Muslim women's agency. The first suggests that agency involves transgression, or the bucking of norms. In order to be agentic, this perspective requires Muslim women to demonstrate resistance against the structures of their religious communities, which are viewed as oppressive. The second approach suggests that Muslim women need not engage in resistance in order to be agentic; instead, scholars suggest that conforming to and confirming structures is also a form of agency (Mahmood 2005). The first perspective, which I call resistant perspective, is rooted in the poststructuralist turn in feminist work (see Bell 2008) and draws on the theorizing of Judith Butler (Butler 1993). This strand of feminist work suggests that actors can resist dominant notions of acceptable behavior or norms by undertaking performances that are out of step with social expectations. In other words, actors resist gendered norms by undertaking transgressive performances (display work that is at odds with conventional modes); by doing so, they sometimes succeed in refashioning these norms.

The agency as resistance perspective was modified in the early 2000s by postcolonial feminist scholars, of whom the most influential is Saba Mahmood (Mahmood 2005). Mahmood, who did her fieldwork with Muslim women involved in the Mosque movement in Egypt, argued that when we think of agency only in terms of resistance, we obscure other kinds of actions and capacities that women might call upon. To sidestep this limited view, Mahmood argued, we should think of agency as embedded within a particular social context. When we do this, when we see agency as shaped by an actor's social context, we can also capture those goals and those actions that may not be aimed at undermining hegemony but that are still reflective of an actor's active engagement in shaping her life. Mahmood's redefinition of agency has been characterized by sociologists as "compliant agency" or a kind of agency that involves actors in an effort not to buck norms but to conform to them (Burke 2012).

***Symbolic agency.*** I label both these kinds of agency, the resisting kind and the compliant kind, as "symbolic agency" because they both involve performance or the activation of symbols. In the first case (i.e., resistant agency), actors undertake performance in an effort to reshape norms; in the second case (i.e., compliant agency), actors work to internalize norms through performance. Both kinds of agency, therefore, involve aesthetic or symbolic effort. They both mobilize signs in service to an objective around norms. Compliant agency works to internalize norms, while resistant agency works to disrupt them, and both use performance to do so. Table 2 summarizes both kinds of agency that I have organized under the rubric of symbolic agency.

There are two problems with symbolic notions of agency. First, an overreliance on these two approaches can create a problem for feminist scholarship on Muslim women. If we see agency as having two registers, compliance and resistance, and assume that in contrast with other women, Muslim women undertake the first kind, we run the risk of reinscribing an Islam/West dualism that feminist work has long sought to surmount. Indeed, it was this very dichotomy that the compliance perspective aimed to overcome. Mahmood's work was groundbreaking because it made visible the agency of Muslim women and, by doing so, helped to problematize the long-standing stereotypes in scholarly work, which had tended to see Muslim women as agentless victims. But by building on Mahmood's work, the recent scholarship on Muslim women and their agency may have overshot its target. Researchers have produced so much work outlining the pious forms of agency that are specific to Muslim women that some scholars have begun to worry that the Mahmoodian framework may now ironically work to revive the impression that Muslim women are "different" from Western women and that Islam is incompatible with Western and liberal forms of life (Husain 2020; Jamal 2006).

**TABLE 2.** Symbolic agency

| Agency | Characterization | Exemplar | Involves | Enacted by |
|---|---|---|---|---|
| Feminist | Symbolic | Butler 1993 | Resistance; bucking norms | Performance |
| Feminist | Symbolic | Mahmood 2005 | Compliance; Internalizing norms | Performance |

A second problem with symbolic accounts of agency is that their focus on aesthetics, or the ways that actors marshal signs in an effort to work on either themselves or on social norms, makes them one-dimensional. Agency, after all, does not involve only actions that actors take for themselves; it also involves actions they take to get others to act on their behalf (Husain 2020; Pugh 2014; Lee 2001), and it is this second, relational dimension of agency that is missing from symbolic accounts of Muslim women's agency. Thus, even though early twenty-first-century academic work on Muslim women has focused explicitly on theorizing and making visible their agency, this scholarship's heavy investment in the discursive, self-making realm of human action has deprived feminist thinking of the relational richness that had characterized the work of second-wave feminist scholars like Kandiyoti, whose notion of patriarchal bargains is fundamentally relational (Kandiyoti 1988). And yet, there is ample reason to include a relational dimension in examinations of agentic performance. Performance, after all, often relies on witnesses or audiences for their success (Alexander 2004; Husain 2022). Yet, this second, relational dimension of agency has not been clearly articulated in feminist discussions that follow Saba Mahmood and Butler's models of agency.

**Relational Agency.** In contrast with the symbolic conceptions outlined above, there are two bodies of scholarship that outline a perspective on agency that is more relational in character—an older body of work in the organization literature (Callon and Latour 1981; Clegg 1989) and a more recent set of writings in pragmatic sociology (Adams 1996, 2011; Reed 2017, 2020). These accounts suggest that being an agent can entail the capacity not just to act for oneself but also to work on another's behalf, as an accountant or an aid worker does. According to the relational perspective, agency involves delegation—recruiting associates who can help us achieve our objectives. This kind of agency provides extension; it allows people to expand the locus of their action over larger swaths of space and time. For instance, imperial centers in the eighteenth and nineteenth centuries, extended their reach in space and time by recruiting company men to administer distant colonies on behalf of the center (Adams 1996). I call this delegatory form of agency "relational agency" because it travels on the back of a relation between the actor and the person that is enlisted to act on the actor's behalf.

**TABLE 3.** Relational agency

| Agency | Characterization | Exemplar | Involves | Enacted by |
|---|---|---|---|---|
| Org theory | Relational | Callon and Latour 1981; Clegg 1989 | Network extension | Enlisting others |
| Pragmatic sociology | Relational | Adams 1996, 2011; Reed 2017, 2020 | Extension; power | Sending and binding recruits |

Table 3 summarizes the theoretical perspective I call relational agency.

Since it involves delegation, relational agency involves a need to accomplish as well as manage recruitment relationships. Agents need not only to enlist others to act for them but also to control recruits, who may be operating at a distant location, outside the direct supervision of their client or patron. Associates need to be sent out to work on the agent's behalf, and they have to be bound to remain true to the agent's interests. Actors who are able to enlist multiple recruits and string them together so as to cover larger expanses of space and time construct what Isaac Reed calls "chains of power," which are vast sequences of actors and agents spread across the globe, like supply chains or armies acting in the name of a corporation or kingdom or state (Reed 2017).

To pull people into a recruitment relationship and potentially craft a chain of power, actors rely on signs, which work like a match to spark binding relationships (Reed 2017). So, for example, we can think of a wedding ring as a sign that signifies a recruitment relationship. A ring tells strangers that a person is already in a binding relationship and cannot be recruited into a romantic liaison. Moreover, when it is exchanged in a wedding ceremony, a ring works to ritually tie people together, to recruit them into a relationship that is binding. In short, relational agency relies on signs to forge agency relationships. And when they are strung together, these agency relationships constitute chains of power—networks that channel capacity over time and space.

The problem with relational accounts of agency is that they underplay the performative component of recruitment. A sign on its own can't summon others to act for us. The meanings contained within signs have to be animated via ritual or performance, as in the case of the wedding ring, which is often exchanged in ritualized ways. And these rituals and performances are often gendered and classed (as in the case of traditional weddings), which means they may require privilege to activate. For instance, research around gender and the workplace has found that women get punished for putting on performances, like aggression, that generate respectful cooperation when men undertake them (Rudman 1998; Rudman and Glick 2001; Heilman et al. 2004). In other words, while the chains of power perspective suggests that agency involves recruitment, which in turn helps constitute power, it does not consider the performative barriers some actors face when they try to forge agency relationships.

To sum up, then, we have three notions of agency in our toolkit that we can use to understand women's agency in the Pakistani police force (see table 4) and expand feminist notions of Muslim women's agency. We have the kind of symbolic agency that involves resistance and the bucking of norms, and we have a compliant notion of agency, which captures actors' effort to conform to norms. And then we have relational agency, which involves recruiting others in order to extend our capacity over time and space. These three perspectives are summarized in the table below.

In the rest of this chapter, I will draw on my observations of Huda and Sana's dismissal from their positions to build on these scholarly perspectives and develop a more multidimensional account of agency, one that helps us understand why even apparently agentic women are unable to move or pierce the glass ceiling at work. By parsing agency's various dimensions, this chapter demonstrates how cultural forces, such as those congealed in the stigma matrix, work to undermine women's agency within state-based occupations. In order to help readers to understand the connection between stigma and agency, however, it is important to first understand the policing context, which embeds women's choices. The policing context in Pakistan organizes women's concerns about stigma and their agentic choices in relation to these concerns.

**TABLE 4.** Toolkit for grasping women's agency

| | | | |
|---|---|---|---|
| Symbolic agency 1 | Transgressive | Bucking norms | Refashions norms |
| Symbolic agency 2 | Compliant | Conforming to norms | Confirms and internalizes norms |
| Relational agency | Connective/seeks extension | Enlisting others | Extends capacity over space and time |

## THE GENDERED ORGANIZATION OF PAKISTANI POLICING

To fully understand how women's agency is shaped by the stigma enshrined within their workplaces, it is important to understand the sociocultural context of the Pakistani police force that embeds their agency. The policing context in Pakistan is gendered in five ways.

First, the organization is gendered in its composition. Like similar forces in other contexts, the Pakistani police force is a male-dominated institution. Women comprise only 1 percent of the total Pakistani police force, even though a 10 percent quota has been reserved for them (Gilmore et al. 2015). In Sindh, the province where Karachi city is located, women comprise a mere 1.5 percent of the police force (*Dawn* 2017).

Second, organizational hierarchies are also gendered. Women are not just few in number, they are also concentrated at the bottom of the police hierarchy. Most are inducted in a category referred to locally as "rankers"—those who do the grunt work of policing the public. At the highest rungs of the hierarchy, the "officer class" inducted via the civil service exam is made up almost entirely of men. There was only one woman at the gazetted officer rank in the Karachi police force at the time of my fieldwork.[1] At the mid-rank level, all but one of the de facto male station houses in Karachi are headed by men. Station houses are also manned primarily by men. A few stations have one or two women assigned to work there, but these women largely serve in auxiliary roles, staying home unless called to work to perform a specific task.

Third, the police force is also gendered through its allocation of tasks and assignments. Women deal primarily with cases involving women and children and are seen as fulfilling the role of chaperone for women citizens who need to engage with the state. When they perform this service, they say they are providing purdah to women citizens. *Purdah* literally means "curtain," and by acting as chaperones, policewomen screen these women from the stigma of being alone in the custody of non-kin men.

Fourth, the police force is also gendered at the organizational level. There are three separate all-female police stations in Karachi, which further bifurcate the organization along gendered lines and also marginalize women at the station house level. Women's stations deal exclusively with cases connected in some way with women, such as domestic disputes, sex workers, or female beggars. The first and best outfitted of the Karachi-based women's stations was inaugurated in 1994 by Prime Minister Benazir Bhutto, Pakistan's first and only woman prime minister, with the aim of facilitating veiled women to access police services and to ensure the safe custody of women (see also BBC 2016). In theory, such stations were meant to enable Pakistani women to access official service without having to forego gender segregation norms. Yet, even as the number of these stations expanded over the years (there are now three in Karachi), they continued to suffer from an acute lack of capacity and unsurprisingly handle only a handful of cases a year.

In Karachi, all three women's stations remain short-staffed and underresourced. Midcity station, described in chapter 2, for instance, was located in a single room on the second floor of a sprawling, intensely masculine station house. It was served by three women constables, only one of whom usually showed up to work. The other constables were deterred from coming to work, I was told, by the fact that the station had no bathroom facilities for women. Chanda, the SHO (station house officer) in charge of this station, said that she had been provided with neither guns nor mobiles (a van used by the police for cruising and other operational purposes).

A similar gendered resource poverty prevails throughout the police force. At the lower ranks, women are almost never issued guns, bulletproof equipment, or vehicles. Most of them do not know how to drive, and while male constables might scoot around on motorbikes, women have to walk, board public buses, pay for rickshaws out of their own pockets, or beg for rides from their male colleagues. While male SHOs are, in general, possessed with larger, better-resourced station houses, more robust staffing, and more and better equipment, women's station heads superintend a few sparsely furnished rooms, an unarmed and slender staff, and sparse material resources.

Finally, the police setting in Pakistan is gendered by cultural ideas that deem police spaces as sexualized, dirty places unsuitable for occupation by decent women. Policewomen I spoke with complained that their family, friends, neighbors, and communities look down on them for working in this vulgar and corrupt profession.

## THE SOURCES OF POLICEWOMEN'S STIGMA

***Policing contexts are contaminating.*** "This is a nice environment," Reema said to me, looking around the room. We were talking at a police training academy located in the south of Karachi. We were seated in an air-conditioned room provided to me by the principal of the academy and were drinking tea that had been served to us by his waitstaff. "This is a very nice environment we are sitting in," Reema said again. She looked around the room in a pointed way. "It's easy to work in such an environment, right?" Reema asked me. "The AC is running, servants are coming and serving tea, you are sitting comfortably," she said, "but tell me, would you be able to sit on top of a sewer lid without getting your clothes dirty? Because that's what we do," she said. "Unlike a sociologist, a policewoman has got to live in a filthy world and yet somehow keep herself clean."

Reema's characterization of her workplace as a "sewer" is very revealing. As structures that literally move excrement out of sight and away from human settlements, sewers represent systems for the ejection of unwanted and offensive material. To be associated with a sewer, to sit on it, as Reema put it, is therefore not only to be seated upon a structure of exclusion, on the very system that ensures the ejection and removal of materials society deems disgusting and abhorrent but also to occupy a contaminating position, one that puts a person at the risk of "getting your clothes dirty," of getting soiled and marked by polluted materials. Reema was not alone in describing her work as polluting. The notion of stigma haunted my work with the police. Women brought it up again and again. 'Our jobs are considered bad,' they told me. 'Because of our jobs, we are seen as tainted women in our communities.' When I pressed them to help me understand why this work would invite so much stigma, women would tell me about the stereotypes that shaped their reception in society.

"People dislike the thana. They are terrified of going to the station," Constable Mehr told me. "For men citizens, they think, if I go to the police station, the cops might ask for a bribe, they might beat me, they might frame me for something I didn't do, but for women who are brought into the station, they think, I will get passed around for sex." Fiza said something similar: "The thana is a dirty space, not suitable for women," she told me. "The cops drink and spit. They smoke and curse, and if they see a woman, the way they stare at her, as if their eyes will make a hole in her garment." The aura of the station house was so gendered and so contaminating, according to these women, that Fiza even feared for my reputation. "You are young," she said. "You are not married. Now, when you keep coming here, after a while people will make assumptions about your decency." Her predictions were not entirely inaccurate. By the end of my fieldwork, I had encountered both unwanted advances from male police officers and unfounded gossip about my relationship with a particular officer.

The policewomen's beliefs about the stigma associated with their profession are backed up by local research, which records a largely negative and very gendered perception of the police force in Pakistan. According to public opinion surveys, 64 percent of respondents describe the police as corrupt and wholly given over to unsavory practices like torture, case fixing, blackmail, framing innocent people, bribery, dishonesty, and a lack of impartiality (Abbas 2020). Local scholars have found that women citizens have especially negative perceptions of the police, viewing them as figures of "horror" due to their "rude, aggressive, irrational" behavior (Hassan 2015).

Policewomen I spoke with were well aware that citizens were horrified by them. "When we round up a woman for questioning," Constable Sehr told me, "she literally becomes hysterical with fear. She sobs and says to us, 'Sister, what is going to happen to me? Are your colleagues going to rape me?'" For ordinary women citizens, the police station is not just a corrupt and violent place but a space fraught with sexual danger. Women caught up in police operations assume that the police will assault or sexually harass them. Their fears are not entirely baseless. One middle-class citizen I spoke with recounted her own experience with the police as a teenager. She was hanging out in a park with her boyfriend, she said, when a constable accosted them. Since they couldn't show him their marriage certificate, the constable threatened to haul the couple back to the station house. He said he would be willing to overlook their illicit appearance together if the woman agreed to let him embrace her.

The sexualized horror surrounding women's perceptions of the station house is also shaped, as I explained in chapter 1, by colonial experiences. During colonial times, British rulers were very concerned about sexually transmitted diseases. So they enacted laws and policies that allowed the police to pick up any indigenous woman suspected of prostitution and forcibly examine her genitals for signs of disease (see Mitra 2020). These policies filled indigenous women with terror, making them afraid of the police and police stations alike. The stigma associated with the police station and women as well as the terror women felt for these spaces persists to this day.

But the sexual terror associated with police stations is shaped also by contemporary women's experiences. A recent local study found that a majority of women who sought police aid said that they were taunted, ridiculed, threatened, and confronted with "cheap words," unwanted physical contact, and demands for sex (Hassan 2015). Many of these women had to return repeatedly to the station house in order to get the police to finally register their case; many accomplished this registration only after paying a bribe (Hassan 2015).

**Policewomen are perceived to be even worse than the men.** Although male police officers told me that they felt that women cops might help mitigate the terrible reputation of the police, women police say that they are often seen in an even worse light than their male colleagues. Women cops are not only assumed to be violent, corrupt, and devious; they are also assumed to be involved in furthering the rapacious interests of their colleagues. "They are all sleeping with their bosses," one journalist said to me, "and they get a cut from the bribes collected from sex workers, massage parlors, and those kinds of activities." Indeed, like women citizens, journalists also appear to believe that policewomen provide their male colleagues with sexual access to prisoners in exchange for a share in corruption money or other resources such as gasoline. Women police are well aware of the rumors that accuse them of colluding with the brutality and rapaciousness of their colleagues. Such stereotypes, they say, make their work extremely unsavory in the eyes of their friends, neighbors, and community members.

"There is probably no job a woman can do that will not invite some gossip and speculation," Constable Seema said. "If a woman has come out of the house to work," she said, "it is assumed that she is open to anything, send a message, flirt, try to start an affair, whatever you want. But when you are in the police," she said, "it is even worse. Then you are assumed not only to be open for sex yourself but also to be a pimp." Other policewomen appeared to believe some of the stereotypes about police rapacity and brutality themselves. "There are some like that," station house officer Chanda, told me bitterly. "Women who lack modesty and do not stay within their limits," that is, restrict interaction with men to official exchanges. Such women, she claimed, "talk with the men, laugh, and joke with the men, and they spoil the whole environment for the rest of us."

Fiza, a constable who worked in a women-only station, also considered some of her own women colleagues to be unsavory women. "I am not saying everyone is good," Fiza told me. "There are a few flirtatious women who use friendship to get favors: 'Get me food. Give me a lift. Buy me gifts.' And because of their behavior, decent women also have to put up with overtures, because such women spoil the environment for everyone." Like Fiza and Chanda, several policewomen worried that the environment of policing, which was imbued with stigma, made it easier for some of the male colleagues to sexually harass them (see also Niazi 2013). They complained that they had endured forms of harassment, including unwanted advances from male colleagues who asked for phone numbers, used terms like "Baby" and "Dolly" when addressing their colleagues, made comments about women's dress and their figures, and even sent unwanted sexual messages and explicit personal pictures to their colleagues (see also Hussain et al. 2016).

### DESTIGMATIZATION STRATEGIES

***Veiled delicacy; purdah-compliant symbolic agency.*** One way that women responded to the stigma associated with their workplace was by enacting compliance with purdah norms. I call this strategy "veiled delicacy." Veiled delicacy performances enacted agency through the use of gestures and signs, such as veils, soft speech, a lowered gaze, physical distancing from men, and snubbing male colleagues who try to get too friendly. Women used such signs to index their fidelity to the norms of purdah or gendered distancing logics. But the signs of purdah are not just gendered; they are also classed. The ability to do purdah is understood as demonstrating a lack of material need, and so purdah is seen by some working-class women as a luxury and a sign of having a good family background. Thus, veiled delicacy performances drew not just on the signs of purdah but also on the gendered signs of class, such as *abayas* (a Middle Eastern full-body veil associated with middle-class people who work or do business in the Gulf region) (see Maqsood 2017), fairness creams (fairness is sometimes associated with an elite background), and body spray. They used these signs to emphasize a middle-class kind of femininity far removed from the brutal, working-class, masculine world of policing.

In addition, these women went out of their way to express a distaste for abusive language, violence, dirt, and sexual immodesty. In one interview, Sharfa, a constable who worked for a women's police station, recounted the following story to help me understand how mismatched police work was to her refined and graceful class background.

"I never, ever thought I would wind up in this disreputable job," Sharfa told me. "I really wanted to go into teaching," she said. "I am very educated, I have an MA, and I read all the time. I have a closet in my bedroom that is full of books, and I read all day long." Sharfa's desire for a government-based teaching career was thwarted by corruption. "Either you need some source," she said, using the local word used to describe a contact who can pull some strings to get you a position. "What they said to me was, pay one lac [one hundred thousand rupees], and the position is yours." Since a teaching position was going to cost more than she could afford to pay, Sharfa said she reluctantly joined the police force. "On my first day after training, I was sent to the women's station. I was shocked," she remembered. "It was so dirty. The women were so coarse," she said. "I felt quite depressed." But as the day went on, things got even worse for Sharfa. "In the late afternoon, they brought a woman suspect to the station," Sharfa said. "My madam, the SHO, said to me, 'New girl, go clean your hands.' I thought she was telling me to wash my hands, so I went to the sink and began to wash with soap. 'What are you doing, you fool?' the madam asked. I said, 'Madam, you told me to wash my hands.' 'Fool, I meant go clean your hands on the suspect, meaning, go thrash her.'" Sharfa laughed about it during our conversation. "'Clean your hands' means thrash someone! I had no idea. I was so horrified. I thought, this is a very bad job, they use an altogether different language here, they want me to hit people."

By recounting stories like this one and using signs like veils, polite language, and fragrant body sprays, women like Sharfa try to mitigate the classed meanings of their working-class, largely masculine jobs, which are tainted with images of corruption and venality. To distance themselves from these stereotypes, women conspicuously signal their connection with a middle-class style of femininity through expressions of delicacy and compliance with the logics of purdah.

Enacting these classed displays can sometimes be difficult, especially as women who adopt this performance claim that they are in a minority and have to manage not just the environment and the overtures of men but also the depravity of other women. For instance, Mumtaz, a constable with six years of service under her belt, recounted the following episode to me as an example of her own modesty and quality in contrast with certain "low-standard" women on the force. Assigned to work with a team, Mumtaz said she climbed into a police mobile (a van that is open in the back) and sat down next to a woman police officer she described as "a low-standard woman," because unlike Mumtaz "she was wearing neither a face veil nor a *burka*," the black gown some women wear over their clothing. To make matters worse, Mumtaz said, "this crude woman" was talking with the men, "using dirty language, all filthy talk with men." This kind of behavior was so unacceptable to Mumtaz that she said, "I, in shame, bowed my head," making it clear to her companions that this kind of talk was not okay with her. "I was thinking, What can I do? Where can I go? Such dirty things they were saying, and the men were laughing." But hunching her shoulders and hanging her head to symbolically withdraw from the environment wasn't enough. "So when the mobile stopped at a red light," Mumtaz said, "I got out and went and sat in the second mobile, which was following behind us."

Although women like Mumtaz felt that they were in a minority, most of the women I interviewed claimed to adopt similar veiled delicacy performances. An overwhelming majority claimed that they would deliberately and consciously assume gestures and aesthetics that would help to signal their respectability in this problematic context. They wore black gowns and face veils when venturing out on the streets; most took off the gown and face veil when inside station houses but kept a scarf on their heads, or a stole around their shoulders. To go without any kind of veil was to signal shamelessness and a low-quality family background.

Veiled delicacy also involved the management of interactions with male colleagues. To avoid being seen as the "wrong sort of woman," some women police officers said that they tried to "act strict" with men, signaling their fidelity to norms of decency by rebuffing men colleagues' attempts at getting "friendly." Laila, a constable who has been on the force for nine years, told me, "I keep myself very stiff," explaining, "if a male [colleague] asks me, give me your contact number or this or that, I answer very briefly that I don't use a cell phone at all." Similarly, Rasheeda said that when she goes out on security assignments, such as crowd management, that require working alongside men, she refuses to make small talk with men colleagues: "If he [a male colleague] says, 'Madam, your name?' I tell him my name. Then to make conversation he will say, 'Madam, are you married or unmarried?' I reply, 'Do you have some business with my personal life? Stick to the duty. Don't ask me personal questions.'"

Women work to project a decent self-image even if doing so requires them to forsake official duties. Farah, a constable working with an investigation unit, told me with apparent pride that she stays out of the interview room when her male boss is interviewing a woman suspect: "They [male police officers] use very dirty language, even with ladies [informants or accused], and they know that I am not the kind who can face such talk, so they tell me, 'Go sit in the other room while we do the interview.'" Since women police are required to serve as chaperones for women citizens during interviews, her pride at abdicating this core responsibility astounded me. I asked her, "Doesn't the *mulzima* [women accused] mind when you leave her alone with the men?" "No," she replied, "they are different types, those women, they know I can't face these things, and the men know I can't face it, because I am not that type, I am from a good family."

Performing veiled delicacy involves not only working on the self and on one's occupation (or abdication) of space; it also requires a styling of temporalities. Women who are loyal to purdah logics also try to avoid night work, if they can. And when it is unavoidable, for instance, when a woman held in custody at a station house requires a woman constable to chaperone her, policewomen bring along chaperones of their own. Mehr, a constable posted at a male-dominated station, said, "When I'm told to come to the station at night, I bring my husband with me." Farzana told me that she brings her husband's younger brother along for protection. And when no chaperone is at hand, Sara says she barricades herself with the *mulzima* in a room latched on the inside, shuttered until sunrise. "We don't even come out to use the restroom," she said. When I asked her why she feels compelled to lock the door, she said, "You know what's going on outside that door, don't you?" "No, what?" I asked. "Wine, parties, the [police] men are not in their right mind. Even the accused woman feels safe only if I lock the door. She says, 'Yes, sister, keep it locked. Don't let them in here.'" Because male-dominated stations are seen as dirty, unruly spaces that are hostile to women's decency, Farzana, like many others posted at de facto male stations, argues that in light of the extreme stigma attached with the station house, she is justified in her wish to stay home, working as a kind of auxiliary or reserve cop who comes in only when there is a woman citizen requiring the reputational cover that a woman cop provides.

In short, most policewomen I interviewed enacted agency by displaying their commitment to purdah norms through a set of veiled delicacy performances. They enacted modesty in dress, gendered distancing in interactions, and decency through spatial and temporal segregation from men.

***Brutal swagger; purdah transgressive symbolic agency.*** In contrast with the purdah-compliant veiled delicacy performances enacted by most policewomen in Karachi, a small minority transgressed purdah norms by enacting a performance I call "brutal swagger," a set of aesthetics associated with mid-level policemen but not policewomen in this context. To illustrate this form of agency, I focus on two women, Huda and Sana, who best exemplified this transgressive strategy. Huda and Sana were posted as the heads of a women's police station in Karachi. In contrast with their counterparts at other women's stations and their subordinates, Huda and Sana cursed frequently, told bawdy jokes, chewed tobacco, spit, spoke very rudely to their subordinates, and boasted about beating suspects.

Both women dressed in flashy civilian clothes, opting for outfits that were seen as immodest by their colleagues: spandex tights worn over short, tight tunics that did little to cover up the shape of their hips and thighs. Neither wore a veil of any kind, instead choosing to leave their hair, which was dyed with blond highlights, uncovered (in the local context, blond highlights can serve as a signal of wealth and status). They both wore a great deal of gold jewelry (also a signal of wealth and status in this context). Although apparently very punctual with their prayers (many Muslims pray five times a day), which they performed with a long cloth (*chador*) wrapped tight around their heads, both Huda and Sana would wind up their prayers by flinging off their veils, tossing them in a corner, and roaming around the station in their tight shirts, making crude sex jokes and coarse references to sex crimes. Both women freely used curse words that I rarely heard other women utter, like *chutiya* (slang word meaning vaginal), *madarchod* (motherfucker), *haramzaada* (bastard). Sana's conversations with me were almost entirely about sex and bathroom talk, fart jokes and sexual innuendo. The first time I met her, she said to me, 'I am so scared of Huda that when I get constipated, I just try to imagine her face, because when I think of her, my shit comes out.' Meanwhile, Huda, unlike the other women who worked in her station house, would sit near the men and crack lewd jokes in their company (a few men were on the staff and male cops from other stations sometimes visited).

While most women I interviewed claimed to dislike the violence sometimes required by their jobs, which they said was incompatible with their gendered decency, Huda described with relish the times when she delivered a beating to civilians. She frequently recounted an incident when she had thrashed a man for ogling her, telling me, "After all, I am police—not lady police, but police—and they should understand police power!" (see chapter 6). Whereas other women told me that it was vital to shore up signs of their decency in the "dirty" police *mahol* (environment), Huda argued that it was more important to signal her authority and *bharam* (reputation, credit, wherewithal). In one conversation with me, for instance, she made the following declaration: 'If you want to be a gentle lady, stay home. Quit the job. If you want to work, then join in with the men. If you are shying away from men, then how will you learn the tricks of the trade? See, if you learn these things, the sky's the limit. You have to leave the *nakhra* and *nazakat* (air and delicacy) at home. To work as police, you have to exude an aura of power.'

To achieve this aura of power, Huda not only worked on her personal presentation; she also worked to style the space of the station under her command. To this end, she appropriated the interrogation room, repurposing it as her "side room" (a private space of rest routinely provided to high-ranking officers by the state), which she outfitted with a bed, food, and makeup. In it, she would recline on the floor at mealtimes. Women stationed as SHOs at other women's stations were envious of Huda's appropriation of this space. Chanda, for instance, bitterly brought up Huda's privileges in a discussion with me: 'Huda even has a side room,' she complained. 'We don't even have a toilet for women here.'

In her "side room," Huda would lie back on a meal blanket and pick up slices of fruit with her fingers and drop them into her mouth. The fruit was washed, sliced, and served by the constables, who grudgingly waited on Huda in imitation of the orderlies officially assigned to higher-ranking officers. Ameera, a constable, recounting her day's routine to me, remarked, "I'm a government servant, not Huda's personal servant, yet all my time is taken up heating food for madam, serving madam, getting water for madam. I don't get to do any police work. I spend all my time responding to madam's bell, which she rings to order tea or to tell me to polish her shoes or press her clothes."

When she wasn't eating, Huda would chew constantly on *ghutka* (a tobacco product), her conversation punctuated by pauses as she spat out streams of red tobacco juice into a jar she kept by her side, occasionally asking her subordinates to fetch more tobacco or to clean out the jar.

Huda's crude gestures began making sense to me in the context of the broader social setting. A male officer I talked to about the aesthetics required to demonstrate *bharam* (credit, reputation, wherewithal) in the policing context, recounted to me his first impression of his first station head: 'This was back in the 1990s, when SHOs were a big *bala* [supernatural being]. I had to bribe one of the lackeys fifty rupees to get me in to see the SHO.' He said, 'They used to be millionaire, billionaire people, big shots, really big shots. It was winter. SHO *sahib* [master] was reclining on a *charpoi* [string cot] dropping dry fruit into his mouth, draped in a red shawl. He was a man of few words. He would give you only one look and a grunt, and you only got a few minutes audience.' This story underlines the kinds of aesthetics these remote superiors deployed to index the magnificence of their office. Huda's aesthetic tactics were similar. The first time I met her, she kept me waiting for an hour outside her office. Later she told me she did this for two reasons. First, she was observing me through the one-way glass in order to get a read on me, and second, she wanted to impress upon me "the power of her office."

In short, unlike most policewomen I interviewed, Huda and Sana enacted symbolic agency by adopting a brutal swagger aimed at signaling *bharam*. This style not only resembled the masculine brutality associated with policemen; it was also transgressive of veiled delicacy performances, which require distancing from men as well as polite and respectful speech.

### STIGMA, SWAGGER, AND RECRUITMENT

While Huda and Sana's aesthetic strategies initially impressed me, they did not appear to impress subordinate women. Constables and head constables I met at Huda's stations, as well as those who were posted elsewhere, spoke disparagingly of Huda, saying that she was incompetent, uneducated, and abusive. At Huda's station, her colleagues acted respectfully in her presence but when Huda and Sana were not around, (they usually came into work late in the afternoon) the subordinates would roundly abuse both of them. Reading Huda and Sana's displays through the prism of gender and class, junior women claimed that the two station heads acted the way they did because they were low-quality woman. Seeing purdah as a form of privacy, working-class women understand its various gestures as a form of class privilege. These women, therefore, enacted agency not by shedding their veils but by asserting their claim to a privacy that their social location and masculine occupation had robbed from them. From their perspective there are only two conceivable reasons for violating purdah norms. One either ventures out of the home because of financial need or in pursuit of vulgar aims. Accordingly, women like Huda and Sana, who jettisoned gestures of delicacy and privacy, were assumed to be low-quality women from indecent backgrounds.

'See,' Meena, a constable, said about Huda, 'she roams around without a *dupatta* [veil], which tells you her background is low standard.' Echoing these sentiments, another constable, Fiza, mentioned a video that Huda had shown me on her phone one day to make a similar point. The video was one Huda's teenaged daughter had sent her mother while on an outing with her friends at Aladdin Water Park in Karachi. In it, Huda's daughter could be seen dancing, her long, wavy hair bouncing as she swung her hips to the rhythm of a Bollywood song. Huda had proudly showed the video to all of us, commenting on her daughter's confidence. The women had looked at it silently, but later they told me, they were shocked at the young girl's behavior. 'Did you see the daughter's *harkatain* [the things she gets up to]?' Fiza asked me. 'She is totally out [of bounds], just like her mother.' When I asked her why the video was so problematic, she explained, 'See, you have come from America so you might not understand, but things like this are not done here. Dancing in public, showing her hair, moving like that. All kinds of people go to that park. Huda's family is out of control. It shows you what standard of person she is.' Similarly, Rani connected Huda's lack of concern for *purdah* to her class position. 'You can tell that her *nasl* [breeding] is bad by her speech and her dress,' she claimed. The use of the word *nasl* is interesting. It suggests a casteist understanding of Huda's immodesty, implying that she behaves the way she does because she comes from bad stock.

The women's responses were understandable; they felt demeaned by having to serve Huda and Sana. Yet their interpretation was also gendered. They read similar behavior very differently when it was enacted by men. In many instances, I saw men deploy brutal aesthetics to very different effect. Right after I heard a woman constable receive a severe scolding, laced with expletives, from her male boss, for instance, she said to me, with evident embarrassment, 'Men get angry. It's okay, I can take it.' On another occasion, a woman constable justified harsh words from her male boss by saying, 'They are *barey log* [big shots]. It is their right to tell us off.' Huda's brutality was not given the same justification, however. Instead of seeing Huda's gestures as springing from her position as a boss, her subordinates grumbled about her treatment of them. Ameera, for instance, complained to me for several days about being made to polish Huda's shoes. 'Is that what I put on my uniform for?' she asked me. Similarly, Fiza grumbled about being made to perform janitorial work. 'I don't even do the cleaning in my own home,' she said, 'I've got a maid who comes in and does it, but here, there is no respect for my uniform. I am treated like a maid or a waiter.' (Maids are inexpensive in Pakistan, charging as little as $30 a month.)

Indeed, at other women's stations, I noticed that women bosses deployed not brutal but conciliatory tactics to coax their subordinates into service. They did this even when requesting official service from women subordinates. Chanda would offer to chauffeur her subordinates to assignments, for instance, as an inducement to perform various duties. Mehr, an

SHO at another station house, told me she sometimes tipped her subordinates with money out of her own pocket in order to get them to perform their duties, a gesture she found "humiliating." Similarly, Nasreen, a woman who had achieved the rank of district superintendent, a status much higher than the one Huda or Sana occupied, told me, "I can't tell you how much sugar and honey you have to use as a woman, call them 'son,' call them 'daughter,' praise them and cajole them to get them to do the work." Another high-ranking woman officer told me, 'Men use abusive language to press their subordinates to work, but we can't do that, we have to use the language of roses, and I suppose that puts us at a disadvantage. But no one will like it if I curse. I wouldn't like it. What would that say about my background and upbringing?'

In short, by mimicking a male-coded brutal swagger in a bid for *bharam*, Huda and Sana violated classed and gendered norms that other women relied on for protection against a dignity they felt was under threat due to the stigma associated with their occupation. While men appeared to be able to use brutal aesthetics to dominate their subordinates in the Karachi police force, for Huda and Sana this gendered performance produced alienation among a crucial set of spectators—their subordinates. Instead of producing recruitment, their purdah transgressive performance produced disaffection and alienation.

The two women's inability to bring symbolic and relational capacities into alignment came into sharp relief in the context of a simple theft and bribery case that went sour. In the following section, I draw on field notes to provide a description of this case. The case demonstrates how stigma empties the agency of women, like Huda and Sana, who eschew the stigma-management performances favored by their subordinates. Alienated by Huda and Sana's transgression of purdah norms, their subordinates withheld their cooperation from the two women bosses and thereby compromised the women's operational capacities.

### THE BOTCHED POLICE CASE

One day I arrived at the station to find Huda and Sana in a fever of excitement. A well-to-do *mudda'ii* (complainant) had handed over custody of his maid to the women's station, accusing her of stealing a large cache of jewelry. Huda and Sana appeared to be very excited by this case, as most of the cases they usually worked involved impoverished complainants and suspects who were unable to pay much of a cut to the police. The police, as several officers told me, need such bribes and payoffs in order to pay for overhead and operational costs. Huda and Sana were convinced that the *mudda'ii* was an easygoing person who would be willing to tip the station for their service so long as he was able to recover the stolen goods.

Moreover, they assumed that the maid was a 'naïve lamb,' that she had stepped out of line only because she was overcome by the lure of opportunity, that she was terrified now that she had been caught, and that it would be easy to secure her cooperation. They assumed that she would lead them straight to her accomplices, enabling the police to recover the stolen jewelry. In addition, the maid would also supply the police with some of the funds needed to cover operational costs, and since her funds were limited, she had offered to provide Huda and Sana with her labor. 'I will clean the whole station for you,' she had told them, 'and then I will cook some food for you as well.' So, in front of my eyes, Huda and Sana allowed Sharifa, the maid, to leave. 'I've got a rickshaw waiting,' Sharifa had said as she was leaving, 'I just need to drop off my identification card at the lawyer's office,' she said. 'Then, after that, my landlord has thrown me out of the house, so I just need to make a few arrangements, but I will come straight back and look after you.' Huda had nodded and called in the head *mohrer* (official in charge of records and communication) instructing him to let Shareefa have her ID card back. 'She's got some work to do and then she will come back and clean the station,' she told him. As she was seeing her off, Sana asked Shareefa, 'Do you remember what we told you?' Shareefa nodded her head emphatically. 'Tomorrow, I will wait for you by the tree you showed me at the courthouse,' she said. Then she left. Later, I learned that she went straight to the railway station upon leaving the police station that day, boarded a bus, and disappeared, never to be seen again.

Huda and Sana had also apparently misjudged the complainant. He visited the station one morning as I was sitting with the constables in the narrow dingy passage that served as their workspace. Huda and Sana had not yet come into the office. The power was out, so the women had left the side door open for air. Constable Raani was gasping and fanning herself with a folded-up newspaper. We were talking about Bollywood movies when we heard a commotion. It was the *mudda'ii*, loudly scolding someone as he marched into the station. He was a small man with graying hair, dressed in a polo shirt and khaki pants. He looked very angry and kept up his scolding as he entered. 'Don't you ever clean up this place?' he was saying. He stomped into the adjoining room, saying, 'I am going to inspect your lockup.' The interior regions of the station and especially the lockup area are ordinarily off-limits to the public. The women protested half-heartedly, 'You can't be here.' But mostly they ignored him, letting him roam around the station, peering in corners, opening drawers, and inspecting the arrangements at the station.

Later, Raani told me that she realized that day that he was not someone you could mess with. 'The behavior lets you know what the *range* of this person is,' Raani said, using an English word that I heard frequently in the police context. 'What do you mean by "range,"' I asked. '"Range," meaning, how far can he reach, who can he phone, what can he achieve through his contacts.' But Raani and the other constables chose not to pass this information on to Huda and Sana when they arrived at the station later that afternoon.

Raani's estimation of the *mudda'ii's* "range" turned out to be correct. After the maid fled, the *mudda'ii* began using his contacts to put pressure on Huda to recover the lost goods. The only way to placate him was to conduct a recovery operation. Quite by chance, I showed up at the women's station on the night that the raid was to be conducted. I had not known it was to take place that night. In the next section I draw on my fieldnotes to recount the events of that night.

I arrive at the station house as the call for the evening prayer is ringing off loudspeakers. I am hoping to interview some of the women on the night shift and I take a rickshaw to the station house. The power seems to be out, and the station house is dark. I knock on the gate until an armed guard lets me in. Two women constables I don't know are sitting in the front yard swatting at mosquitos. One of them jumps up as soon I enter, barring my way into the building. I am surprised by this unusually inhospitable reception. The other constable runs in to inform Huda about my arrival. Huda comes out almost immediately, expressing surprise at my appearance. Has she forgotten that she was the one who had suggested I come tonight? 'Let's sit here in the garden,' she says.

There is no garden. The gloomy yard is made up of dust and mud; a few trees lean languidly against the boundary wall. Pitch dark, swarming with mosquitos, and throbbing with the noise of the generator, the "garden" is not a comfortable place to sit. Huda appears agitated, but she does not ask me to leave. Sitting down next to me, she tells me to send out for tea for everyone. I dig out some money from my pocket and give it to Razia, one of the constables who is sitting with us, so she can order tea from the nearby *dhaba* (makeshift tea shop).

A little while later, a police patrol van, known locally as a "mobile," heaves into the driveway. It is packed with people, most of them wielding large rifles. Three of them, unarmed women I know, climb out. Three unshaven, rough-looking men dressed in civilian clothes jump out after them. Huda calls over one of the women, Meena, a constable I know, instructing her to 'keep the researcher entertained.' Then Huda follows the rest of the crowd into the station, leaving Meena with me alone in the dark.

Once Huda is gone, Meena begins pouring out confidences. She claims that the station is in a state of tension tonight because Sana has 'accidentally lost sight' of a *mulzima* (accused woman) in our custody, Shareefa, a maid accused of stealing a large cache of gold jewelry from her employer. 'Now Huda has got the men involved in order to conduct a raid,' she says. 'Today they have to recover the *maal* [loot].' Other women cops have told me already that 'losing sight of" a *mulzima* can be grounds for dismissal. This is a big deal. It is rare for a government employee to be dismissed from service. Those who are removed lose not just their jobs but also their pensions and other benefits. So getting caught for a rare fireable offense is no small matter.

But the situation is actually much worse than a simple matter of "misplacing" a suspect. That is just how Meena put it at first, but after we have been chatting for a while, she inches closer and whispers, 'Huda and Sana took a bribe and let the *mulzima* go,' she says. 'She fooled them. She said she would come back to the station in an hour, but as soon as she got out of here, she caught a rickshaw to Cantt Station and got on a bus to Punjab and vanished.' Meena says, 'Now they are pretending that she broke out.'

As Meena and I talk, the local tea shop supplies the entire station with three more rounds of tea and cookies. Trays of tea go into the dark station. The generator hums. Meena appears both awed and thrilled by the trouble her two bosses are in. 'We've got the rickshaw driver's testimony,' she says. 'The suspect is gone.' But now, Meena explains, things have gotten really hairy for Huda and Sana. 'The *mudda'ii* is someone important, and he's got Huda by the neck. He is not going to let this go. Huda should have known he was connected.'

Meena and I are huddled together and speaking in whispers. Huda suddenly bursts out of the station looking angry. 'That was a long interview,' she says. Meena darts out of her chair and into the station house. Huda sits down in the chair that Meena has vacated; a male cop who has accompanied Huda out of the station takes the other seat, the two flanking me on either side. A tall tea shop waiter wanders around with a round metal tray carrying empty teacups. He looks scared and lost. 'Come here, *bharwa* [pimp],' Huda says rudely. 'Make sure you get your money because I want give you what other people owe.' Taking this as a hint, I give the tea shop man whatever cash I have in my pocket.

'You left your pot here the other day,' Huda says to me rather roughly. I had brought home cooked *haleem* (a lentil stew cooked with chicken) for the women to share. 'I'll go and get it,' I say, thinking this is a good excuse to get my stuff and leave. 'Stay where you are!' Huda barks at me. 'Oye. *Madarchod* (motherfucker), why are you sitting there like an idiot?' Huda calls out to a shabbily dressed elderly woman who is sitting on her haunches by the entrance to the station. She is a complainant who came in earlier in the day seeking police help against domestic abuse. 'Go fetch Fauzia's pot,' Huda commands the careworn-looking complainant.

A large man comes out of the station and stands before Huda grinning. 'You're not making a *chutiya* [pussy] out of us, are you?' Huda asks him sternly. 'No, madam, your work will be done!' he replies, grinning.

'They all made *chutiya* out of us, now the *mudda'ii* [complainant] has gripped Sana in a vice,' Huda says, shaking her head. 'Are your 'formants reliable?' she asks the man, 'because the *mudda'ii* has really got his foot on Sana's throat.'

The man grins at her but says nothing. She continues, 'Of course, a little *oonch neech* [give and take] is normal,' she said, 'but now we have to get their stuff back, or we are done!'

'We will get it tonight. Half was sold off; half is there,' the man says, 'but madam, I have spent a lot of money on gas, and we've got twenty men working this raid. Twenty men!'

Huda looks bitter. 'Twenty men have been rounded up,' she said. 'Now all we need is Ali Baba,' referencing the story of Ali Baba and the forty thieves.

'We've got the middleman,' the man reassures her. 'Shareefa has run off with her share, but today you will get the rest of the booty.'

Huda looks agitated. She turns to me. 'What were you talking to Meena about for so long?' she asks. 'Your workers are so brilliant,' I reply. 'I learn so much from them.' I am trying to placate her. At this the male cop sitting beside Huda asks me plaintively, 'Why aren't you interviewing men?' I reply that I intend to do so but that 'I just want to get to the ladies first.' At this Huda comments, 'Why do ladies always have to come first?' (a play on the phrase "ladies first"). '"I think the concept is left over from colonial times,' I reply. At this the male cop launches into a lengthy tirade against the hypocrisy of Westerners. 'Islam is the perfect religion, but they try to make us look like beasts,' he says, arguing that Islam treats women very well, but the West is always trying to make it look like Muslim women are treated badly. I am itching to leave, and Huda is clearly getting impatient with both of us, but his speech goes on for several minutes. As soon as he pauses, I dart out of my seat, bidding Huda a hasty goodbye and rushing out of the gate to find a rickshaw to take me home.

### AGENCY AND THE RELATIONAL MEANING OF SWAGGER

Huda's behavior during the night shift so alarmed me that I avoided her station for several weeks after that visit. A month later, I was visiting another women's station when I learned that Huda and Sana had been removed from their posts at the women's thana and were now relegated to desk jobs at one of the headquarters. When I discussed this episode with other senior women, they told me that Huda and Sana were removed from their positions not because they engaged in corruption but because they failed to do so in an effective way. According to these women, competent corruption is a crucial pivot ensuring the rise of police personnel to good postings. Sameena, a high-ranking woman, said that she was consistently relegated to lowly postings because of her reluctance to engage in corruption. 'Some of the grandeur you see in these offices, doesn't come from the state,' she explained, 'our bosses keep the operational budget for themselves,' she explained, 'and we are expected to outfit the office through our own resources.' When I asked her where they expected her to get the money, she laughed, 'you know where,' she said, 'I don't do it, that's why I don't get good postings, because when I come into a place, I jam everything up. The wealth stops flowing because of me.'

Echoing Sameena, a senior male officer explained that in order to achieve plumb postings, "like a car jack you have to get fitted" into the corruption circuit, relaying money, resources, favors and connections up and down the hierarchy. These circuits don't just enrich individual officers, but also help to furnish offices, fill petrol in cars, expedite police work (e.g., by providing payments for informants) and provide food, transport, and other kinds of aid to low-ranking cops (see Wade 1982; Gupta 1995; Jauregui 2014 on similar operational and collective uses of corruption money by police in other contexts). To get plumb postings or to avoid getting ejected from good ones, a cop must serve as a competent conduit for these informal circuits, relaying money, contacts, and information up and down the chain to bosses and subordinates alike.

As Arif, a male police superintendent, explained, the swagger—the cursing, beating, and spitting—is aimed not just at fashioning an image of the self as a powerful figure but also to communicate corruptibility, a desire and an aptitude for corruption to bosses, subordinates, and clients. Cops use such signals to recruit and get recruited into the larger web of informal exchanges that help compose "chains of power" in this context (Reed 2017).

Put simply, the engines of agency run on two motors in this setting. One employs symbolic dimensions of agency—spitting, cursing, and bullying—in order to create a presentation of self as formidable figure. But this image is crafted also in service to that other kind of agency, which I have called relational agency. Cops use such signals not only to indicate *bharam* but as an invitation to potential recruits and recruiters, associated with the larger web of illicit exchanges that help compose a corruption chain of power in this context. Indeed, without the added torque of this second motor, recruitment, the apparatus of agency circulates empty signs, rendering the wielder into an emperor openly remarked upon for his lack of clothes. In short, an agency that relies exclusively on refashioning norms through aesthetic effort, for instance by jettisoning the signs of purdah, is an empty agency, one unable to dislodge the glass ceiling. It is not enough to give off signals by performing swagger; actors also need associates that are willing to buy into, subscribe to, and extend the meanings of their displays.

Successfully recruited associates could have aided Huda and Sana's efforts in the maid corruption case in three vital ways: First, they could have provided valuable information to their bosses; as an example, Raani could have shared with Huda her estimation of the complainant's wherewithal, an assessment that turned out to be accurate. Such information may have made Huda and Sana more cautious about letting the maid go off and run her errands. Indeed, at other police stations, I observed subordinates communicating in detail to their bosses everything that occurred in the bosses' absence.

Second, a loyal subordinate could have accompanied the maid when she left the station, making sure she did not flee. But if they had been asked for such a service, Huda's subordinates would have come up with excuses. Her best constable, seething over being made to polish the boss's shoes, was constantly feigning illness to get out of work.

Third, successfully recruited subordinates could have done more to control the complainant when he dropped in to "inspect" the station, instead of allowing him, in Huda's absence, to roam freely around the station, gathering more information about how poorly things were run. But Huda's juniors made little effort to stem the flow of damaging information out of her station; instead, they spread gossip about their bosses. I often heard the stories they told about Huda and Sana from women posted at other stations and at headquarters. Such tales did not seem to come out of the stations of more conciliatory women bosses, who abided by purdah aesthetics and adopted conciliatory recruitment styles rather than brutal ones.

In short, cooperative subordinates could have provided Huda and Sana with extension—they could have helped the women to increase their capacity over time and space by protecting their domain in the two women's absence, guarding information by eschewing gossip, and supporting the two women in their operational pursuits. Cooperative subordinates could have extended Huda and Sana's ability to maintain control over the station even when they were not present. But alienated by Huda and Sana's purdah transgressive styles, the constables withheld their support, which caused Huda and Sana's control of the station to fracture.

### THEORETICAL IMPLICATIONS

***Lessons about Agency.*** The case of Huda and Sana's dismissal from the women's police station provides several key insights about agency and stigma.

First, the case demonstrates that agency is multidimensional. Women in the policing context responded to stigma by employing different kinds of agency. The constables who served under Huda and Sana enacted a compliant form of symbolic agency I have described as veiled delicacy. In contrast, Huda and Sana responded to the stigmatizing environment by embracing the signs and gestures that were seen by others as polluting. They enacted agency by violating the classed and gendered norms of purdah. "I'm not lady police. I am just police," Huda declared. Huda and Sana were not alone in adopting this kind of agency. I observed other women at various levels who also adopted this style, but it was the less common response to stigma.

Each of these symbolic kinds of agency, brutal swagger and veiled delicacy, were tied up with relational dimensions of agency. Purdah-compliant women bosses used mollifying modes of recruitment. They employed kinship language by calling constables "daughter" and offered caring gestures, such as sharing food or offering rides, to cajole their subordinates into compliance. In contrast, purdah-defiant actors, like Huda and Sana, tried to adopt more masculine-coded styles of recruitment by bullying and belittling their subordinates into submission.

Second, the case illustrates how women come to be marginalized in the Pakistani police force. Women are marginalized in this context because their agency is hobbled by stigma. When women bosses adopt forms of recruitment that are congruent with their associates' preferences, e.g., by employing kinship language and polite address, they succeed at recruitment but fail to symbolize corruptibility, which rests on the more assertive signs and swagger associated with a can-do form of masculinity in this context (e.g., violence and sexualized language). But when women bosses like Huda and Sana adopt the masculine-coded signs and swagger that signal corruptibility, their performances alienate women subordinates, who are preoccupied with signaling decency in a male-dominated and stigmatizing environment. Thus, women's agency is compromised, this case suggests, because stigma inhibits their ability to bring two distinct kinds of capacities (symbolic and relational) into alignment. Veiled delicacy allows women to secure women associates but bars them from becoming the associates of powerful men in the corruption circuit. Brutal swagger allows women to send signals to the corruption circuit but blocks their ability to recruit women associates.

Recruiting is complicated for women not only because the agency of women leaders is hamstrung by stigma but also because the agency of their subordinates is constrained by the need to combat stigma. When confronted with the dignity dilemma of working in a stigmatized profession, junior women work to recoup their damaged respectability by enacting performances that may mitigate stigma but that also compel women to engage in various forms of professional retreat. Junior women rebuff male colleagues, stay out of the interview room when a suspect is being questioned, and request auxiliary positions so they can stay home unless specifically called to work for a particular assignment. These gestures allow them to buy some gendered respectability, but this purchase comes at the cost of professional competence. By undertaking veiled delicacy performances, women enact agency not by asserting themselves in a male-dominated profession but by laying claim to a privacy that their social location and masculine occupation robs from them.

But even though veiled delicacy is a prominent strategy subordinate woman use in pursuit of dignity, it isn't the only one. Interview data suggest that another pathway to stigma mitigation lies in simply doing police work. Ameera complained that she had not put on a uniform in order to polish shoes. She wished to learn how to conduct investigations, but her lowly rank and her assignment at a women's station made the desire hard to achieve. Fiza, who resented being made to wait on her boss, spoke enviously of women she knew that were employed by the navy. "Their uniforms are so graceful," she said. "They are provided with proper workplaces and treated with respect." Yet the opportunities for acquiring honor through police work were limited for women. Instead, low-ranking women across the policing context said they were denigrated in various ways. They were spoken down to and asked to sweep, clean, and serve tea. Many said they were harassed by their male colleagues and mocked by their superiors. In short, junior women opted for a form of agency that reinforced their subordination in the police force because they were provided with insufficient pathways to honor. Denied opportunities to mitigate stigma by undertaking competent policing, they preferred to retreat as much as possible from visibility, indeed to stay home if they could.

These findings advance feminist thinking in two ways. First, they suggest that agency is made up of two analytically distinct capacities—displaying and recruiting—that must work in tandem for actors like Huda and Sana to accomplish their goals of upward mobility. It is insufficient, therefore, to think of agency as just about doing; we must understand performance not only as a vehicle for mobilizing culture to remake meaning but also as a medium of enrollment, an invitation to audiences and interlocutors to buy into, support, and extend the meanings that actors advance through their displays. And it is at the intersection of these distinct capacities, doing and recruiting, that stigma disrupts women's capacities in the workplace.

Second, the findings also point to the relationship between recruitment and the glass ceiling. In the police case, the women's gendered inability to invoke particular meanings doesn't just keep them out of chains of power; it also shapes local perceptions of women's capacities and their leadership. I opened this chapter by highlighting local explanations for women's marginality in the police force. Women cannot ascend to positions of authority, senior men claimed, because of their need to adhere to the norms of purdah. But how precisely do purdah norms limit women's competence? The empirical case outlined in this chapter suggests that women's perceived need to abide by the aesthetics of modesty and delicacy keeps them out of corruption chains, which run on brutal and violent signals. Since they are unable to slot into the informal networks that channel power in this context, women formally provided with leadership positions are read as dead switches. Their inability to elicit favors, generate money, or mobilize resources renders women into poor conductors of power, forced to undertake placatory modes of recruitment that undermine their operational capacities.

In this chapter I have shown how stigma shapes women's opportunities in a male-dominated, male-coded profession where women are not only few in number but also concentrated at the bottom of the hierarchy. Next, I turn to a context, that of lady health workers, where the workforce is exclusively made up of women, and the work, providing primary health support to expectant mothers and young children, is coded as feminine. How does the stigma matrix operate in this alternate environment? Do women enjoy better opportunities for accomplishing relational agency in a terrain where the workforce consists only of women? Do the symbols they draw on in this woman-majority, female-coded arena provide better purchase for accomplishing extension through recruitment? As we will see, even when women are in the majority and the workplace is saturated with signs and symbols associated with women, the stigma matrix still hobbles women's agency and creates problems for their destigmatization strategies.

## 4 | SACRED CONDUITS: STIGMA AND THE AGENCY OF HEALTH WORKERS

**ON A BALMY WINTER'S DAY** in Karachi, I head out to meet Shazia and Shaheen at a government hospital located in Shamsheer, a working-class district situated in the north of Karachi and inhabited largely by factory workers, vegetable farmers, fishermen, and migrants from the north and the west of Pakistan (names of places have been changed).[1] Shazia (43 years old) and Shaheen (30 years old) are both lady health supervisors (LHS), and they have invited me today to observe a meeting they are conducting with the lady health workers they are tasked with supervising. LHWs are a women-only community health force employed by the Pakistani state to control child and maternal mortality, circulate contraceptives, push vaccine compliance, and help clients manage diseases such as tuberculosis.

Shazia meets me in the yard of the government hospital where the women will all collect today. The hospital, set back from the road, is hard to locate. The rambling old building stands in a large mud lot shaded with trees. Draped in peeling paint and caked in dust, it must have been an elegant mansion in the 1940s, when it was built, but the local government appropriated it a few years ago as an abandoned building. According to Shazia, her boss, a government-appointed district doctor, asked his various health workers, including Shazia and her family, to occupy the building as an initial step toward seizing it for official use. He had promised her, she says, that she would get to stay on after he secured control over it. "He said he would allow me to live with my family in the servants' quarters built in the back," she says, "but then he changed his mind."

In a mud lot outside the building, Shazia introduces me to her sons, who are carrying plastic chairs they have brought from her home. Shazia points to the chairs. "See, I have to arrange for chairs on a personal basis," she says to me laughing. I follow her inside, and we make our way down a dusty corridor and then come to an abrupt stop outside a closed door. "The room is occupied right now," Shazia says. "There's a vaccinators' meeting going on, but once the meeting is over, the room will be free for the rest of the day, and we can use it." The boys leave. Shazia and I stand around outside the door. Shazia fans herself with an envelope she has pulled out of her bag. She is perspiring heavily. "I'm glad you're here," she says to me. "I told them [the people in charge at this hospital] that doctor *sahib* [the official who permitted me to do my research in the field] sent you, that you have come from America," she says, grinning, "so because of you, they will let us have the room."

Some fifteen minutes later, I follow Shazia into the room. Expecting a conference room, I'm surprised to find a roomy office dominated by a very large desk draped in green fabric and covered with files. There are six chairs arranged around the desk, and several more stand like sentries against the walls. A troop of about twenty women trail in shortly after; some seat themselves in the available chairs, and some sit down cross-legged on the floor. The women pull files out of plastic shopping bags that they are using as tote bags. A few of the women have purses, which they place on the floor beside them. Two women have balanced tiny babies on their knee and are bending down to fuss over them. Shazia introduces me to the room, although many of the women already know me. I sit down next to Shaheen, my co-host, while Shazia rushes off to find a bathroom.

The room soon fills with the sound of several concurrent conversations. Appearing to be in a cheerful mood, the women are laughing and shouting over one another. Zeenat, a particularly shrill and exuberant young worker, is explaining why women in her "catchment area" are unable to comply when Zeenat, following official prescriptions, instructs them to deliver their babies in hospitals. "Listen, in the homes in my area," she tells me, "there are days when the stove never gets lit, the women have to turn to handwork [stitching, knitting] in order to eat, and it's hard to make the rent, so they say to me, '*Baji* [sister], to go to hospital I have to pay taxi fare, then registration. Then they [the doctors] write prescriptions. These things are not in my capacity. . . ."

But Zeenat's narration is suddenly cut off. The door opens with a bang, and a large man bursts into the room, storming, "*Hanh jee* [yeah], what business do you all have here?" he asks very aggressively. "We're from the National Program," several women reply in chorus, referring to the official title of the lady health worker program in Pakistan. "Ask madam," one voice calls out. "The vaccinator meeting is over" another says.

"But here, I don't have the capacity for you," the man shouts. He puts a lot of emotion into the word "you" as if it is particularly these women he can't accommodate. Another man is cringing behind the large man in the hallway, trying desperately to placate the first man. "Sir, they are from Aman," he says. "They've gotten permission."

"No, no," the women protest. "We're from the National Program," one clarifies. "Where did Aman come from?" another asks angrily. The large man doesn't seem to care. "I'll see to all of you," he says, in what sounds like a threat. He stalks out of the room. The women start rising and collecting their things. Raised male voices continue in the hallway. The second man is telling the first one, "Sir, I'll arrange a place over there. Sir, I'll move them." The first man continues shouting, but I can't make out what he is saying.

The women start filing out of the room, many of them muttering under their breath. I'm not sure what to do, so I stand up to follow them. Shaheen, my co-host, looks embarrassed. She says, "The problem is that we have no place to sit." "Many people have been telling me that," I reply. "Even when we are given a room, officially, it is soon snatched from us," Shaheen says. "We get to enjoy it only briefly. We get maybe fifteen days of happiness. We come into the space; we put up charts on the walls,"

"Spend our own personal money to do it up," Zeenat, the health worker I'd been talking to, interjects.

"Spend a thousand rupees on it," Shaheen continues, "and they come and snatch it from us. Along with the decorations we put up."

"We all get together and contribute donations," Zeenat interjects again. The donations pay for chart papers and other trimmings.

"It [the room] is snatched along with the decoration," Shaheen continues. "Okay. At least return our trimmings!" she says, laughing. "And the proof of this, there's a room in the back here, even now, I can show you, it's got charts up that we made by hand."

Shazia, my host, reenters, and Zeenat says to her, "Madam, go again and speak. Sir was here right now, raging that 'you people have no business sitting here.'"

"I heard the shouting," Shazia replies.

"Go and speak again," Zeenat insists.

"I heard what he had to say," Shazia replies, more firmly this time. I assume that she doesn't want to face the man's wrath any more than she has to. Another male doctor comes sheepishly into the room. He comes directly up to me and says apologetically, "You carry on, Madam. There's no problem."

"Why was he raging?" Shazia asks.

"I'll arrange chairs for you," the doctor says to me, ignoring the question. "Thank you, sir," Shazia says, humbly.

"No worries," I say to the doctor. "I understand, people are very sensitive about chairs in Pakistan." This is a meager attempt at a joke because a chair can refer also to a post such as a seat of government.

"No, we don't want chairs," Shaheen says emphatically. "We want a room!"

Several women take up this chant. "We want a room! We want a room!" The doctor leaves. Eventually, we are shunted to a covered verandah in the back of the building. It is a tiny, dusty, empty space without chairs or tables. Shazia's "personal chairs" come in handy after all.

### PLACELESS WOMEN

While jarring, this encounter was not altogether unexpected. In the year that I spent observing lady health workers (LHWs) and their immediate supervisors (LHS), these voluble and cheerful women quite literally occupied the margins of the health offices I visited to meet with them.[4] Even though I was a visiting scholar with no connection to the state, I was provided by the doctors at the local district hospital with a room (and attached bathroom) to carry out my research. In contrast, my participants, actual employees of the state, typically hung around in corridors, sat in groups on stairwells, loitered in parking lots, or perched on public benches when they came to these offices for meetings or other business. "We are not given any room or space for our work," they complained to me. "If we want to have a meeting, we have to do it in my house," Shazia said. Laila, a 40-year-old LHW, said something similar in an interview. Although she is required to visit various clinics and health offices in the course of her work, she told me angrily, she is given neither space to work in nor a seat to sit on while she is there. "Sometimes they sit us in the corridor," she said, "or, if we are friendly with someone there, personally, if we get along, for instance, with the vaccinator, then she may allow us to sit in her office, but everyone else will say, 'You can't sit here. You will disturb our work.'"

This lack of provision is compounded by what women describe as their humiliating treatment at the hands of their various bosses. "They think of us as dust on their shoes," Ayesha, a middle-aged supervisor, complains. "They think we are equivalent to slippers," she says of her bosses. Women complain that bosses speak to them curtly, yell at them, fling files at them, leave them cooling their heels for hours despite having set up appointments, and worse, that they occasionally harass them sexually.

This treatment is surprising not just because lady health workers work to protect this developing country against the ravages of disease and overpopulation but also because in addition to these onerous duties, LHWs expend considerable effort going door to door administering the polio vaccine to Pakistani children. As frontline forces in the global battle to eradicate the polio virus, Pakistani lady health workers are therefore vital links in the transnational aid circuit that facilitates sizable flows of foreign currency into Pakistan via the GPEI (Global Polio Eradication Initiative), a billion-dollar-a-year global project seeking to purge the world of the polio virus by vaccinating vulnerable children. Pakistan is one of the last countries in the world to still host the crippling and incurable polio disease. And LHWs are crucial agents in the state's efforts to eradicate it. Accordingly, national and transnational policy documents describe LHWs in glowing terms as "the backbone" of both, the Pakistani health system and the GPEI project in Pakistan (e.g., Kayani et al. 2016; Khan et al. 2009).

So how does the backbone of a country's public health system come to be treated like a heel? The stigma that lady health workers experience is shaped by the intermixing of local and global forces and processes, a churn that is captured by employing my framework of the stigma matrix. In earlier chapters I have described how stigma is constituted at the macro level by colonialism, neoliberal Islam, and securitization. I have also explained how these macro-level forces are mediated at the intermediate level by organizational arrangements, which give rise to specific meanings and feelings around gender and class. In this chapter I examine how the matrix shapes women's experiences and their agency at the micro level—how they describe the stigma they experience, how they respond to it, and how their strategies fare in the various settings they occupy.

Health workers experience the stigma structured by local and global processes in many arenas and interactions. They experience it in the racialized distribution of risk, whereby certain bodies are safely removed from a field of work that is the target of terror threats, while other bodies are sent out into the dangerous arena to complete global objectives. They experience it in the classed distribution of physical exertion and financial compensation, whereby certain bodies are renumerated handsomely, while other, harder-working bodies are not. They experience it in the gendered and classed meanings assigned to their work by their own families and communities, where LHWs are seen as abject figures, evocative of poverty and desperation. And they experience it in the pollution of their gendered identities and reputations.

Lady health workers contest these different experiences of stigma by laying claim to a new morally laden identity that is simultaneously militaristic and maternal. Drawing on various local and global idioms—quasi-mystical healer, mother, holy warrior, they enact agency by mounting a destigmatizing performance that seeks to reframe the meaning of their work, their wages, and their contravention of gender norms. Adopting the role of forbearing woman, quasi-mystical healer, mother, and holy warrior, lady health workers deploy a quixotic presentation I call "martial motherhood," a moral performance that not only aims to sanitize their problematized identities but also acts as a social emollient, helping ease LHW efforts to cultivate connections with clients, a connection that they can leverage in service to their professional goals.

But while their martial motherhood performances work to further LHWs' relational agendas with poor and working-class clients, these destigmatization performances cannot overcome the local and global hierarchies that work to widen the class breaches between workers and elite actors in the arena of community health. Thus, as in the case of policewomen (chapter 3), the agency of health workers is also compromised by class structures. However, in this case, the connection between women's symbolic and relational agency is more complicated. On the one hand, LHWs' symbolic efforts help to improve their efficacy in forging connection with the poor and working-class citizens they serve. But on the other, the classed character of their symbolic agency also winds up amplifying women's marginal status within the state.

The case of health workers, like that of the policewomen examined in the last chapter, helps to illuminate the mechanics of the stigma matrix, which employs multiple structures (e.g., class as well as gender) to hamstring women's agency. In both cases, women's symbolic efforts are constrained by issues related to class, which undermine women's relational agendas at work. Before I describe how class acts as a stumbling block for the destigmatization performances of lady health workers, however, it is important to understand how health work came to be stigmatized in this context.

## THE SOURCES OF HEALTH WORKERS' STIGMA

*Global Imperatives and the transformation of LHW work.* One important way that health work became degraded, LHWs say, is because of globalization. The agendas and interests of "white" people, they claim, transformed their work, eroded their reputations, and obliterated the joy they had previously derived from their jobs. In the old days, health workers say, when the National Program first began in 1994, the work was relatively easy, and it was comparatively decent. The original mandate of the program, when it was first conceived during the tenure of Pakistan's first woman prime minister, Benazir Bhutto, was to stem child and maternal deaths. "Before that, there was no program like this one," Shaheen tells me. "We were the first of our kind, and they [the doctors and officers] had a very hard time convincing women to join the ranks of the force."

To get the program off the ground, doctors working in peri-urban and rural communities in the 1990s sought and recruited local resident women who had had some schooling and who displayed leadership qualities. These women were then coaxed, in the name of compassion and community-mindedness, to join the program. Hiba, an LHS who works in a peri-urban community on Karachi's border with Baluchistan province, recalls, "I had no interest in working. My husband is a building contractor, and he was doing quite well, financially," she tells me, "and I was very busy with housework. I had children and I was happy staying at home." "How then did you wind up in this line of work," I ask. "There was a doctor in my neighborhood," she says, "on the lookout for an educated woman. People told him that I had completed matric [ten years of education], and he got after me to sign up. I told him, 'Sir, I am not interested in working. Women in my family do not work outside the home.' But he argued that as an educated woman, it is my duty to spread knowledge among the illiterate women in my neighborhood. That's how it was described at the time. They said to us that first, we will train you and teach you good things about health and then you will go and impart this information to the women in your community."

The program was sold to early recruits not as a job but as a government sponsored education initiative. "They told us that after you have finished your housework, in the afternoon, when you are done with cooking and all that, then for just one to two hours, you will visit a neighbor and tell her good things about health," Roshan, an LHW who works in Karachi's district east, tells me. "So, we thought, this is very good, I will learn good things, and then I will share good things with others, and my home responsibilities will also not get disrupted," she says.

Since it was not quite a job, the work could be conducted discreetly. Women went quietly to their neighbors' homes, as if they were simply making a social call, and they offered advice and information about health and hygiene, childcare, and female health. Since they were better educated than many of their neighbors, and now, thanks to the program, also better informed about health, they were greeted with enthusiasm. "I made a name in the community," Shireen from central Karachi recalls. "All the ladies knew me, and some people started calling me doctor *baji* [sister]," she says, laughing. "And although I was not a doctor, for them I was better than a doctor because I was giving useful information but without the supercilious attitude of a doctor." Since she looked and talked in ways the clients found familiar, Shireen says, they were very comfortable with her and were pleased with her visits. Similarly, Rehmat says, "People used to point me out when they saw me at a gathering, they would say, this *baji* [sister] tells us very good things about health, they appreciated it a lot, the things that I told them." Like Shireen and Rehmat, many first-generation LHWs who began their jobs in the 1990s said that their work provided them with a lot of joy. They relished the chance to help their neighbors, and they enjoyed the respect and honor this service generated for them in their communities.

The easy and discreet intimacy of the National Program was rudely disrupted, LHWs say, when polio was "shoved on our shoulders." The National Program was founded in 1994. Polio vaccination, LHWs say, was not our concern back then. "We were concerned primarily with women's health," Shaheen tells me. "That is the bread and butter of this program. We care about young mothers, women of childbearing age, and young children. We had *nothing* to do with polio." The mission to promote maternal health, Shazia says, was "the main motivating factor for many of us. We wanted to help the mothers in our community, *our own community*."

But then in 1999, polio vaccination modalities in Pakistan changed in response to global pressures. "White people," Shazia says, "were suddenly struck with the motivation to eradicate polio, and they started pressuring Pakistan to step up its vaccination efforts." The polio program stopped relying on fixed-point campaigns, such as polio camps (mobile vaccination units set up in various locations, where children could be brought for vaccination), and instead decided to take the vaccine to peoples' homes. This onerous new mode of vaccine delivery required a large force of workers, "and for that," Mona says bitterly, "they had a ready-made force, right here, to draw on—the lady health workers."

When they do polio work, LHWs are paid a stipend of five hundred rupees a day (roughly five dollars at the time of my fieldwork) over and above their health work wages (20,000 rupees or $200 per month). Polio work, which involves long hours of labor, usually continues for several days each month. On campaign days, women often head out of their homes at dawn and don't return until well after dark. They trudge on foot from door to door, carrying coolers containing the vaccine. If they ring the bell at a particular house and no one answers, they have to circle back later in the evening or the next day. Sometimes people don't answer because they're sleeping. Sometimes, clients say, they are simply fed up with the dogged frequency of the program.

Door-to-door work would be easier, LHWs say, if they only had to do it in their own communities where people know them. But for polio, women are sometimes sent to work in distant communities where they are strangers. Since people in those areas don't know them, women say, they are sometimes hostile and rude. "People slam doors in our face," Laila says. "They abuse us. They say, 'Doesn't the government have anything better to do?'"

Officially, participation in the polio program is voluntary. LHWs can refuse to work on polio, and some do. But unofficially, they say, they are compelled to participate. "I was told if you don't do polio then we don't need you as an LHW," Ramsha says. Local supervisors and district-level doctors who are pressured by global agencies and local elites to efficiently conduct polio campaigns shift some of this pressure on to the LHWs under their command. "They just put everything on the LHW," Shala says bitterly. "Polio also, put on the LHW. Measles also, put on the LHW. If you want someone to sit in the audience at a political event, call your LHW. If you need to do a community health event, LHW. If you want to have your house painted, LHW. If there are flood victims to see to, LHW. Whatever you need, just call the LHW. Here is a ready-made army for all your problems."

Polio also makes community health work more onerous. While the National Program had initially required only a couple of hours of work done over a few days a week, polio work adds several more hours of labor to the LHW's slate and goes on for several days, leaving women with less time to complete their other duties. "In a month where there is polio," Mehnaz tells me, "our regular work suffers. We have to scramble to do our visits, collect the data—how many births, how many pregnancies in our catchment area, who has had what injection," listing some of the duties her regular work requires. "Then we prepare the data for submission to the office," she says, showing me the files she prepares each month. "I work very long hours, believe me, it's a morning till night job."

Once polio work was added to their slate, being an LHW was no longer about finding a few hours in the day, whether morning or evening, to visit known neighbors. Instead, it required setting out at dawn to work all day in unfamiliar communities, begging and cajoling people to accept the vaccine for their children. There were more meetings now and more people to report to and satisfy and get signatures from and a lot more interface with strange men. Yet, workers tell me with chagrin, neither their salaries nor their status changed. Despite their increased contributions to public health work, LHWs were seen, they said, not as government employees on salary but as community members who support government initiatives in exchange for a *wazifa* (a stipend).

When they were pulled into doing polio work, LHWs suddenly became more visible within their own communities and in the public imagination at large. Rather than wise local women discreetly offering advice to their neighbors, they began to be seen as forlorn laborers trudging on the public roads and interfacing with strangers. Their new visibility also drew attention to the content of their health work. Where previously neighbors had not given much thought to the nature of the advice these women offered, now they began to focus on just what it was that LHWs were peddling—not only a vaccine widely believed to cause infertility and impotence in boys but also birth control aids and advice. Suddenly, LHWs became unwelcome visitors.

Despite what first-generation LHWs say, however, the degradation of their work was not shaped just by the addition of polio to their list of duties. Changes in the broader economy also produced changes in the composition of the workforce, the motivations of the workers, and, therefore, the perception of the work in the community at large. While first-generation women were cajoled into a quasi-job they did not need to perform, second-generation women were pulled into this occupation by their financial situations, and unlike the first-generation LHWs, these newer recruits were relying on their wages to make ends meet.

**Neoliberalism and the transformation of women's work.** Global health imperatives were not alone in transforming health work. The occupation was degraded also as a result of the impact of global processes on Pakistan's economy. As I describe in chapter 1, in the late 1980s and early 1990s the Pakistani state signed on to the Washington consensus, and as a consequence became the tenth-largest recipient of World Bank and IMF loans. In compliance with the structural adjustment policies required by these loans, the country began to enact various neoliberal measures. It began deregulating business, worked to reduce government spending on social programs, allowed increases in the prices of petroleum and electricity, and eased away subsidies that had made commodities such as flour and cooking oil affordable for the working-class and poor segments of the population.

By the end of the 1980s, these policies had caused the public-sector share of industrial investment to fall from 73 to 18 percent (Brown 2016). The state began to sell off its stake in mills, factories, and other manufacturing units; by 2005 it had privatized 160 public-sector companies. One hundred and thirty such enterprises collapsed in the wake of their sale. Hundreds of thousands of previously secure state-based jobs simply vanished even as the policies of structural adjustment continued to amplify the prices of basic necessities such as food and fuel (Sajjad 2014).

People who were able to hold on to their jobs following the sale of their public-sector organizations faced a transformed work context. In contrast with government jobs, private-sector jobs rarely provide job security, pensions, or other perks like health care. While employees in government jobs are able to unionize in order to press for reform, such collective bargaining is not possible in private-sector jobs, where production processes are often too fragmented to allow for unionization.

These changes had a disproportionate impact on male workers. Men not only formed a larger share of the labor market in Pakistan compared to women, but they also formed a larger proportion of the workforce in the institutions and sectors, such as the Karachi Electric Supply Corporation, Pakistan Telecom, and the National Refinery, that were undergoing divestment by the state.

The job loss and the inflation brought about as a result of neoliberal policies disrupted the gendered dynamics of urban working-class families. As jobs became scarce and insecure, working-class urban men, finding it increasingly impossible to meet their family's economic needs, were forced either to seek supplementary sources of income or to accept the financial contribution of their wives (see also Shaheed and Mumtaz 1990). These financial disruptions disturbed family dynamics as male headship in the family had previously been tied to men's breadwinning role. Through their capacity for financial provision, men protected women from the hardships and privations they would otherwise encounter in the world of wage work. Their ability to maintain this traditional arrangement of male protection and women's privacy underwrote their family's claim to decency.

The disruption of these normative familial arrangements was evident in lady health worker narratives. The women I interviewed fell into two categories. One group of women, which I have been describing as first-generation health workers, joined the program in the 1990s. These women were confident in their husbands' breadwinning capacities and said that their recruitment was motivated not by financial considerations but by a desire to engage in social welfare work.

A second group of women, the second-generation workers, joined the program after 2000 (n=25). These women said that their recruitment into this line of work was motivated primarily by financial necessity. The men these women had relied on for financial support (fathers, brothers, husbands, and sons) had failed to find steady or adequate sources of income. These women had therefore felt compelled by their *majboori* (compulsion, constraint, helplessness) to take on the lady health worker jobs.

While first-generation women complained about the added pressures and insults that polio drives had put on their plates, many of them were sanguine about their status and their roles within the health work sector. Since a large proportion of these women came from families that were financially secure, many of them successfully resisted polio work and instead chose to focus primarily on the women and children who resided within their own neighborhoods. These women said they were motivated not by money but by their desire to serve their community. For them, health work was a source of pride and honor.

Second-generation women, in contrast, were unable to resist polio work for fear that their much-needed jobs would be withdrawn in retaliation for the refusal. When their bosses pressed these women to volunteer, they said they were too afraid to resist. These women relied too urgently on their incomes, which they used to pay rent and children's school fees. These women expressed grief and bitterness about the humiliations they encountered in the course of their work. They felt that they were forced to weather mortifications because of their poverty. Second-generation health workers railed at the injustice of a patriarchy that is unable to protect them from enervating work but nevertheless continues to subject them to the dishonor of transgressing into masculine-coded spaces for work.

### THE SETTINGS OF HEALTH WORKER STIGMA

The degradation of health work impacts women's interactions and experiences in several arenas of their professional and personal lives. It shapes their experiences and encounters within the family and the community, where they say they are stigmatized in various ways. And it mars their interactions with local bosses and global actors, who they say humiliate them at every turn. In each of these arenas, women say that their interlocutors shame and belittle them in various ways. In this section I describe each of these stigma arenas in turn.

*The family.* "This work is not considered decent," LHW Shiza's 20-year-old daughter Sara tells me. Shiza, a second-generation LHW has four children. Her husband, when he was alive, worked as a sweeper in a local madrasah, earning wages that were insufficient to provide for his children's education. To plug this gap, Shiza took up LHW work, because, she argued, unlike other jobs she may have chosen, in this job "it's just ladies, we have no interaction with males, even our LHS [supervisors] are ladies." In their community, she and her daughter explain, it is not considered decent for a woman to step out of the house for work. "If you are going out of the house, people assume that you must be coming into contact with all kinds of people," Sara explains. "They think you have lost your morals and become a woman of loose character." But what if a woman needs to earn a living, like if she is a widow?" I ask. "In such cases," Sara says, "women try to work from home, they take on stitching or ironing, or if they can't do that, and if they are educated, they will try to pick a job that entails very limited contact with men, like teaching girls. Teaching is still seen as somewhat decent." She and her younger sister, both primary school teachers, have been helping their mother financially, since their father passed away a few years ago. "But to tell you the truth," Sara says, "even teachers are not spared the gossip. Even about teachers, people say things." "What kind of things do they say?" I ask. "They say, 'Look at Shiza's daughter. She goes all alone and stands at the bus stop, then God knows where she goes, she comes back late in the evening. Where has she been? Who was she with?" Sara works at a school some distance from her neighborhood, and sometimes it is dark by the time she gets home. "If you come home after dark, again, people are making assumptions about your character," she says.

"That's the thing about LHW work," Shiza says. "We picked it because at first, we were told, 'You will be working within your own neighborhood. You will just work in the houses in your immediate neighborhood. You will work only with ladies. This is a ladies' program. It has nothing to do with men. And you can set your own time." So Shiza had assumed that the LHW work would not compromise her respectability. But she was in for a rude shock. "Within a month or two, they told me to go and do polio," she complains. After that, she says, it was impossible to do her LHW work discreetly. Her neighbors now saw her as a government agent and began to make her feel a great deal of shame. "Why do you come here to incite my wife?" one neighbor would tell her each time she showed up. Others would shout at her and call her names, she tells me sorrowfully. "They would say, 'Our women are not like you! They practice purdah!'" she says, explaining that her polio work in particular had made it seem like she was a loose woman who went to strange communities knocking on doors.

Once they saw her in the light of a purdah-defiant woman, Shiza's neighbors were no longer happy to let her "influence" their wives. Whereas first-generation LHWs had gone quietly into homes and spoken discreetly with the women residing there, women like Shiza now had to deal with families, especially men, who were indignant about the content of Shiza's work. She didn't just provide women with advice about nutrition and hygiene; she was also collecting private, intimate information about birth control preferences and practices, which she entered into a log to submit to the district health office. She distributed advice on very personal subjects, like how much of a gap women should aim to leave between the birth of their children. And she offered women contraceptives, which they sometimes requested she do secretly, without letting their husbands know.

Once they became aware of her role as a government agent, thanks to polio work, people also became aware of the sexualized content of her main job, Shiza says. Because of the visibility lent to her by polio, Shiza's health work also became shameful in people's eyes. "Going from home to home to talk about condoms and family planning is not deemed decent or respectable behavior," she says. Lady health workers like Shiza came to be stigmatized by their own neighbors not only because some of them considered it vulgar to openly discuss topics related with sex but also because contraceptives have been described as incompatible with virtuous behavior by some religious leaders who claim that birth control represents unwarranted interference in divine providence (see Hafeez 2019). Because she was going from house to house providing women not only with advice but also with actual condoms, pills, injections, and other contraceptive aids, some people saw her as a source of corruption who would pollute their families with her ideas.

Still, these small indignities are bearable, Shiza says, but polio work is not. "Whatever indignities we suffer with LHW work," she says, "it is still done among our own [community]." LHW work only involves working within Shiza's own neighborhood, and while some of her neighbors are critical of her work, others do appreciate and support her. "There are homes I go to where I am greeted warmly," she says. "They offer me tea and friendship, and I look forward to these visits." But polio work regularly adds a whole new field of injuries to Shiza work life. "For polio," she says, "I walk like a machine all day. I tell my daughters, 'These are not legs, they are wheels, I'm not a human, I'm a rickshaw,'" she says. "Sometimes, I'll go to a house, and someone will come out and scream at me so harshly that I can't stop weeping. The tears just roll out, I can't stop them, and I think to myself, 'Really, it's like I am not even a human anymore.'"

Despite these troubles, Shiza says, she has always exercised patience in the face of her work. She has learned to tolerate the shame and humiliation. "My skin has thickened considerably over the years, but what breaks my heart now," she says, "is the shame my job is causing for my daughters." Shiza's daughters Sara and Myra recently got engaged to men their mother had selected for them. Sara's fiancé is from an educated family, she tells me, but "in our society, unfortunately, even the educated class thinks this job [LHW work] is indecent." For this reason, Sara tells me, her mother's job has created considerable consternation among her in-laws. "Some people went to my prospective in-laws," she says. "They were taunting my in-laws and saying, 'Her mother walks the roads. Where are you getting your son married?'" The comments caused embarrassment for Sara, when her in-laws repeated them back to her. She tells me, "I have never been against my mother's work, but obviously when I hear such comments, I feel a lot of pain." Shiza listens to Sara's comment with evident sorrow. "I have had to raise these father-less girls alone," Shiza says. "And I did it through this job. It was such a moment of pride for me, when I got them, both engaged, but when I come to hear that my job is causing problems for them—." She breaks off, weeping, and in between sobs says, "My heart just breaks."

*The community.* When Hajra first began polio work in 2010, she tells me, some of her more conservative neighbors reacted so badly that she and many of her colleagues began doing their work covertly. They would pretend that they weren't LHWs at all but only state agents collecting innocuous data. "People would say to our faces, 'Polio! Such contemptible, dirty work! Can't you find anything else to do?'" she says. The National Program's association with polio, she explains, worked to stigmatize their regular health work. "For polio," she says, "we don't just work in our own catchment areas, we are sent to alien places, unfamiliar places, where we don't know anyone, nor does anyone there know us." This foray into unknown places has made her neighbors see Hajra as immoral and sexually available. "I go out from morning to night, and I am forced to face all kinds of taunts during my workday, and these things makes them think poorly of me."

When they go on foot from house to house for their polio work, Hajra says, they are harassed and humiliated. "Such dirty things people say to us. Men will come out and try to lure us into their homes as if we are providing some other kind of service," she tells me angrily. "They make kissing noises at us, and they say, '*Aaja, aaja*' [come, come]," as one would to an animal. "Sometimes, a man will come out and say, '*mujhe pilla day janeman*' [let me sip it, darling]." Encounters like these make polio work not only appear disrespectful but also feel like an injury to honor. "From inside, you feel, your respect is withering," Hajra says, adding that she would much prefer to do just the work the program was originally tasked with. "Women used to die in childbirth, and we helped to bring that number down," she tells me proudly. "The whole world was impressed by our results, that this poor country has done so much to reduce maternal mortality." But any pride she might feel for her work has diminished, Hajra says, by the injuries polio work produces.

"I've been pelted with shoes and stones," Hajra says. While working in a remote neighborhood one time, "children came out of somewhere and started throwing stones at us." Hajra says, "It felt like we are not even humans, like we have come from some other world." "They threw stones at you?" I ask her incredulously. "Yes," she replies, "as soon as we got down [from the bus] a racket began. People were chanting, 'Polio workers have come! Polio workers have come!' I don't know where this *lashkar* [troop] of children came from and began throwing stones at us," she recalls. "I was scared that a stone might get me. One girl [polio worker] passed out from fear."

**Local bosses.** In addition to the humiliation they face from their communities and their families, LHWs say they are subjected to severe degradation at the hands of their bosses. Mehr, a supervisor, would frequently bring up the behavior of the doctors who oversaw LHW work. On one occasion, Mehr and I were gossiping in a verandah outside a district hospital in north Karachi, where supervisors from all over the city come each month to attend a meeting. Mehr, a supervisor who has worked for the National Program for more than ten years, was discussing the recent drama I had witnessed in Shamsheer, where a doctor had rudely ejected lady health workers from a room they were using to meet in. She didn't seem surprised. 'Doctors hold LHWs in very low estimation,' she remarked. 'Like an object to be used or like a piece of furniture.' She drew closer to me and whispered, 'The one you met yesterday, the fat doctor, he came to me one time, after a meeting, and he says, "you have to get me Naheed's phone number, she is a ripe one."' Mehr was not alone in making such a disclosure.

Fazeela, a supervisor I met in her home, told me that after a recent meeting, a male doctor in attendance had caught sight of one of the LHWs in Fazeela's charge. 'I brought Komal with me that day, and he saw her,' she says. Komal is an attractive woman in her thirties and has what Fazeela describes as 'an especially good figure.' 'She is tall, and she sticks her chest out,' Fazeela says. I have met Komal and know that Fazeela doesn't like her. Komal is one of the very few LHWs who arrives at the health office with her head uncovered. She wears a fashionable bob cut and trendy, short and tailored tunics. Fazeela frequently brings her up in conversations with me, describing her as a pain in the neck: 'So the doctor came and sat down next to her, and he kept touching her arm and talking to her.' After the meeting,

Fazeela says, the doctor came over and said to her, 'Fazeela, either give me her number or give her mine.'

This demand enraged Fazeela. "I was outraged," she says. "I'm not a pimp.' But she isn't angry with the doctor alone. Komal shouldn't have gotten Fazeela mixed up in such a situation, she says. But then she relents a little. 'Can't blame her entirely. The doctors are scoundrels,' she says. 'Do you know what we say about them?' 'What?' I ask. 'We say that if a *dupatta* [a veil] gets caught in a shrub, the doctor will get a crick in his neck from craning to catch sight of a woman,' she says, laughing. 'Just give him a suggestion of a woman and he loses his mind.' We both laugh. Then Fazeela grows somber. 'I also have had a lot of indecent proposals,' she tells me. 'Doctors say to me, if not you, then send us one of your girls,' she says, growing angry again. 'This is something I could put on the media even.' She says, 'I know journalists. I could go on TV and tell all.' Then she adds, 'But why rock the boat? Who knows what reprisals there may be?' Fazeela was afraid to go to the media, as doing so would require her to disclose her identity. She said she was glad I would write about her experiences. 'You can give me a different name in your book,' she suggested.

**Global elites.** On a lazy afternoon, I've been hanging around the health office all day and am tired. In a room set aside for meetings, the health workers are sitting at tables arranged in a large circle. The afternoon session hasn't started yet. It's running late. I sit down next to a bespectacled woman I have spoken to a few times before, and we begin talking about global actors. A trio of women sitting across from us is listening in curiously. They're whispering and nudging each other. Suddenly, one of them calls out to me, 'Are you talking about WHO?' She means the World Health Organization. I nod at her. She gets up and charges across the room. 'I will tell you about WHO!' she says. The other women giggle and clap. 'No, I am not afraid. If you want the truth, get it from me,' she exclaims. I get up and join her in the center of the room where she is standing. She appears to be talking not just to me but to the room: 'I will tell you about it in front of all these women. They will back me up.' The other supervisors grin and nod. Her name is Kanwal, I learn. She has been a supervisor for over ten years. Today, she wants to tell me about a specific incident that she thinks will reveal all I need to know about the WHO.

A little while back, Kanwal says, she had been supervising a polio vaccination drive in a catchment area I will call Steep Hill, a settlement of refugees and people from the north of Pakistan, an area that borders Afghanistan. Steep Hill, Kanwal says, is known as a "no-go area," a term that health workers and cops both used to describe a neighborhood considered dangerous to work in. I am familiar with the neighborhood. It is popularly imagined as a wild and untamed settlement outside of the civilized zones of the city. The settlement consists of crude, unfinished huts precariously erected up and down a steep, rugged hill. To get to the settlement, Kanwal says, one has to walk up a steep, unpaved trail, balancing files and paperwork along with other vaccination paraphernalia such as a large cooler containing vials of vaccine.

During the last polio drive, Kanwal was busy with her team going from door to door vaccinating children. It is routine, she tells me, for WHO representatives to visit the polio team as it conducts its business. They check and verify the team's work, their data collection, and their coverage. But when she arrived at the foot of the hill, the WHO representative assigned to check the work of Kanwal's team 'refused to even step out of her air-conditioned, luxury car. Forget about climbing the steep path.' Instead, Kanwal says, 'she called me on my cellphone, commanding me to come to the car.' Kanwal says she felt humiliated and outraged. 'I had to abandon my work and trek all the way down the hill to the car so that the madam could sign the papers.' Kanwal says the woman made her walk up and down the hill not once but several times. 'This story,' she said, 'should convey to you how little the WHO thinks of us and how badly they treat women workers.'

There is a great deal of hooting and clapping at this angry speech. Other women chime in with their own thoughts about the WHO. Ramshah, a well-dressed supervisor, says that she and her workers are offended by the salary disparity between UN workers and themselves. The difference rankles because UN workers, she says, have no local knowledge and are rarely willing to step out of their luxury offices and cars. 'Right!' says Yasmeen, another supervisor, 'and whenever local conditions become too risky, UN workers are pulled out of the field. Who does the work then?' she asks. A chorus of voices takes up this refrain: 'Who does the work then?' Kanwal answers, 'At such times and in certain high-risk localities, it is LHWs who must brave the threat of bullets to ensure that the vaccination work continues.' While this acceptance of risk appears to be a source of pride for LHWs, who describe themselves as soldiers in an army, they also read it as a sign of their less-than-human status in the eyes of global actors like the WHO. 'When we are killed,' Ramshah says, 'the compensation we receive is so low, it feels less like reparation and more like insult.'

As this conversation winds down, I go and sit outside in the large corridor and begin to write notes. Rafya, a supervisor I have met a few times, comes and sits down next to me. 'There are some things I want to tell you,' she says, 'without the recorder on.' I make sure my recorder is off, and she says, 'Then I can tell you what no one else would have the courage to tell you.' She wants me to write what she has to say, so that those in America can hear it, but she doesn't want her voice on tape, in case someone is able to compel me to play it. She claims that the town (meaning the local government) and the WHO collude in corrupt practices. The local representatives, together with global agents, don't just embezzle the money that comes into their accounts to pay for materials such as "chalk" and "photostats" but they also falsify salary records. 'On paper, they show something else, and what they hand out is something else,' she tells me. When I ask for an example, she says, 'My driver's salary was recorded as 4,000 rupees on paper, but he was paid only 2,800 rupees in hand.' 'And does the WHO know that this kind of falsification is going on?' I ask. 'The big WHO bosses are aware of this corruption,' Rafya says, 'but fail to take action.' Rafya insists that it is my job to report such abuse. 'Now that I have told you, I have placed my trust in you,' she says. 'You must be my voice in this matter.'

### WOMEN'S EFFORTS TO MANAGE STIGMA AND RECUPERATE DIGNITY

Women contest the humiliation and degradation inflicted upon them by their families, their communities, and their local and global supervisors in several ways. Their collective responses to the stigmas they encounter because of their work are described in chapter 6. But women also make more personalized efforts to sanitize their problematic identities. Drawing on various local and global symbols and scripts—veils, jihad, motherhood—they attempt through performance to reframe the meaning of their work, their wages, and their contravention of gender norms. I call the moral performance they produce in pursuit of these meanings "martial motherhood." Since it draws on idioms and symbols that are more legible and therefore more meaningful for their working-class and poor clients, "martial motherhood" serves not only as a salve against stigma but, as I show below, acts also as a social emollient that helps ease LHWs' efforts to cultivate connections with clients that they can leverage in service to their professional goals.

But while these martial motherhood performances work to further LHWs relational agendas with clients, as classed and gendered enactments, they don't do much to boost women's status in the fastidious, rational, bureaucratic offices where LHWs go to receive orders and submit their reports and findings. In their interaction with the elites in charge of local and global health initiatives, LHWs' performances reinforce their marginalized social location. The very cultural idioms that enable LHWs to connect with poor and working-class citizens serve also to expand the devaluation of their work.

### MARTIAL MOTHERHOOD

Mehrunnissa claims she has always been extraordinary, even as a child. "Where other children liked to spend their money on candy," she tells me, "I would spend my pocket money on books and notebooks." Hajra says that "nature" (*qudrat*) has endowed her with a singular kind of civic sense, one that prompts her to go so far as to pick up a broom and clean the local parks in her area. Saima says that she is endowed with extraordinary domestic prowess; an uncanny ability to stitch and embroider, to clean, organize, and manage the home. "When you come to my house," Saima tells me, "you will be amazed. You will ask me, how can one woman accomplish all this? A to Z, everything I do, but I don't even need to think about it, I just do it automatically." Shazia claims she has inherited a mystical power for healing (*shifa*) from spiritually elevated women in her family.

Such claims to exceptionalism form the staging ground of martial motherhood performances. By describing their difference as a sign of an essential, natural, transcendental character, health workers recast their gendered deviance as a quasi-mystical singularity bestowed upon them by nature. They do not breach the norms of purdah, interface with rude men, trudge for hours in the sun because they are desperate or immodest women. They take on these labors because they are driven by a transcendental call to service. Their homes and their children do not suffer from the women's wage work; rather, their magical motherly and housewifely capacities encompass the entire neighborhood. Their work is motivated not by greed for money but by a provident and maternal logic. Health workers embrace the hardships that work imposes on them because they are mothers, providing and taking care not only of their own children but of the community. Their contravention of gender norms for work, therefore, is reframed not as deviance but as a maternal sacrifice. Health workers' exceptionalism, their extraordinary sacrifice, their exemplary maternity are passports that authorize and validate their transgression of socially set gendered boundaries.

*Mothers.* Hira, a mother of five, says that she was forced to work when her husband, a bus driver, suffered a spinal injury that caused him to become bedridden. At first, Hira says, she began working out of her home, stitching bows for a bra factory at 10 rupees (roughly 10 cents at the time of my fieldwork) per bow. But even though she worked until there were "holes in my fingers" she was still unable to cover the cost of rent, school fees, and other household expenses. Conditions became so bad that, Hira says, she was forced to accept charity from neighbors and siblings. One day, she tells me, she fed her children "stale" food, "so at least their belly would be full, even if the food had gone bad." Having arrived at such a pass, she says, she saw the LHW job as a divine favor, albeit one that required her to embrace a great deal of suffering, "because my training was from 9 to 4, and it took me two hours to get there on the bus, so I was away from home from 7 to 6. And at the time, my children were small, so it was very hard," she recounts. "But because of all that suffering," she says proudly, "look at me today, eight people sit daily at my *dastar khwan* [meal blanket] and I am able to feed them all. I can help my siblings, and I am the one now who sends food to neighbors who are in need." Rather than disrupt her children's well-being, Hira says, "my job has given me the capacity to look after all the children, to save everyone's children from things like polio, and to help the mothers and children in my catchment area."

Unlike Hira, Mona anchors her claim to motherhood by talking about her stillborn child. In the wake of the devastating event, she tells me, health work allowed her to become a mother to her entire community. "I started [working as a health worker] because, let me tell you the true story, Allah knows, whatever I will tell you, it's a heart-rending story," she says. "I was in a desperate condition, I had been married and I gave birth to a baby, but it died, and that caused some disagreements with my husband, and I got divorced. And because of these worries my mother had a heart attack, my mother died. I became completely mad." These desperate circumstances, Mona says, made her contemplate suicide, but a local lady health worker, Isma, took Mona under her wing. "She knew me, she knew my mental state, so she began forcing me, first to come with her on polio rounds." After Mona had done a few rounds of polio work, Isma convinced Mona's father to let his daughter serve the community by doing health work. The job, Mona says, was a godsend. "I needed to be busy," she says, "and I also needed money so bad. My father was in so much debt." Mona's father's weaving business had been flailing; he was unable to pay his workers, who were consequently drifting into poverty. By taking on health work, Mona was not only able to help her father financially but was also able to provide for his employees. Side by side with her health work, she says, she began to sell crocheted purses and cell phone cases made by artisans who had once worked for her father. The profits went to the men who had lost their jobs when her father's business closed down.

Now in her forties, Mona tells me proudly that she houses an impoverished cousin and his family and also helps neighborhood children with their studies. She says, "Now I no longer yearn for death. Instead, I desire to serve. So I got courage from this job, and because of my work, from inside my conscience woke up." Thus, Mona sees her job not as a form of wage work but as a source of social service and provision. "By doing this work," she says, she is able to be a mother to those who are in need of aid or succor. "When I visit a woman who is in trouble," she says, "I tell her my full story. She [the client] starts crying. She grabs my hand and exclaims, 'Sister!' and I reply, 'Yes, I've been through such trials, and if I came through it, you will too. And like me, you too will become [strong like] iron."

**Quasi-mystical healers.** The exceptionalism of martial motherhood performance turns not only on LHWs' maternal instincts but also on their quasi-mystical healing abilities. These abilities, LHWs say, make them better than doctors. "The thing about doctors," Shazia says, "is that people think they are unpleasant." Hira offers a similar characterization: "My clients don't like doctors. Doctors send you for too many tests. Any symptom they see, they first want a test, how can poor people manage?" Worse, Fazeela says, "doctors don't take women seriously. They say, 'You are fine, stop wasting my time.'"

In contrast with doctors, whom LHWs describe as arrogant, supercilious, and disconnected, lady health workers claim to possess innate and holistic healing skills that have particular utility for women and are also beneficial to the broader community, including animals and the environment. This quasi-mystical healing ability incorporates an empathy and a thoughtfulness that doctors are incapable of. Because of their compassion, LHWs say, they are better than doctors at making diagnoses and at performing simple medical procedures. Farzana, for instance, reacted indignantly when I suggested that perhaps the reason nurses receive better pay than LHWs is because they receive more training. "We study the same amount as them, do you know?" she asked me angrily. "Just by looking at a person, we can tell what disease he is suffering from. We are able to diagnose the illness, which even doctors are unable to do until they perform tests. We can do complete vaccination, complete. And some LHWs are even able to perform deliveries [i.e., assist with childbirth]. They are trained, our LHWs are." In a similar vein, Reema claimed that at training sessions and other encounters with doctors, she had come to feel she was more competent than them: "Recently, there's a clinic, I went there for training, and we had to take a test, and even the doctors that were there were copying from me. I always get good marks, always."

The exceptional healing skills women claim derive not only from their innate talents but also from their interest in and connection with people in their community. To illustrate this care and concern, Samreen, a middle-aged LHW, produced a long reenactment of the tone of voice she had recently used and the kinship terms she had deployed to wheedle an aged grandmother in her catchment area to comply with medical interventions, "Ma," she said. "Come on, Ma. Look, your son is here. Your grandson is here. We all love you, Ma. Take your medicine, Ma. Don't quit on us, Ma. Our hearts will break, Ma."

Other LHWs observing Sara's performance told me that innate talents made LHWs better than nurses and doctors at simple tasks like "giving injections" and "inserting the cannula" for aged or very sick patients. Shaheen took this line of argument further, arguing that God had given her healing hands. "Many thanks to Allah, I am known to cure even those people who are childless couples. I won't exaggerate," she said, "from here [Karachi] till Punjab [a neighboring province] I am well known. People send for my medicines, and by Allah's help, hundreds of thousands of those who were childless were able to conceive." When I asked her what she used to treat these couples, she replied, "I have some, my own homeopathic and herbal formulas. And it is just God's blessing. It is Allah's will. I am only a conduit. I work as a conduit. The power is Allah's. Allah is very benevolent to me." By describing themselves as conduits of a higher power, women emphasized the moral and the vocational character of their work.

Women also underscored the transcendental nature of their work by invoking religious terms surrounding trust and responsibility. "Like doctors," Salma tells me, "we also take an oath. Therefore, we are both keepers of trust [*ameen*] and guarantors [*zaamin*] of public health," she claims. "You can think of us as mobile, portable doctors available in every home." But, she argues, "we are not like those doctors that just provide medicine. Instead in the shortest time, and at cheapest cost, LHWs will provide such cures, as to spread joy and happiness everywhere." When I ask her to give me an instance of these distinctive cures, she says, "For instance, take mothers who breastfeed. We call on them at home, and their mind is made fresh by us, and we are able to explain things to them in ways that doctors cannot." When I press her to elaborate, she says, "For example, we get complaints. Women say they are suffering from back pain. Then I'll ask, 'How many months old is your child?' If he is two months old, and she can't carry him on her hip [because of the pain], believe me that in such a case, breast feeding can actually help, so long as it done in the right way." I asked her what the "right way" to breastfeed was, and she demonstrated, explaining, "The correct mode is that, first, you should sit up straight, drink some water yourself, one glass, then from one side give him to drink for fifteen minutes, then from the other side for ten to fifteen minutes." By offering this kind of advice, Salma says, she soothes and reassures harassed young mothers.

Such women can sometimes be starved of company and kindness, she says. "But when I sit with them and talk to them in a soothing voice, I take seriously their complaints and ailments. I offer them compassion, and then they feel refreshed and they feel light."

As natural and holistic healers, LHWs say, they provide their clients with compassion that not only soothes their nerves but also makes them more hospitable to health worker visits. "Sometimes, it happens," Hajra says, "that we will knock at a client's door, and she will open it looking very irritated." At such times, Hajra says, "I say, '*Baji* [sister], you look very unwell,' and then she will reply, 'Yes, I am not well.' She is irritable. Then I say, '*Arre* [oh], you don't take stress, tell me what is wrong.' Now she gives me details about her illness. I give her a bit of advice, and whatever I have at hand, I give it to her there and then. I say, 'Take this, and go lie down for ten minutes.'" "What kinds of things do you give her?" I ask. "Now if she is a blood pressure patient, and she is getting irritable, I ask her, 'What's going on?' She replies, 'My B.P. is up. Don't talk to me.' I don't say anything. I say, 'Do you have cucumber in your house?' See, cucumber is a useful thing. Most people have it, coriander, green coriander is also present in every house. Plums, you know the ones we use to cook biryani, so if there is nothing else available, I'll say, '*Baji* [sister], suck on this plum.' Coriander also works, not the leaves but the stems. Put it in your mouth, keep chewing it, keep chewing it. It becomes fiber, right, so spit out the fiber, all the juice you got, you didn't even notice, and you're fine."

Such homespun cures, health workers acknowledge, work not just because of the efficacy of the remedy but because of the concern displayed in the interaction. "She is alone, she is tired, she has no one who cares how she is feeling," Hajra says, "But I have asked her how she is. I have responded to her mood, and I have told her one or two things [i.e., remedies], and because of all this, her attention toward me has increased. Now she has forgotten her ailments, she starts talking to me, she might say, 'My daughter is going through something.' When she begins to tell you such stories, then you know you have unlocked the safe of her heart. Then I turn my focus to her children. '*Mashaallah*,' I say, 'your children are very beautiful. You are taking good care of them. You are a good mother.' Then the mother is pleased, and when you praise her children, the mother is even more pleased."

By claiming innate talent, employing compassion, and wielding natural remedies, health workers reframe the meaning of their work and simultaneously cultivate connection with their clients. They sometimes refer to their clients as sisters (*baji*), and they sometimes call them *beti* (daughter) and take on the role of mother. They style themselves as healers who are a conduit for a higher power and as guardians who can be trusted with the keys to the human heart. Their care and concern, their trustworthiness, and their communitarian approach, they say, makes them better than doctors, and they are accordingly loved and respected in ways that doctors are not. "Women come up to me at social events and community gatherings," Shazia says. "They say, 'Sister, that remedy you gave me did wonders!' They praise me and they hug me." Shazia wipes a tear as she concludes: "I have to say, they are very lucky, those women, who fall into the hands of an LHW instead of a doctor."

**Veils and holy war.** "A few years ago," Farzana, a 48-year-old health worker, tells me, "polio workers became a prime target for terrorists." Therefore, she says, "when I am setting out to do polio work, I stop and remind my children about where my important papers and documents may be found in case I don't return." "And how do they respond?" I ask. "They get very angry with me," she says. "They say, 'Why do you always tell us such things?' But I say, 'Who knows anything about life, where and when it will end?'" Shocked, I ask her if she routinely sets out for work with the expectation of getting killed, and she replies, "Absolutely! But I envelop my body in a *burka,* and I set out with the *durood shareef* [an Islamic prayer] on my lips, and I go do my duty."

While the National Program requires LHWs to work within their immediate communities, polio work often takes them into unfamiliar localities. Unlike routine health work, polio work is also hard to camouflage. When doing a vaccination drive, the women travel as part of a team. They carry the vaccine in coolers, and they record each vaccination on papers attached to a clipboard. When they knock on doors, they loudly introduce themselves as a polio team. The distance and the strangeness of these communities combined with the visibility of polio work make women feel afraid. Their fears are justified. Over a hundred polio workers have been targeted for killing by terrorists in the last two decades. In 2012, the Pakistani government briefly halted its polio campaign after terrorists killed nine workers in three days. Employees of the WHO and UNICEF, which support and oversee polio immunization efforts, were withdrawn from the field. After a brief respite, however, lady health workers say, they were sent back into a field that global actors were too afraid to return to.

Hajra provides a particularly vivid account of this period. "The first murder that occurred," she tells me, took place in the territory under her supervision. "After the killing, work stopped there, for three months," she says. "Neither WHO nor USAID were willing to continue, out of fear. No one worked, believe me, for three months, the [polio vaccination] work stopped altogether." But then, she says, a highly placed official in Geneva called up a Pakistani official. "He said, no matter what it takes, I want polio [work completed]." The authorities were especially concerned, she says, about the high-risk locality she was assigned to work in. "Polio virus is very high in this area," she says, "but no one had the courage [to do it]." In desperation, the commissioner in charge asked Hajra if she was willing to brave the breach. "I said, 'Sir, I will do it.' He said to me, 'Look, if you do it, it will be at your own risk.' I said, 'Sir, I will do it.'"

The next day, Hajra says, she "filled three cars, with Baloch and Pathan girls [local ethnic groups] and got out in that same area," the one considered a security threat. It was "so dangerous [that] no one from WHO ever, ever steps out of their vehicles in those areas," she says. "They refused to send their staff to help us, saying 'They can't work *there*,' but I said, 'Sir, we will do the work, when it is a problem for *our country's children*, when we are working in all of Pakistan, all of Karachi, if one area gets left out, then it's like all the rest of our work in other areas is rendered useless, I mean, it will be like we did nothing, right? If even one child is left out, how will polio finish? We have to wipe it out, we have to save our children." So, she continues, "They said, 'Daughter, it's like jumping into the well of death.' I said, 'Sir, I am willing to plunge in.'" I asked her how she gathered the courage to step out of her vehicle, and she replied, "I just went and did it, what I said to everyone was that the time of death is already fixed [i.e., fated], the day that is written for death, right? I have stepped out for a good deed, if I die in a virtuous deed, in a *jihad* [holy war], then I will be a *shaheed* [a martyr], and no one dies before the time of destiny. Believe me. I salute my workers, really, who worked shoulder to shoulder with me. We would board the bus, and every girl would recite *darood shareef* [an Islamic prayer] and blow it on herself [i.e., as a ward], and we took the name of Allah and got down in the battlefield."

By using the idioms of jihad (holy war) and martyrdom, women like Hajra reframe the meaning of their work and their status as workers. Vaccination is no longer a labor performed in exchange for stipends or wages, it is a holy war waged in service to "our country's children." Lady health workers are not just laborers, they are soldiers. In place of weapons they rely on faith, veils, and Islamic prayers. Their claims to the status of holy warrior rest not only on the value of the deeds they perform (i.e., defending children) but also on their willingness to face a risk that others, who draw far greater salaries and enjoy a higher status, are too afraid to confront.

"One time the DC [deputy commissioner] came with me on my rounds," Laila tells me proudly. "We got to one house, knocking, and no one was answering, so the DC says, 'Okay, let's go. They're not answering,' I said, 'Sir, I have to administer the drops. I have to do my duty.'" Laila says she kept knocking until a man came to the door, rudely shooing her away, "The DC got scared. He was afraid that it might be someone connected to the Taliban, and he went to stand far away, on the other end of the street, but I stood my ground, saying [to the man], 'Brother, please,'" she says in a wheedling tone, "I kept pleading, until he said to me, 'Mother, I don't speak Urdu,' so then I plunged in. I went into the house, which we are not ordered to do. I said, 'Vaccine, child, sick, dead, finish,' and I did it, I administered the drops, the DC was shocked."

Through their descriptions of risk and bravery, women not only lay claim to the sacred identity of a holy warrior, but they also transform the meaning of wage work. Wages become *halal* (legitimate), they claim, only when a person is willing to cross all limits in the completion of her duties. "Our work, we make it halal," Shehnaz says. "The rest of these all, WHO, government, they are too scared to do their duty." Even the cops who accompany health workers, says Shehnaz, are nothing but cowards. "When a certain home in an area refuses to answer the door, the police that are with us, they get scared. They say, 'Leave it, *baji* [sister]. To hell with them. Let's keep going," she says. "But I say, 'No! I won't move until I get an answer to my knock.' Why? Because we know we have to make our work halal because if we don't," she argues, "then when we are sitting with our family and eating the food we have earned, we will think, Oh Allah, we made our work into a lie." Similarly, Reema connects the legitimacy of her earnings to the significance of the work. "People think all we care about is money," she says. "Of course, we do need the money, but we also understand the purpose of what we are doing, why it is important."

The purpose, in the LHWs' telling, is not simply a globally driven vaccination project but a sacred struggle. Farzana describes it this way. "Take it that we are doing jihad, for our children, for our families, for our husbands," she says, suggesting that her polio work is in part a struggle to provide for her family's well-being. For Shazia, polio work is not just a personal jihad waged in order to ensure her own family's well-being but a higher-level sacred battle fought in service to the community. She laughs as she says, "No, if it had been your duty, and you had seen what the disease is like, if you had seen an affected child, you would not be able to sleep for two days."

The idiom of holy war, usually associated in the popular discourse with men, does not dislodge the gendered language of veils and motherhood that health workers frequently deploy but instead is powered by these symbols of womanhood. Shehnaz recounts her encounter with Asifa Bhutto, the daughter of the assassinated prime minister Benazir Bhutto, who serves as a spokesperson for polio eradication in Pakistan. "Asifa Bhutto asked me, 'You keep doing polio even after getting shot at?' and I said, 'Yes! Because I am a mother,' I said to Asifa. 'I am a mother, if one child gets left out, how many others will die? So, I am a mother, so I won't stop. If I get shot, I'll get shot, so what?" While Shehnaz says she derives her courage from her motherhood, other women say that their veils provide them with the pluck to carry on their dangerous work. Mehr, for instance, assigns an almost magical power to her abaya, which she sees as a kind of cloak of permeability. "I am known for entering even into no-go areas, where the police are scared to go," she tells me proudly. "So, for instance, here is a road," she says, sketching a map on a piece of paper. "On that side of the road is Ali Raza Colony. A person who belongs on this side of the road cannot go there. The person from that side cannot come here," she explains, saying that ethnic conflicts render certain localities off-limits to outsiders. "But I, I always put on an abaya, and I go into that community." She goes even though she belongs to a rival ethnic group. And when she arrives, she tells me proudly, "they treat me with utmost respect. In fact, they send an escort back with me so that I can pass safely out of their area." "And how do you manage to win them over like this?" I ask. "I use my abaya," she says. "I wear an abaya, and I say to them, 'We are all Muslims. I'm a decent woman. I'm a mother. I'm here for the children and because you are my brothers in faith and I wish to serve my Muslim community.'" "And they respond to these arguments," I venture. She replies, "They have come to realize that I'm a mother, a sister. I have no political motives. I am just doing welfare work as a Muslim." The pious, filial, and militaristic idioms that animate martial motherhood performances help LHWs to generate respect and to cultivate connection with their poor and working-class clients.

Martial motherhood performances not only reframe the meanings surrounding women's work, their transgression of purdah norms, and their wages, they also provide LHWs with a permeability and a capacity for connection. These capacities amplify the women's effectiveness at work. Their veils, their claims to motherhood, their compassion for working-class and poor women, their descriptions of sacrifice and suffering all make LHW work more legible, more relatable, and more meaningful for their clients. When counseling women about birth control options, for instance, LHWs take on the role of mother or elder sister. Such idioms of kinship foster trust and intimacy where the cold, dispassionate performance of a government servant would create distance and wariness. The familiarity of the roles and idioms LHWs draw upon in their performances make their clients' more receptive and more willing to comply with the policy measures LHWs push. Women's veils, the sacred language they use, and the kinship claims they make also facilitate their ability to penetrate into zones that other state and transnational actors cannot or will not enter. In sum, the moral meanings of their martial motherhood performances not only provide unarmed and vulnerable LHWs with the courage to breach "no-go" areas but also provide them with safe passage and respect within these unfamiliar localities.

### THE CLASSED BARRIERS TO RECOGNITION

The very symbols that amplify the resonance of LHWs work with their clients, ironically, undermine their authority with the local and global doctors and experts who superintend their work. In the bureaucratic offices that superintend their work, LHWs' martial motherhood performances amplify their classed mismatch with the rational bureaucratic state. Here, the feisty, colorful, and compassionate LHW appears not as a wise woman with a service vocation but as a poorly educated and financially constrained peri-urban woman with little knowledge or competency to manage the complex workings of the state or its partner agencies. The language of kinship and sacrifice cannot be deployed in these contexts. Bosses must be addressed as "sir," not "brother." The knowledge and experience LHWs so proudly share with their clients around the efficacy of coriander for blood pressure, for instance, or the correct way to breastfeed a baby, can hold no water in the local or global health office. Instead, in these spaces, such tools of connection act as signs of LHWs' working-class background and therefore work to block their ability to gain recognition as agents of the state.

Sharmeen said this lack of recognition was not just humiliating, it sometimes compromised her relationship with her clients. "One of the women from my catchment area needed to go to the hospital," she tells me. "She is not educated and is afraid to speak with medical staff, so she asked me to go with her." Since Sharmeen knew the woman's case history, she thought she would be able to help speed things along at the hospital. "When I got there, I told them [hospital staff] that I am an LHW, that Zaiba has been my client for fifteen years, but they shooed me away. There was no recognition. They had no idea what an LHW is, what work she does, or that she is also, like them, an agent of the state," she complains. The hospital staff ignored Sharmeen, refused to listen to her, and gestured at her to go sit in the waiting area like everyone else. "So, my client saw their attitude and she said to me, 'What is the point of you?'" The whole episode, Sharmeen said, made her feel very embarrassed. "I have worked for the government for decades," she says, "and I can't even get recognized in a health setting as a health worker."

The state's unwillingness to recognize LHWs, Mehnaz argued, can be gleaned from its unwillingness to make any provision for them that could help boost their authority or at least help them prove they are who they say they are. "We have no place to sit, no badge we can show to let people know that we are agents of the state. We don't wear a uniform, like cops do, and the hospitals and clinics have no idea who we are." Even when community doctors are aware of health workers, LHWs say, they see them not as agents of the health department but as tools that carry vaccines and medicines into homes and bring data out of them. "When they want to organize an event, like a measles awareness campaign, then they call us, they tell us to gather the community, to fill the seats," Farzana complained. "Otherwise, for them, we are nothing, just a shoe you put on when you need to go out."

While some offices and actors failed to acknowledge or recognize LHWs as legitimate agents of public health, others went further and actively marked them as unwelcome and unwanted outsiders. Indeed, many of the interactions I witnessed between workers and officers were like the one I described at the beginning of this chapter, where doctors at a district hospital aggressively demanded that LHWs vacate an office they were using to hold a meeting. Through much of my fieldwork, I observed that bosses did not speak to LHWs; they yelled at them. They tossed files at them. They threw them out of their offices. They questioned them in sharp, commanding tones. They did not wait to hear their responses. When they spoke to LHWs they refused to look at them.

This steady humiliation, LHWs told me, was partly inspired by the officers' rage against the protest activities the LHW union had organized. To contest their poor treatment by the state, LHWs had organized a series of protests (see chapter 6) and after years of effort had eventually moved the Supreme Court to instruct the health office to regularize health workers and reclassify them as full-time employees of the state. When I met the women four years after the court had rendered its judgment, its orders were at last getting implemented; the women's jobs were finally on the way to becoming regularized.

"They [the officers in charge of LHW work] are enraged," Shazia explained, "because they all told us, your status will never change. You will never become regular employees. But then we did it, we achieved the impossible, and they hate that." State officials were so hostile to the idea of regularizing LHW jobs that, Fiza said, they were now dragging their feet and making every effort to stall the process. "Over and over again, they say, bring your credentials," Fiza said, "bring your birth certificate, your ID card, all the things. Over and over again, I bring it, I submit notarized and certified copies, and they still say, 'I have not got it. It's lost, It's not there.'" Likewise, Sameera said that data she'd had verified and entered into the government's computer systems had mysteriously disappeared and she was told to resubmit it, again and again. When women did bring in their documents, they said, they were told that a particular and vital paper was missing or that their files had been rejected because of filing errors or because they were stapled in the wrong order or required an even further level of verification.

On one occasion, I witnessed an encounter that exemplified the humiliating bureaucratic fastidiousness LHWs were complaining about. One morning halfway through my fieldwork I walked into a room set aside for my use at a local health office, only to find that it was already occupied. A woman government servant dressed in very stiffly starched, expensive-looking clothes was sitting in an armchair in a corner of the room. She was wearing a great deal of perfume and jewelry. A group of LHWs stood cowering around her armchair. As I approached the door, the officer flung a file out of it; it went sliding down the hallway, the papers inside fanning out across the floor. A nervous-looking LHW darted after it, whimpering apologies. "These papers are not in the right order!" the officer shouted. She then turned to the next LHW in line, "Where's your ID card?" she yelled. The LHW looked terrified. Virtually bowing in terror, she opened a plastic folder and pulled out her national identity card and handed it over to the officer. The officer looked at it, comparing it with a paper in the file on her lap. Again, she flung the file out of the door, "The birthdate on your ID card doesn't match your school certificate," she said. The LHW began to say something. "Madam," she said, but the officer turned her face away. "Next!" she said, turning to the next person in line.

Seeing that the room was occupied, I went and sat on the staircase in the hallway outside. The LHW with the mismatched birthdates came and sat down next to me. She seemed very upset. Her name was Nissa. I asked her if she would like some water, and she explained the scene I had just witnessed. Since the LHWs had been regularized as state employees, she said, their paperwork was now undergoing fresh scrutiny. "It's my mistake," she said to me about the encounter with the officer. "Why should I lie?" After she had finished school, Nissa said, her father had wanted her to take on a particular job, which had had a minimum age requirement, so to get her inducted, she said, he had bribed the school to falsify her birthdate and make her seem older. She had been too young to have an identity card then (the minimum age for acquiring an ID card is 18), so it had been easy to falsify her age via her school documents. But now, she said, the birthdate on her ID card did not match the birthdate on her school records. The school records made it seem like she was two years older than she was. This discrepancy was very important because Nissa was only 58 years old according to her ID card but 60 according to her school certificates. At 60, state employees are retired from their jobs, which meant that Nissa would not be able to reap any of the benefits, such as increased salary, that regularization was to provide LHWs. In any case, she told me, the state has decided that only those who retired after the year 2022 will be able to draw pensions and retirement benefits. "Imagine," she said to me. "I've given more than thirty years of service to this organization and now at the age of 58, I can't even hold on to my job."

Nissa was not the only LHW to be brutalized by a bureaucracy that underlined her unsuitability for a government position. Hira, another LHW in her late fifties, was having difficulty meeting the state's exacting procedural requirements. Hira had grown up in a village located a couple of days drive from Karachi. When she was a teenager, she said, the local river flooded, sending water gushing into Hira's house and into the trunk she had used to store her credentials. "Nowadays," she said, "in other countries, what a good system they have! Everything is computerized. If someone has a problem, it is like, 'Okay, let's see, what is this person's problem?' Then they will use the computer to solve it. But here even schools and colleges, who knows if they even maintain records, they will never provide you with anything." Since the state had initially not required LHWs to have more than a primary school education (eight years of schooling), many of the women had not passed what are locally called "board exams" and therefore had no diplomas, which are centralized within provincial matric and intermediate boards and therefore can more easily be reissued if the original is lost. Hira, therefore, had no way to furnish the government with the school records they were demanding as part of the regularization process. Even though she had worked for the state for more than two decades, they were now telling her that she was not qualified to be an LHW and therefore could not be regularized or receive benefits. Her service was ignored: all the children she had vaccinated, the births she had recorded, the women she had counseled, and the data she had collected meant nothing. The state was not looking at the paperwork she had produced to fill the cabinets and computers of the health department. They were interested only in her credentials.

In addition to school records, LHWs struggled to produce other necessary documents the state demanded. One document that created insurmountable difficulties for LHWs was the national ID card. The National Identity Card (called the NADRA card) periodically expires and has to be renewed. The paperwork requirements to have an ID card issued or renewed, women said, are draconian. ID card offices ask for birth certificates, property papers, marriage certificates, and a document testifying to the support of a male guardian. "Don't even talk to me about the NADRA card," Muzna says. "If you ever go there [to the ID card office] and visit, you will realize what we go through. People start lining up at 11 p.m. in the night. You will see, they are standing on the roads and footpaths. Poor things. All night they are in line. They don't even sleep. In the morning, they are given a token. That too, only fifty tokens will be issued, otherwise they have to come stand in the line again."

But without the ID card, she explained, one cannot get a job, a phone line, or a bank account. The requirement of male guardianship in particular caused enormous difficulties for women. Rizwana, an LHW in her fifties, for instance, wept during her interview, as she described the plight of her youngest daughter, Rida. "Her financial situation is not good," she told me, Rida's husband was addicted to drugs and did not work. Rida, who had had an arranged marriage entirely engineered by her father, now had two children, a son and a daughter. When Rida first got married, her mother told me, sobbing, "Even on the wedding night, he was high, and he peed on the bed." The man was also violent, the mother said: "He beat her. He pulled her hair, but she didn't tell me. It was her friends who told me, eventually. She hides it from me. She says, "You've got so much on your plate. I can't burden you further.'" But Rida was unable to leave her husband, because, as her mother put it, "she can't get a job because she doesn't have an ID card. Now she is married. Her husband has control. He won't give his ID card to her [to support her application]. How can she make it without him? If I make it for her, on her father's name, then how to explain where she came by children?" By requiring women to get either a husband or a father to support their application, the state created insurmountable difficulties for women like Rida, whose husband had no interest in helping her achieve financial independence.

When women did manage to collect the extensive list of documents that the regularization process required, they were told they had not filed them correctly, that they were not in the right order, that they did not make enough copies, or that they had not gotten all the necessary signatures. Women interpreted these demands as attempts at stalling the regularization process. In their view, the officers were not just doing their job, they were deliberately trying to humiliate the women to remind them that, as women from working-class neighborhoods who lacked college degrees, they lacked the status and the caliber that is required of those who wish to occupy regularized positions within the state.

Yet the very qualities that made LHWs "unsuited" to state-based positions were also the qualities that helped them excel at their jobs. It was precisely because they lacked the formal and sophisticated credentials their bosses possessed that LHWs were able to connect with their clients. Even the obstacles LHWs encountered at identity card offices made them more relatable to their clients, who faced similar hurdles and difficulties whenever they interacted with government institutions.

Unlike LHWs, their bosses were able to rely on the perks of their offices to get past some of the bureaucratic hurdles that ordinary citizens must overcome. When they needed a signature from an officer of a certain grade, they could simply ask one of their colleagues to provide it. Bureaucratic hurdles are in any case not as onerous for middle-class citizens. When I needed to renew my NADRA card, for instance, I was able to go to a NADRA office in my elite neighborhood, where the lines were shorter and where I was able to pay a larger fee for quicker service, described officially as "executive" service. I was also able to vault past some of the more onerous documentary requirements because my mother owned property in Karachi, which was taken as evidence of identity. When they asked me to produce my father's identity documents, I told them firmly, in English, that he was dead and that his card had expired and that since they were the government, I expected them to have his information on file. They did not ask me any further questions. Elites who cannot intimidate these officers with their English-speaking skills can also rely on friends and contacts to speed up their documentary processes.

Because of their working-class background, LHWs are often unable to get past bureaucratic requirements with the speed and dignity that middle-class people do. Without easy access to the classed credentials and documents that elites possess, such as school certificates and property ownership documents, LHWs find it much harder to craft the requisite performative entitlement in the government office. Even though they work tirelessly for the state, they are still treated like outsiders within its offices. The work they have done cannot make up for the papers they have failed to obtain. Their labors on behalf of the state provide them with no special consideration, nor even a basic dignity. Despite their exemplary, death-defying service, they are doubted and brutalized by a state that for several decades has relied on the very classed characteristics that it stigmatizes as being beneath the dignity of the regularized, recognized state agent.

## THEORETICAL IMPLICATIONS

In this chapter I have shown how stigma shapes women's opportunities when they work as part of a woman-only force, doing work that is seen as feminine work and under the direct supervision of women supervisors. To manage the stigma associated with their contravention of purdah, LHWs craft what I call a martial motherhood performance. They draw on a set of symbols usually associated with men, such as holy war and martyrdom, and juxtapose these with the gendered symbols that provide women with honor, such as motherhood and modesty. In doing so, LHWs craft and inhabit a quixotic identity of warrior mother with healing power. This performance makes LHWs more legible to their clients, who more willingly accede to the wishes of their health workers. Clients surrender information about their family that they would not give to anyone else, including information about the number of people in their household, their sexual habits, and their living arrangements. Clients also go along with LHW prescriptions. They accept condoms or agree to receive birth control at the clinic. They hand their babies over for vaccination, they agree to take tuberculosis medication, they participate in public health awareness campaigns, and they agree to make an effort to learn about hygiene. This recruitment of clients is accomplished through the use by LHWs of gendered and classed symbols like their veils, kinship language, and maternal concern.

Although martial motherhood performances allow LHWs to successfully recruit their clients to the state's various health objectives, these classed performances do not provide them with dignity, authority, or relational purchase in the bureaucratic offices that superintend LHW work. In the bureaucratic context of the state, women's symbolic agency crashes into classed obstacles, such as school certificates and identity documents. In these contexts, veils and motherhood, compassion and holy war are contrary tokens that reinforce women's marginal status as outsiders. In these settings, it is classed credentials that matter, not grassroots knowledge or community connection. Lacking the necessary symbols of middle-class status, health workers are brutally marked as outsiders who can never truly be part of the state's official, regularized machinery. Their inability to obtain the credentials and documents that are systematically inaccessible for working-class people, especially women, serves as a barrier that obstructs their efforts to manage the stigma associated with their job.

In the next chapter we will look at a case, that of airline work, where women are able, through their jobs, to access classed symbols that suggest their connection with elite and cosmopolitan lifestyles. Moreover, unlike the policewomen we met in chapter 3, airline attendants work in an occupation that is culturally constructed as feminine work. How does the stigma matrix shape women's agency in this context? Are women better able to accomplish recruitment and inhabit authority when they work in a setting that provides them with easier access to both gender and class symbols?

# 5 | MAVENS OF MOBILITY: HOW AIRLINE WOMEN NAVIGATE STIGMA

A FEW MONTHS INTO MY fieldwork I was having tea with some former high school friends and complaining about traffic. I described the difficulties I had faced recently, when a protest organized by a politician had shut down Shahrah-i-Faisal, an important thoroughfare that leads to the PIA office where I was interviewing airline attendants. No one said much, but later a U.S.-educated former classmate sidled up to me and said, "I can't understand how you can work with such dirty women." Surprised, I asked her whom she meant. "The PIA air hostesses," she said. "They are really dirty women." In the moment I was taken aback by the apparent intensity of her feelings toward these women, but over time I got used to this kind of reaction. Friends, relatives, and even strangers I met outside my field sites would display a mixture of disgust and amusement when they heard that I was working with PIA's airline attendants. "Why would you want to talk to *them*?" people would ask. "I imagine you hear some titillating stuff," people would say. The stigma around airline work was so strong that it even rubbed off on me. People simply could not understand how the experiences of these women could possibly be of interest to a sociologist and implied through their comments that my interest suggested there was something "off" about me as well.

The stigma I faced in interactions with elite and middle-class interlocutors paled in comparison to the humiliations I witnessed airline women face. At the PIA head office one morning, for instance, Bee was complaining about the conditions at the PIA women's hostel where she lived. 'There was no water [in the taps] again this morning,' she said. 'And the place is so dirty,' she went on, 'can't anything be done about the cleaning?' 'I have the perfect solution for you,' Faisal, a steward and a senior officer in the airline attendants' union, replied. The room went quiet. Two other airline attendants turned to look at Faisal. 'I've decided I am going to arrange an apartment for two to three air hostesses,' he said. 'It will be located in an affluent area, in Defense or Clifton, with one bedroom for each woman and all the necessary facilities: water, generator, the works,' he said. 'Really?' Bee asked, looking interested. 'Yes, really,' he replied, 'but the condition will be that I will live there with you.' Everyone laughed, but Bee looked annoyed. 'Very funny,' she said. She did not laugh.

Such off-color jokes and propositions are, airline women say, a routine part of their job. "This job is not considered a decent job for women to do," Sehr, an attendant with more than twenty years of flying experience, told me. Air hostesses, as they are called in Pakistan, complained that passengers feel perfectly entitled to ogle them, make rude comments in their vicinity, and even take photographs or videos of airline attendants without their consent. Zara said that her fiancé disliked her job so much that he was going to make her quit once they got married. Reham said that her brothers were so angry with her when she joined PIA that she had had to move out of her family home and take up residence in the PIA hostel. "They've thawed a bit now," she said, "but I keep my contact with them to a minimum," she explained. "Like right now, one of them is getting married, and I am not attending the wedding, only the after-wedding reception. I just said to my family that I can't get time off, even though I do have some leave I can take. I just don't want to go."

Like Reham, several women said that their job had caused rifts and disagreements in their family. The stigma of air hostessing work didn't just disrupt family life; it made women vulnerable to harassment from the broader community. Farah, for instance, complained that someone at her neighborhood gas station had deliberately punctured her car tires while she was inside the store. They did this, she thought, because they knew she was an air hostess and therefore deserved to be harassed.

Despite this degrading treatment, air hostessing jobs are also seen as very desirable opportunities. When Safiya, a police constable I met through fieldwork, learned that I was also studying flight attendants, she begged me to help her get a PIA job. "I'll do anything to become an air hostess," she said. I asked her why she would give up a job she had held for eight years to start again at the bottom of a new field, and she replied, "They get to go out of the country, and they look pretty, and they dress nice, and their salary is good, and it was just always my dream since I was child, to fly like that." Her description accorded with what I heard from a seven-year-old child at a working-class boxing club in one of Karachi's working-class neighborhoods, Lyari. After the girls had finished their boxing class, I asked the littler ones what they wanted to do when they grew up. Sania, a young girl with wiry hair piped up, "PIA air hostess!" Taking a cue from her, some of the other girls also started chanting, "Hostess, hostess!" I asked Sania what she liked about the air hostessing job, and she replied, "They are pretty, and they are kind, and they go out of the country!"

## BOUNDLESS WOMEN

While some people might think they are dirty, promiscuous, or "loose," for working-class girls and women, air hostesses represent a dream of literal mobility, a chance to rise above their working-class situations and to travel abroad. Airline attendants make something like three times the salary that policewomen with comparable educational qualifications make. While health workers and women police officers are constrained to walk, hail rickshaws, or travel on overcrowded buses, airline women are picked up from home and dropped off after their flights in air-conditioned passenger vans. While health workers trudge for hours in the hot sun and policewomen deal with those accused of prostitution, theft, and murder, airline women travel to places like Toronto and London, where they stay at luxury hotels. Policewomen and health workers rarely have access to drinking water at work, and they have to pay for tea or food out of their own pocket. But airline women receive generous travel allowances, paid in U.S. dollars, which they often use to sample foreign treats like lattes and chocolates. In short, airline women are able to consume experiences and products that are well beyond the reach of most working-class Pakistani women.

Yet the same spatial and economic mobility that makes flying a dream job for working-class girls also spoils airline women's image and identity. It is precisely because they fly long distances, alone and without chaperones; spend nights away from home; and offer hospitality to hundreds and hundreds of strange men that airline women are seen as dirty by many. To achieve the dream of class mobility—international travel, consumption, beauty—working-class women have to surrender something of their respectability. In exchange for the dollars and the donuts, the MAC makeup, and the high-heeled shoes that their jobs enable them to obtain, they are required not only to undertake physical, aesthetic, and emotional labor (Hochschild 1979) but also to manage the "spoiled identity" of "dirty women" (Goffman 1991).

How do airline attendants balance these complicated moral and material pressures? How do they navigate the stigma that compromises their identity? And what do their efforts tell us about agency?

Unlike policewomen and health workers, who draw on gendered symbols, such as veils and motherhood, to navigate the polluted meanings of their jobs, airline women's symbolic agency draws on the trappings of class to contest stigma. While policewomen and health workers draw on the symbols circulating in their immediate environment, such as veils and kinship language, to forge an agentic response to stigma, airline women import symbols of luxury, like designer bags and makeup, from abroad. Airline women's propensity to draw on globalized symbols for destigmatization is instructive. Although the recent scholarship on Muslim women and their agency has tended to prioritize the local contexts that embed women's action and subjectivities (see Sehlikoglu 2018), this chapter suggests that the sources of Muslim women's agency can be multiple and global. Just as stigmatizing actors draw on global signs to humiliate or denigrate their victims (as in the case of LHWs in chapter 4), stigmatized actors also are able to draw on globalized signs and discourses in their destigmatization efforts.

To contest the stigma surrounding their occupations, airline women draw on the classed affordances of their jobs and perform a cosmopolitan identity—a sophisticated, fashionable presentation of global citizenship. Understanding this cosmopolitanism as a sign of modernity and cultural superiority, they distinguish themselves from those who would stigmatize them. Unlike the "backward," "childish," and "thoughtless" people who denigrate them, airline women say that they are agentic, autonomous, self-reliant, and thoughtful, all signs, they say, of a more evolved personhood, one that is focused not on denigrating others but on creating a good life—a life that is beautiful, rational, and independent. Thus, unlike the policing context (chapter 3) and health work setting (chapter 4) within which women's agency is hamstrung by class structures, the aviation context provides women with the ability to vault over class obstacles.

But although global symbols, like makeup and handbags, do allow women to create new meanings around class, these symbols still limit the efficacy of airline women's destigmatization efforts. Airline women's agency is limited, as I show in this chapter, because of the gendered meanings associated with the symbols airline attendants invoke. These meanings became apparent when I observed women interacting with their male colleagues. In these collegial interactions, women appeared to enact more conventional, deferential, and dependent gender performances—seeking guidance from male colleagues, deferring to men's ideas and opinions, and turning to them for help managing professional problems and relationships. These gendered dynamics are shaped, this chapter argues, by the character of the cosmopolitan scripts airline women draw on to craft their symbolic agency, which are also postfeminist in their composition. Postfeminism refers to a distorted neoliberal form of feminism that equates women's emancipation with consumerism. If women are now able to buy and wear expensive and sexy accessories, postfeminist discourses suggest, then obviously we have accomplished the liberation that earlier generations of women sought and therefore feminism is now a passé project.

Since postfeminist sensibilities involve heightened forms of femininity and consumption, their integration with cosmopolitanism shapes the relational outcomes of airline women's symbolic agency in two ways. First, by enacting cosmopolitan consumption, airline women distinguish themselves from the "poorer," "less sophisticated" clients and family members who denigrate them. Describing these interlocutors as unsophisticated and boorish, they fend off stigma by disparaging their stigmatizers. Second, at the same time, the post-femininity associated with their cosmopolitan consumption allows airline women to uncritically enact a patriarchal bargain with their male colleagues. A patriarchal bargain is a pact some women make with patriarchy; it involves bartering small privileges in exchange for ongoing inequalities in the broader system (Kandiyoti 1988). In airline women's case, the bargain involves offering male colleagues deference and subservience in exchange for help accomplishing various personal and professional objectives. The aid women receive comes at the cost of an enduring subordination to their male colleagues.

In short, although airline women's symbolic agency allows them to negotiate the stigma of their polluted identities through a classed performance of cultural superiority, it does not enable them to escape the gendered hierarchies that continue to organize their workplace and that are reinforced rather than replaced by postfeminist scripts. Unlike policewomen and health workers, whose agency is hamstrung by the structures of class, airline women's agency is undermined by the structures of gender. Thus, the chapter shows that while globalized signs and discourses can serve as a resource for Muslim women's agency, they can also serve as vehicles for the transport of globalized forms of inequality.

Of the three occupations examined in this book, airline work is considered the most sexualized, and it is therefore the most stigmatized. I have described some of the sources of airline women's stigma in chapter 1 and 2, and in this chapter I dig deeper and explain why airline work is considered worse than the other jobs examined in this book. Next, I describe the performances that airline women mount to combat the stigma of their work, and I parse out the relational consequences of these performances. Understanding the broader consequences of airline women's destigmatization efforts helps us to better understand the mechanics of the stigma matrix.

Unlike policewomen and health workers, airline attendants are able to vault over the class impediments that restrict women's dignity and their authority at work. They are able to do this because their work provides them with resources, like money and travel opportunities, that allow them to claim a refined, modern sensibility that resembles elite dispositions. But class mobility alone is not sufficient for getting past stigma, as this chapter shows. Although they are able to get past the classed barriers that animate the stigma matrix, airline women are unable to circumvent the gendered barriers that also enliven stigma in this context. The matrix, therefore, continues to obstruct even the relatively affluent airline women from inhabiting authority at work. By highlighting the tenuous agency of airline women, this chapter shows how global, imported scripts and structures can serve to restructure, rather than mitigate, the effects of the stigma matrix for frontline women.

## THE SOURCES OF AIRLINE WOMEN'S STIGMA

***Beyond the pale.*** While Pakistani society is largely critical of women who leave their homes for work, airline work, attendants claim, is seen as much worse than other jobs. Since it involves hospitality and requires women to look beautiful, airline work is seen as sexually degrading. Since they have to travel vast distances and spend nights away from home, airline work is seen as morally compromising. "If a girl steps out into [the world] for any job, any job at all," Nazli, a 50-year-old air hostess said, "then she is anyway categorized as fast or loose," but this characterization is amplified for airline women, who are seen as not just fast but worse, morally ungrounded. "People do understand," Nazli explained, "that in some cases, a woman has to work, like a widow may have to work"; in such situations, she said, women's work is palatable to society, so long as it doesn't transgress the bounds of decency, "they are all right if you do teaching, take on work you can do within your home, such jobs may be acceptable, but air hostessing, no!" Decent women, the thinking goes, may be compelled by circumstances to work, but only indecent ones are willing to endure the extreme moral compromise that airline work demands. And if they are willing to compromise so much, then that must mean they are immoral. "I am working," Zebunnissa complained, "because of my *majboori* [constraint]. Most of us are working because of some constraint. Someone has lost her father, someone else is supporting a widowed mother. We are all here because some necessity has compelled us to work. But this necessity does not cleanse our position in people's eyes, because they think, if she is willing to go to this extent [i.e., take on an air hostessing job] then she will go to any extent, she will do anything." If women are willing to cross the line of decency in their choice of job, the thinking goes, then that must mean they have no boundaries at all. They are so far beyond the pale that their behavior is no longer governed by any moral codes or norms. This logic, airline women argue, is compounded by the perks of their job, which inspire shock and jealousy.

"People say things like, 'Couldn't you find something better to do? Wouldn't it be better to endure poverty than this?'" Afshan says, arguing that the luxury and opportunity airline work affords makes it look like too good a bargain. "People see the money we get, the travel we do, going abroad, the things we buy, and they ask to see our things, 'What all things have you purchased?' they ask. And it seems to me that they begin to think that it can't be about financial constraint, no, she must be a good time girl, she does this because she wants a good time, and she is having a too good time."

Misha makes a similar argument, suggesting that the affordances of airline work inspire jealousy as well as misogyny. "In our society," Misha says, "people would rather watch women suffer. They are happy if a woman is getting a beating at home or starving, but if she goes out and does a glamorous job, then they think she is a bad girl." The glamorous trappings of airline work—the makeup, the beauty, the international travel—eclipse ideas about financial need and make airline work seem like a pathway picked not out of necessity but for vulgar ends. Instead of a job done for wages, airline work is seen as an activity that women undertake in pursuit of less savory impulses. "They think we are flirts, we are materialistic, we are fickle, that we are having affairs and that is why we picked this job," Zebunnissa says, "so we could sleep with the pilot, the male attendants, the passengers, we do it for gifts or for time pass, we are wild, just party girls, partying."

***The taint of political interference.*** The stigma of airline work is compounded, women suggest, because of political interference. "Political actors have destroyed PIA," Roshan, a 50-year-old airline attendant, says. She is not alone in blaming politicians for the airline's negative image. "It doesn't matter which party, which government is in power,' Sharmeen says. 'They have all contributed to the degradation of this once-prestigious national institution.'

In claiming that political interference and "VIP culture" have ruined PIA, airline women are like policewomen, who also have a lot to say about the impact of VIPs on police efficiency and professionalism. "VIP culture" refers to the special treatment some people are able to get because of their office or their connection with someone who holds an important office. VIPs, women suggest, are able to flout laws and order the police around. And they are able to get special privileges from PIA.

Politicians technically have little to do with the airline, which is only partially governmental. But those with political clout, the women told me, do manage to use their power to interfere in the airline's workings in two important ways, which I outline below.

1. *Operational interference.* Politicians have ruined PIA, women said, by interfering with the airline's operations. Those who are located in influential positions in the government are able to delay or reroute flights and demand special privileges on board. "They'll bring in huge bags. They will show up hours late, and the flight is held back, so the rest of the passengers will be getting irritated and taking it out on us. When they do show up, they treat us like servants," Neera complained. Such delays make the airline look unprofessional and disorganized. "Passengers don't realize that the delay is caused by a VIP. They think that we have messed up, that we are incompetent, and the airline is a joke and a disgrace."

Operations are compromised not only through direct interference but also through indirect meddling by politicians via the union. Many union officials, I was told, are also affiliated with major political parties, and that affiliation plays a part in their election to the union. Politically affiliated union actors compromise PIA by using their political connections to rig the airline's workings. They dictate flight schedules and assignments, have disciplinary infractions overlooked, and go on extended leaves with pay. This interference has negative effects on PIA, women said, because it creates an extra burden for those employees who don't have influential friends. Moreover, well-connected colleagues can get away with harassing attendants, as Faisal did, when he offered to solve air hostesses' problems with the hostel by cohabiting with them.

2. *Interfering in recruitment procedures.* VIPs were also accused of interfering in the airline's recruitment procedures. Women complained that powerful political actors routinely use their clout to obtain jobs for their preferred candidates. "All kinds of strange people have joined the airline," Roshan complained, "thanks to this minister or that minister." As a semi–state job, airline positions are very attractive opportunities, providing incumbents with job security and other benefits and perks, including free travel, grooming, travel allowances, and transport to and from work. Thus, according to PIA crew members, political leaders reward their supporters and party workers by promising PIA jobs to their friends and family members. "So, our image is worsened," Bee told me, "because these political appointees who get inducted without merit are weird and strange." I asked her what she meant by "weird." In response, Bee told me the following story:

"When I came for my first interview," she said, "They [the recruiters] really liked me because I had done a business degree, so I was very professional. I knew how to give an interview, I knew what a CV is, and so I made a very good impression on them," she said, clarifying that "I am not just boasting, but I am telling you this, so you understand how political influence has become a big problem in PIA." I asked her how political interference was connected to CVs. "Very strange and weird types of people get inducted into PIA because of political interference," she said. "Some politician pushes for a particular candidate to get recruited," so induction is done not on the basis of merit or professionalism but on the basis of favoritism. "These *sifaarshi* [people appointed on the basis of political favor]" are "totally unprofessional," she said. "They don't know how to dress, talk, make a CV, do an interview or do anything in a professional way." This lack of professionalism, she said, had depressed the recruiters she met during her own recruitment process. "They told me, 'You won't believe the kinds of people we have had to interview; they are just weird.'"

*The disgrace of weird and strange people.* When I first heard airline attendants refer to political appointees as "weird" and "strange," I assumed that I was witnessing the class prejudice of urban, big city, working-class women against poor, rural, or small-town workers appointed in an effort at affirmative action by politicians aiming to provide opportunities to a broader swath of the electorate. But when I brought up this assumption with airline women, they became angry with me. "You think we are prejudiced," Tara, a 50-year-old senior bursar (head attendant), said to me. "You are not understanding what we are saying. You are failing to recognize and acknowledge that we are talking about corruption," she said. I asked her to give me an example of she meant by "weird." In reply she brought up the case of an airline attendant who had recently made the news. "The girl who was caught shoplifting in Toronto" was a political appointee, she said, referring to a highly publicized case of an air hostess who had been apprehended by Canadian police for shoplifting luxury items in a mall. Coincidentally, I had met this woman the day before. She had been standing with some union men in the corridor outside the union office. They were huddled together in an intimate conference. She was smoking and looking upset. When the men left, she approached me and told me about her plight. 'I've been dismissed without a trial,' she said. 'I don't know what I am going to do.'

I told Tara about this encounter. "She told me that she had been dismissed without due process," I said. "She told me she was devastated." "Nonsense," Tara said irritably. "She'll never be dismissed, I can tell you that." I said I had been told in the office also that she had been dismissed, and Tara argued, "If they're saying it. . . ," she broke off, then she shrugged. "But it doesn't happen," she went on. "The airline is getting a bad name, but they will still try to keep such political types safe [from disciplinary action]." Since the case seemed to upset her so much, I changed the subject. But after a few minutes, Tara brought up the shoplifting case again. "Even if she is put on trial and her act is confirmed, they still won't dismiss her," she said bitterly. "She'll come back, you watch and see. That's what I'm saying." I asked Tara how this disgraced employee could possibly return, and she replied, "A phone call will come from the President House or the Prime Minister House or some Minister or Senator or other big shot, someone will do something. Someone from the board of directors will rescue her. That's how things are done here," she said. "That's just how it is."

When women with political connections used their networks for professional advantage, air hostesses argued, they didn't just distort the operations and procedures of the airline, they gave airline women a bad name. "Then people assume we are all like this," Bee said. "We all have this kind of a boyfriend, who will get us out of trouble. And why do we get these kinds of favors? How do we get out of hot water? What do you think is assumed about this arrangement? What is the powerful person supposedly getting in return?" she asked me. "It makes us all look bad," she said, leaving the assumptions about what was offered in exchange for rescue hanging in the air.

In sum, just as political interference disrupts police work, according to policewomen, who complain that cops are able to get out of work and get good postings on the basis of political connections, it also disturbs the working of the airline. The prevalence of corruption creates reputational dilemmas for the women employed in both these fields, who are assumed to also be involved in the informal and extralegal exchanges between VIPs and workers. In these exchanges, women are assumed to trade sex for favors. Policewomen are assumed either to provide their colleagues and other influential actors with access to the women in their custody or to participate personally in vulgar gatherings where men are engaged in boozing and cavorting with women colleagues who rely on men for gifts like burgers and gasoline. Airline attendants are assumed to exchange sex for favors and gifts from colleagues, or worse, it is assumed that they are the mistresses of influential men, who have provided them with these glamorous jobs in exchange for a sexual relationship.

How do women negotiate the stigma associated with these shameful assumptions? They draw on the resources provided by their work to enact a set of performances I call postfeminist cosmopolitanism. In the next section, I provide details of this agentic performance and parse out its different dimensions, symbolic and relational. What kinds of symbols and aesthetics do women draw on and what kind of identity do they craft in their efforts to manage stigma?

### POSTFEMINIST COSMOPOLITANISM

In contrast with policewomen's veiled delicacy and LHW's martial motherhood, airline women's postfeminist cosmopolitanism involves a defiant and reconstructive form of symbolic agency. While health workers and policewomen draw on symbols imbued with honor from their immediate environment, such as veils, motherhood, and jihad, airline women import a set of symbols (e.g., expensive lipsticks) that index norms circulating in global discourse (e.g., postfeminist ideas about women's freedom as a sign of modernity) to stigmatize their stigmatizers.

But agency, as I mention in chapter 3, runs on two motors. It doesn't pursue meaning alone; it also seeks relational ends. By animating symbols through performance, actors don't just create or perpetuate meanings about themselves; they also seek to recruit others who can help them to extend these meanings, as well as their capacity over time and space. Senior women in the police, for instance, use sweet talk and kinship language to cajole their subordinates into work that is onerous, such as night shifts. Successfully recruited junior women protect their boss's reputation and authority even when the boss is not around. And they travel at the boss's behest to perform various tasks the boss cannot undertake on her own. Similarly, LHWs use signs of caring to coax their clients into providing information to the state and complying with state policy. By enacting the role of loving mother, LHWs recruit their clients, getting them to cooperate with policy imperatives. What kinds of relational affordances does postfeminist cosmopolitanism permit for airline attendants? How does symbolic agency in this case fire up relational capacities?

In contrast with LHWs and cops, airline women's performances help them to pursue distinction and distance rather than connection. Actors don't just use signs and symbols to forge connection, but as this chapter shows, they also sometimes deploy symbols in an effort to disconnect and disengage with actors they dislike. In this case, symbolic agency operates as a motor of severance, allowing actors to break off or at least to constrain an interaction or an affiliation. By performing distinction from their stigmatizers, airline women attempt to limit the claims that these people can make on them. They try to cut off passengers who are rudely demanding too much attention and they distance themselves from family members who humiliate them or seek to take advantage of their affordances.

In what follows, I provide a detailed account of postfeminist cosmopolitanism, including a description of the symbolic and the relational aspects of this stigma-management performance. Although postfeminist cosmopolitanism does allow airline women to address the stigma associated with their jobs, it also works to reinforce two sets of hierarchies that are connected with other kinds of stigma: (1) the hierarchies circulating in stigmatizing discourses that construct Muslim majority countries, like Pakistan, as backward and inferior to so-called modern contexts on the basis of gender arrangements; and (2) the gendered hierarchies that disadvantage women at work, constructing them as less independent, less autonomous, and less competent than men.

### SYMBOLIC AGENCY AND POSTFEMINIST COSMOPOLITANISM

Airline women manage stigma by laying claim to a set of capacities they have developed through their jobs. These capacities, including access to freedom and choice, access to knowledge, and the cultivation of cosmopolitan taste and interactional competence not only generate feelings of accomplishment and dignity but also provide airline women with distinction, a term the sociologist Pierre Bourdieu uses to describe tactics people, typically elites, use to set themselves apart as superior and more deserving than others (Bourdieu 1984).

*Airline women are free.* When I first showed up at the PIA offices for my field work, I dressed as I had in my other field sites. Aiming for a nondescript, unremarkable appearance, I wore a pale blue knee-length tunic I had purchased at a local boutique, with straight black pants and sandals that strapped around my feet. I clipped my hair in a bun and wore no makeup. I also brought along Surraiya, a chaperone I sometimes hired to accompany me on field visits, in imitation of the policewomen I had worked with, who would bring younger brothers or parents with them when they came to work at the police station. The airline attendants I met in my first few days at PIA were quick to protest against my aesthetic practices. "You don't need to bring a chaperone here," Ambreen told me on my first day. "This place is not like the other places you go to," she said.

Other women lectured me on my appearance. "You should blow-dry your hair and wear it down," Kausar said. "You should wear lipstick," Shama declared. "Is this how you dress in Virginia, so shabbily?" Zeba asked me. "You need to do yourself up nicely. It's a mark of respect for your interlocutors. It's a mark of your self-respect."

The question of aesthetics, I soon learned, was tremendously important to airline women. They took pride in their appearance and expressed great distaste for those who didn't. A well-groomed appearance was not just about looking good but about feeling good, a sign of their freedom and therefore of their access to dignity. PIA, they told me, was not like my other field sites. I didn't have to worry for my safety here. "Policewomen and LHWs," Rana said dismissively, "are *beychaari* [poor things]. Their colleagues are rough and crude. Their workplaces are coarse and dirty. This place is not like that. Here, you can imagine that you are in a foreign country. You can behave freely here."

For airline women the distinctiveness of PIA rested on the connections that they drew between feeling free and looking good. Both of these aspects of airline work relied in turn on the transnational mobility airline work provided. PIA work was different from other workplaces, safer, and more conducive of dignity, because it involved transnational travel. And the safety and the travel together furnished women with the freedom to look good and the ability to achieve a well-groomed appearance that shored up their dignity.

"If I worked in an office, I would have a boss," Nazli said. "Now suppose my boss was not all right, meaning if he was not a decent person, still every day I would have to put up with him. Daily I would have to listen to him. There would be no escape." An airline job was safer, she argued, because it involved moving and meeting a continuously changing set of people. This constant motion made it difficult for someone to take advantage of the familiarity fostered by daily interaction to impose unwanted intimacy upon her.

PIA work provided safety in another way too, airline women argued. Unlike the women in my other field sites who worked in "strange" and insecure situations, airline work provided women with luxurious and secured work environments. "See, if you are working in an office," Rida argued, "then one man can hit on you with lecherousness. But when four hundred passengers are traveling along with you, okay, sometimes it does happen that one will try to come on to you, but they hesitate also, they worry that 'if she snubs me, in front of all these people, it will be insulting for me.' So, you see, it is up to me. If I want to get with him, I can encourage his advances, but if not, he can't exceed the line. Therefore, it's a safe job, safer than office jobs, where women have to face the same people all the time."

But safety for airline women was ensured not only through the constant motion of airline work and the presence of other people but also by the luxurious nature of airline jobs. "From the airport, we go to the hotel," Bee told me. "The airline puts me up in fancy hotels," she said with evident pride. "In such hotels, you know, there is full security for me, and no one can enter my room—until and unless I permit them to do so." For Rida and Bee, these provisions of safety not only ensured protection but also provided the women with dignity by safeguarding their right to accept or reject flirtatious advances. Unlike cops and LHWs, who largely viewed any kind of sexual advance as a threat and therefore as a source of indignity and humiliation, airline attendants felt safe to engage in flirtation because they felt that in any such interaction, they were free to reject an advance they were not interested in.

Together, the various forms of safety provided to airline women supplied them, they said, with a feeling of freedom and tranquility. "Like here [in Karachi] right now, if I am feeling bored, I cannot go out alone," Sana explained. "If I do go out and sit somewhere alone, like on a bench at the seaside, passersby will stare at me curiously. This is a big issue in our Pakistan, women cannot roam at will in public spaces." Sana went on: "But abroad, wherever you sit, whatever you do, there is peace." The freedom to inhabit public spaces in peace, free from harassment and the intrusive gaze of passing men, women said, allowed them to feel "normal." In contrast with LHWs who described the frequent sexual overtures they confronted during their door-to-door polio vaccination work as making them feel like "we are not even human," airline women said that their ability to travel to places where no one looked at them, let alone approached them with unwanted advances, made them feel as if they were human.

"With this job I get to go to America," Seema told me.[1] "Which otherwise I wouldn't be able to afford. But [working] here, we get to go, at least once every two months," she said. "When we go there, PIA puts us up for a four-day stay at a hotel. Then we roam around. This is where we get our enjoyment, our down time to rest and relax. That is how you become normal, like if you are feeling fed up due to some family issue you are facing, you get some freedom, some alone time you can use to start feeling normal again." So accustomed to the feeling of comfort and relaxation they got from being alone abroad, airline women had begun to equate the feeling of freedom with feeling "normal." The stress that is generated from being around family or compatriots who are too intrusive and inquisitive about women's actions and their movement had become, in their mind, an abnormal feeling. The sense of unfettered freedom they felt when abroad, women said, gave them a feeling of dignity. "I can go anywhere I like," Zara said, "and no one can ask me where I am going, or what I am going to do. The only requirement PIA places on me is that I have to be available in time for my flight. So, you can do it with dignity also. You can do it your own way." The ability to make one's own choices provides women, in this case, with a dignified feeling.

**Airline women are knowledgeable.** In addition to safety, freedom, and tranquility, airline women claimed, their work provided them with a rare and expensive form of knowledge that even elites would be hard pressed to access. "What I say is that even billionaires can't manage the education we get," Mona said with apparent pride. "We get to learn, see, and explore the world in ways that others simply cannot." The extensive foreign experience that airline work provides, Nazli argued, constitutes a "real education." "Most people get their education from books," she said, "but that kind of knowledge can be forgotten." But "personal experience," on the other hand, is more durable. "What you see with your eyes, that thing you can never get anywhere else." I asked her to give me an example of things she had learned. "I cannot forget the blooming time of the tulip garden," she said in a dreamy voice. "It was in Amsterdam. When I went there the tulips were in bloom, so I was lucky, and to this day I remember it, how amazing it was, so I haven't been able to forget it."

Such rare sights and experiences, airline women argued, made them different from "ordinary Pakistani girls and women." "I have to say, I have known the cherries of Damascus, the pyramids of Egypt, the Black Sea of Jordan. I have known Rome and Venice," Sarah said to me. "How then can you compare me to the average, the ordinary girls of this country?"

Their distinction from ordinary girls, airline women claimed, rested not only on the superior knowledge they had gained through travel but also on the financial strength they derived from their work. For instance, Rida told me that some of her colleagues had been pressed into work because of a *majboori* (compulsion, constraint). Since I had heard women in all three field sites use the word *majboori*, I said, "Yes, many people have a majboori of one kind or another." "But this a very good majboori," she replied, laughing, "it brings about so much good. You are getting such good exposure and such good pay, so I think it's a very good job, why not? Do it!" I asked her what the pay was like, and she replied, "So you can say that a person who is doing full-fledged flights, between 80 and 90 hours and has accumulated about five years of experience, that person can make between 100,000 and 150,000 rupees [$1000–$1500 at the time of my fieldwork] per month. Now bear in mind many of these girls are do not have college degrees," she said, "so it's very good that they get this kind of salary. Who else will keep them at that rate? You tell me."

Policewomen with comparable education make roughly 25,000 rupees a month. Lady health workers were promised 20,000 rupees but only after they had engaged in strenuous protest over their low monthly wages (roughly 12,000 rupees). Shiza, a health worker I knew, had asked me to help her find a beauty salon job for her daughter, Mehr. The salon near their home was offering only 15,000 rupees a month. Mehr would have to work ten-hour shifts six days a week to earn her 15,000 rupees, and she would have to share her tips with the rest of the staff at the salon.

While airline work invites a great deal more stigma than police work or health work, it pays a much higher salary. Airline women referred frequently to their higher pay and said it opened up a whole new array of vistas and experiences to them that ordinary women simply could not access. "I am the kind of person," Zara told me, "if I am in Paris, I feel I should go see the Eiffel Tower, I should see the Champs-Élysées. I should purchase souvenirs, so I can say I bought something in Paris. And I try out the local cuisine, at least, like crepes in Paris or bagels in New York, so I can know what the food is like." She makes this effort to see, taste, and know New York and Paris, she said, because it is a form of education. "We may not have college degrees," Zara said, "but believe me, we are much more sophisticated than women who have MBAs even."

*The cosmopolitan tastes of airline women.* "I used to be a little, naïve village girl," Shagufta told me. "This job has transformed me," she said. "What's the biggest change you've noticed?" I asked her. "She's learned the difference between MAC and Medora," Hassan, a male crew member who was listening in, said. (MAC is a well-known international makeup brand, while Medora is a Pakistani cosmetic brand primarily aimed at working-class women.) Shagufta burst into laughter, smacking him in a friendly manner on the elbow. "He's so naughty but he is right. I learned the difference between MAC and Medora," she said, giggling. "I've learned a lot about grooming," Shagufta went on. "I've learned how to walk, talk, how to present myself."

While Shagufta talked about her acquired sophistication in a lighthearted and humorous manner, other women, like Sarah, were much more serious in their discussions about what this cultivation meant. The taste and the sophistication a PIA woman acquires through her travel, Sarah suggested, raises her status. "A PIA woman," Sarah argued, "becomes an international figure." She cannot be "compared to an ordinary girl" who "teaches, or works in a bank." A PIA woman's "mental approach," her "mental level is totally different," she said. "If you talk to us, you will see from our conversation, that our mental level, always, always, will be at a higher level, because we've seen the world, we've seen different cultures, we have seen them in a way that ordinary people don't get to see them, we have become through those experiences, an international woman." This cosmopolitanism that airline women claimed was reflected, they argued, not just in their conversation but also in their appearance. "When I speak of an international figure," Sarah explained, "I mean someone who moves, speaks, and behaves in line with global ways and protocols." In contrast to this globalized woman, the average Pakistani woman, Sarah claimed, has "no sense of fashion, style, protocol, or correctness." She will show up, Sarah said with apparent disgust, "in mismatched outfits—the pant doesn't go with the shirt, doesn't go with the shoe, doesn't go with the accessories or the hairstyle." Whereas airline women put thought into their overall look, ordinary Pakistanis had no sense of putting together a "finished" or "polished" look.

"When you travel abroad," Sarah explained, "you go to places like casinos or hotels or theaters and you learn that there is a dress code, which has been established for those who want to visit such places. You can't show up in jeans or slippers there." There are some places like that in Pakistan too, Sarah acknowledged, "like the golf club," where "slippers, jeans, and sweatpants are not allowed. So, I suppose, that that sense is gradually coming here too," she remarked. But airline women already have this sense of grooming that Pakistanis are, according to Sarah, only just beginning to acquire. (Elite spaces like the Sindh Club have had dress codes and other rules surrounding comportment for decades, but the airline attendants appeared to be unfamiliar with these elite locations and lifestyles in Karachi).

In keeping with Sarah's aesthetic argument, airline women appeared to be very careful about their appearance. Unlike policewomen or health workers, airline women never wore headscarves. Their hair always appeared to be blow-dried. When out of uniform, they wore recognizably branded Pakistani clothes paired with expensive-looking handbags and shoes. They used large smartphones; wore chunky, flashy watches; and wore expensive-looking sunglasses. When hanging around the office together, they spoke to each other and to me about branded perfumes, mascaras, and lipsticks. Laila, for instance, laughed as she told me about the famous Pakistani makeup artist, who at a training workshop had encouraged airline women to buy Kryolan TV Paint Stick, a foundation used by television professionals. "I'll stick to Bobbi Brown, thanks," Laila said to me, implying that her own standards were higher than those of this renowned Pakistani stylist. In a similar lighthearted manner, Seema joked with me that the makeup allowance PIA provided "couldn't even cover the cost of one nail polish—I mean the kind that we wear."

**Airline women are complete persons.** Airline work, the women claimed, didn't just transform their outward appearances and tastes; it also altered their "internal makeup" and personhood. "Personally, if I consider my own person," Naz claimed, "then I feel I am complete." Because of her job, Naz said, "I have learned the difference between being a human being rather than just a being." Whereas a being just exists, a human being, Naz said, is reflexive, agentic, and autonomous. Such qualities distinguish airline women from average, ordinary Pakistani women. When I asked her to elaborate, Naz brought up the issue of fatalism. Pakistanis, she said, unlike Europeans, have a tendency to leave things to fate. This propensity, she said, made them beings rather than human beings:

> We [Pakistanis] have this attitude. We will say, "Leave it to God." God is in charge, but then if we leave things to God, then obviously, they will remain suspended because . . . God is not going to come and save your

spectacles—if you left them too close to the edge of the table, they will fall. He has set a system in motion. He has given me the reasoning skills about how to wear things, how to place them on the table, how to take care of my things. . . . He has given me command, how I should speak, how I should interact, how I should complete an action, how I should sit, how I should manage myself—that is all up to me.

Feeling possessed of a distinct, more European mode of existing in the world means exercising both reflexivity and projectivity. It requires not just going through the motions dictated by culture but thinking about where one has been and where one is going. Meera, a 30-year-old air hostess who has been flying for several years, put it this way: "I lived in Abbottabad before I joined PIA. I lived in a normal, ordinary way—got educated, primary school, middle school, and all that but when you go out [abroad], you learn a lot about life." "What do you learn?" I asked her. "You learn that that was not life, what we were living before. Because it was not what you had chosen. It was just flowing on a set path. You did not arrange it; you just followed a pattern." She paused and then added, "I mean that when you begin flying, you get to see where you were and where you have to go. You begin to set goals. You begin to think about the distance you have to cover."

Having goals and being deliberate meant choosing the kind of life one wanted rather than following a pattern established by others. When I asked Shazia, a single mother of two teenaged boys, what she had learned from her job, she said, "I learned how to live life. In short, I learned how to live." "And what does that look like?" I asked her. "Life should be easy, convenient, and beautiful," she said. "In our culture," she remarked, "people are so bogged down in a particular way of living, they don't think about the style of their life. They don't think about how to design life, how to make it simple, elegant, and enjoyable." I asked her to give me an example of this elegance. "I don't allow fuss to ruin my life," she replied. "I have learned to make things easy. I buy frozen foods, like chicken nuggets, or you can get rotisserie chicken at the mall, and then, instead of washing dishes, I use disposable paper plates. To clean the house, I use a Swiffer. You can't get those here, it's a very convenient tool for cleaning. So I have learned to make things easy at home, to get it done with a minimum of stress." Rather than follow the script that ordinary mothers used, cooking food, washing dishes, and cleaning the house in conventional ways, Shazia claimed she had chosen to design a lifestyle that was convenient and easy and that left her time to enjoy herself.

***Airline women's superior interactive competence.*** Airline work, women said, didn't just transform their subjectivities; it altered their interactions. "Because of this job, I think, I have become, like an out-of-the-ordinary, outgoing type," Seema said. I asked her to give me an example of what she meant, and she recounted a recent experience she'd had while dining out with her fiancé. "Like, in Pakistan we have this norm that girls should be modest. They should not talk too much," she said. "So recently, I went out to eat at *Do Darya* [a local restaurant by the creek] with my fiancé. So, when we got there, I went ahead and began placing the order. This is my habit, so, instead of showing any hesitation, as a normal Pakistani girl would do, I began instructing the waiters. I began telling them, 'Don't do it this way, do it that way, tell chef to cook it like this, not like that,' and my fiancé was staring at me aghast," she laughed. "After the waiter left, my fiancé says, 'I am here, right? I can do the talking. Why are you doing the talking?'" "Your fiancé didn't like you taking charge?" I asked. "No," Seema laughed. "Actually, we air hostesses have become so accustomed," she said. "I don't mean, I'm not saying we do something wrong, but we have so much passenger dealing under our belt, I've gotten into the habit of being outgoing and that causes problems for me sometimes." Although she described her newfound boldness as a problem, Seema seemed simultaneously proud of it. She described several other instances of times when she had taken charge and left the men in her family baffled at her confidence. "They will get used to it," she said with a smile. "They will have to because it is a part of me now."

Like Seema, several airline women claimed that because of their frequent dealing with droves of passengers they had acquired a cosmopolitan interactive style, one that, in contrast with Pakistani women's modes, is outgoing, firm, efficient, and in control. "From what I've seen," Afshan said, "this crew has this habit that even if a random stranger, a passerby is falling, tripping, for example, we will plunge forward saying, 'Oh, you didn't get hurt, did you? You are okay, aren't you?' I mean, customer relations has seeped so deep within us now that we tend to forget that this is not how things are done here in Pakistan," she said. "Such outgoing behavior is not disliked in foreign countries, but it is disliked in Pakistan. This is something that I have noticed a lot." "Is such outgoing behavior frowned upon when men do it?" I asked. "It is disliked only for ladies," she replied. "They don't mind that much if men are outgoing, but they mind it with the ladies." "What is it that people dislike about helping a tripping stranger?" I asked. She laughed, saying, "They say things like, 'Look at her, she is uselessly taking tension on his behalf. She should mind her own business. Why should it matter to her if someone falls or not.'"

Besides an outgoing style, airline work, women claimed, has provided them with an interactional style that is efficient and controlled. "The main thing about this job," Mehreen said, "is that you learn to manage yourself very nicely. Like, we do the meal service. We do it within the time frame of one hour, right?" she said, explaining that each crewmember has fifty passengers to serve. "You have to handle feeding fifty passengers in one hour. And managing the tempo of interactions like that, it teaches you everything." "What have you learned, for instance?" I asked. "Learning, like if you fly two or three times, you learn how to keep yourself firm. If you speak firmly to someone, then that person also speaks to you from a distance. If you don't speak with them firmly, if you don't have knowledge of your job, you speak to them in a casual attitude, then they too will speak to you in a casual attitude, which may create problems that you will then have to face." I ask her what she meant by "the knowledge of your job." "Knowledge," Mehreen explained, refers to the perceptiveness airline women have acquired from experience. "We have learned how to read people, and then how to tailor our manner to that person in such a way as to control the outcome of the interaction."

This interactive competence aids women not only in speedily handling large numbers of passengers but also in handling unwanted flirtations during voyages. "The thing is," Bee said, "many people try to approach us [i.e., flirtatiously], so if we appear to be even a little bit weak, then take it that people start approaching us like flies." Managing this kind of interaction, Bee said, required inner strength, and confidence. It meant having the self-control to put up a particular, unapproachable kind of front. "See, there are all kinds of women here," she said, referring to her colleagues.

"Desperate and foolish ones and also smart ones. Now, if you encounter a passenger who knows how to leverage someone's desperation, because you were unable to mask it, he can take advantage by showing you gold-tinged dreams, for instance," she explained, "a girl can fall under the spell of his words." To fall under someone's spell, Bee suggested, implied that such a woman "doesn't have willpower when people try to butter her up with their talk" and that she will fall prey to their promises. "Those who have acquired perception, have learned to read their interlocutors, are able to put up an appropriate front, and therefore exercise more control over their fate."

These perception skills were important not only because they helped women to do their jobs quickly and efficiently but also because marriage was seen by many women as an important exit strategy, a way to get out of flying. Many of them looked up to Roshan, a striking 25-year-old flight attendant who told me that she was serving out her notice period. She had met a German man on one of her flights and they were to wed at the end of the year. While Roshan's colleagues weren't necessarily looking for foreign men, many stated candidly that they did wish to settle down with someone who was "open-minded" and able to "take care" of them. "This job," Bee explained, "comes with an expiry date. It takes such a tremendous toll on your body that it is rare for people to be able to keep doing it at 50, 60. You have to have an exit strategy."

To pursue romantic possibilities in the course of work meant being open to men who were sincere in their interest while shutting down those who were either insincere or undesirable. To deal with the undesirables, Seema said, women knew when to adopt a more confrontational style. They boldly shut down unwanted advances while welcoming those that seemed promising. Their confrontational style, airline women boasted, set them apart from "ordinary," "shy," and interactionally inept Pakistani women. Nazli argued, "There is a lack of awareness in our society. Basically, my own experience, what I've seen is that we are all about words here, not about action. I'm sorry I'm being a little bit blunt here," she said. "Now what is the definition of bluntness? Here in Pakistan, they see a truthful style as insolence," she said. "Whereas in the west, they do things openly, here it is preferred to be clandestine, and if you are open, they say you are blunt, and it is disliked."

Other women similarly argued that firmness should be distinguished from rudeness. "The word I use is 'assertive,'" Sarah said. "See, assertive, firm, not rude." Airline attendants have to be assertive, she explained, "because flying is a very risky form of travel. I mean it is safe, but I mean, you are not on the ground, you're in midair, so naturally I have to behave firmly. Safety standards are extremely important." In a similar vein Bee argued that she works not in hospitality, as some ignorant people might characterize her job, but "in aviation," and that involves a controlled, careful, and firm mode of interaction.

***Failure is a sign of inferiority.*** While women's claims of "perceptiveness," "awareness," "self-control," and "assertiveness" provided them with a sense of professionalism, they also made women responsible for any bad behavior they might face from others. Each of the qualities that women prized implied the exertion of individual control and therefore supported the notion that negative and invasive interactive outcomes are ultimately women's own fault and their own responsibility to manage. "See, a human creates the atmosphere herself," Bee argued, echoing an axiom I heard in all of my field sites. "You will find good and bad people everywhere," she said, "but you should have a lot of willpower inside you to handle both kinds." Sana put the same argument more succinctly. "If you don't exert willpower and control in your life," she said, then "you will have to pay the price." Through our abilities, Sana explained, we create a kind of music, "because there is a music, right, each action generates its own music, so people who don't have self-control will have to face the music and those who do exercise control, who keep their life streamlined, they will face a good kind of music."

By arguing that women were ultimately responsible for the encounters they faced, that they had to be clever, perceptive, strong, and in control in order to ensure positive encounters, airline women deployed a neoliberal postfeminist logic that suggests the importance of personal empowerment, personal choice, and personal responsibility over structural issues or systemic problems. They made stigma a problem that individual women must find it within themselves to manage. Handling flirtatious or difficult customers required drawing on a personal well of willpower. Those who got carried away by the false promises of fickle men were "weak" and "desperate" women, unable to exercise perception or self-control. Those who spoke up may be considered rude but ultimately were reflecting a Western, cosmopolitan kind of bluntness, which suggested their professionalism and their competence and their ability to exert control.

**Postfeminist cosmopolitanism and inequality.** Although postfeminist cosmopolitanism allows airline women to enact dignity in a performance that combats the stigma associated with their work, their assertions also reinforce a set of problematic binaries that circulate in global discourses about Muslim contexts. Muslims have long been represented in stereotypical ways in scholarly and mediated discourses in the Global North. These "orientalist" discourses portray Muslim societies as stagnant and unchanging in their culture and oppressive in their gender arrangements. As discussed in chapter 1, such orientalist narratives helped imperial powers in the nineteenth century to rationalize and justify colonial rule. In the twenty-first century, orientalist ideas were invoked to justify the War on Terror, a conflict that relied on longstanding stereotypes about Muslim backwardness and ideas about Muslim women needing saving from Muslim men, in an effort to generate support for action in Afghanistan and the Middle East.

When they describe their stigmatizing interlocutors as culturally backward, airline women reaffirm stereotypes about Pakistan's lagging modernity. In suggesting that Pakistanis are less thoughtful, less organized, less independent than airline women who have gained their own autonomy, thoughtfulness, and organization in part through their exposure to western contexts, airline women reinforce the idea that there is a problem with Pakistani culture, which is reflected in Pakistanis' unreflective behavior and in their oppression of women. To negotiate stigma, in other words, airline women engage in stigmatizing their stigmatizers. They try to defuse the negative meanings of their work by importing a set of stigmas that denigrate their own culture on the basis of gender arrangements. Yet gender-based stigmas are not exclusive to Pakistani culture. Pakistani women are not unique in having to contend with stigma for their occupation of public space. Certainly, in other contexts, the content of the stigma may be different. Yet, frontline women face degrading interactions in many other contexts, including those that are not Muslim majority. During the COVID-19 pandemic, for instance, frontline workers in Brazil were stigmatized as they were seen as vectors of the disease. As a consequence, they were faced with increased physical and symbolic violence, gossip, and verbal abuse as well as denial of services and housing. At times, even their families faced secondary stigma for their connection to health care workers. In their study of this stigma, Wenham et al. suggest that gender and racial inequalities contributed to the stigma that health workers (who are mostly women and Black) faced during the pandemic. Since the occupation is composed mostly of women and people of color, it was already devalued in Brazil prior to the pandemic, which only aggravated workers' experiences of stigma (Wenham et al. 2021). Meanwhile, in Canada, Phillips et al. found that staff at a service catering to sex workers experienced "stigma by association." Since their work involved helping a stigmatized category of actors—"the prostitute"—workers at the Peers Victoria Resources Society were also seen as polluted through association (Phillips et al. 2012). In short, gender and sexual stigmas are not unique to the Pakistani context, and Pakistani people are not alone in denigrating frontline women for the nature and content of their jobs.

Airline women's use of stigmatizing global stereotypes is interesting. It suggests that despite their inaccuracy and injustice, global stereotypes may in some contexts serve as weapons of the weak. While orientalist ideas produce a flattened and incorrect portrait of places like Pakistan, painting an image that global powers can use to promote policies of domination and interference in this context, they also serve as tools for some actors, like airline attendants, to contest their marginalization within their own society. Yet fighting stigma with stigma leaves a crucial mechanism of inequality intact. When marginalized actors use the tools of their oppression to challenge it, they leave the engines of inequality churning undisturbed. By challenging their stigmatizers with a new set of stigmas, airline women keep an important set of global hierarchies intact—those that construct some places and people as superior and modern in contrast with others. Airline women's performances suggest that places like Pakistan have yet to catch up to the more evolved western cultures and contexts, where gender norms are less restrictive, and women are freer. Thus, postfeminist cosmopolitanism uses signs of class to reaffirm a set of imported scripts around gender, which come with their own baggage and inequalities. It neither questions the class system nor examines the ways that gender acts as a vector of inequality outside Pakistan, just as it does within.

In the next section, I examine another set of gender hierarchies that is also shored up by airline women's destigmatization performances.

### RELATIONAL AGENCY AND POSTFEMINIST COSMOPOLITANISM

Airline attendants' cosmopolitan presentations—their assertions of heightened autonomy, independence, and freedom—didn't always accord with my field observations. Their performance of competence wobbled and fell apart during their interactions with their male colleagues. In these interactions, women enacted a deference and a dependence that belied their claims of autonomy, independence, and self-reliance. In everyday operations and interactions, women sought guidance from their male colleagues, deferred to men's ideas and opinions, and turned to men for help managing professional problems and relationships. Naz, for instance, interrupted her interview with me several times to poke her head out of the cubicle where we were sitting and ask her male colleagues what they thought she should say to me.

On one such occasion, she had been telling me that in the 1990s PIA constrained women from marrying until they had completed at least five years of service and, further, that the airline had at the time disallowed women to fly after the age of 40. I asked her what the current age of retirement was, and she got up, stuck her head out of her office cubby and called out to her male colleague across the hall. "Saleem," she called out. "Should I tell the truth, or should I lie?" she asked him. "Truth!" he hollered back. "The truth always wins!" "But," she yelled, "you always instruct me that it's better to lie." "Yes," he replied, "but Fauzia has come here for her research, so she should learn things, right?" He walked over to where we were seated before continuing, "Now if Fauzia decides to lie, then that is up to her." Apparently, emboldened by this exchange, Naz sat back down and delivered a diatribe against "the rot" that political influence had ushered into PIA. "The rules about appearance and self-presentation have gone by the wayside," she said angrily, "because women with political influence are able to get around them and do as they please."

I witnessed such dynamics not only in the context of my interviews but also in my observations at the union office where airline attendants socialized over tea and meals. Although several women served the union alongside men, doing what they called "welfare work" (i.e., helping airline attendants manage various issues with management), it was the men who acted as brokers, rallying various connections to further the women's personal and professional requests.

On one occasion, for instance, I observed Bee asking her male colleagues for help obtaining data she needed to complete an assignment required for the completion of an MBA course she was taking. She told Saqib, a union officer, that she needed printouts of PIA's balance sheets over the past five years and didn't know where to get them. Her confusion was not surprising. It can be very hard to obtain such data without help from a personal contact willing to do it as a personal favor. "Shall I go to the stock exchange and look for them?" she asked Saqib, who was busy completing a report for the general manager's office. "Do you know Yasir Khan?" he asked. "He can get them for you." Bee shook her head to signal that she didn't know Yasir. "I'll speak to him for you," Saqib assured her. "Will you get me the data?" Bee asked. "Don't worry, I'll get it for you," Saqib said. This exchange was not unusual. Women relied on men to complete tasks that required *jugaar*, a local word for jerry-rigging or using ingenuity and personal connections to complete tasks that could not be completed via formal or official channels. The data Bee needed could not be obtained without the use of a personal connection or favor. Men who had personal connections with political parties, as Saqib did, were even more adept at doing jugaar.

Women sought men's aid not only for help with tasks requiring jugaar, such as obtaining hard-to-access financial data for their degree programs, but also with more formal operations, like handling written communications with management. For instance, Razia, a senior bursar (supervisor of crew on a flight), ran into trouble with a pilot on a domestic flight one day. In her words, the pilot became enraged with her over the appearance of one of the crew members, a young male flight attendant she was supervising. Razia claimed that the pilot had asked her "very rudely" why Waseem had not shaved properly. "I told him, 'Oh, really, I hadn't noticed he is unshaven. Let me put on my glasses.' I did not see anything objectionable without my glasses." This response apparently angered the pilot, who, Razia says, had already come on board in a bad mood, which had only worsened in the course of the flight and which he unleashed upon her in the end. When the flight ended, she said, the pilot told her, "You better not fly with me again. You are not a professional. Don't ever dare set foot on my plane again!" She said, "I told him, 'It's you who are unprofessional!'" At this, he stepped forward with his hand raised as if to hit her, yelling, "Get out of my plane!" "He came to hit me," she said to me, her voice shaking. She then turned to the entire union office and said, "I'm going to use the Women's Protection Bill against him," referring to a piece of recently passed legislation aimed at protecting women against violence. "I won't put up with this treatment." Then she turned to me and went on: "He was the one who was unprofessional," she said. "He has no consideration, complaining about the boy's shave, does he realize what time Waseem had to report to work? Even if I had noticed his growth, which I didn't, because it was not visible without glasses, I couldn't have sent him back home. Does the pilot not realize we are short-staffed?"

The pilot didn't just yell at Razia. He lodged a complaint against her with the management, who put the complaint in her permanent file and also asked her to tender a written explanation for her part in the episode. Razia, clearly very angry, turned to the union for help. The union staff were worried that in her heightened emotional state, Razia would make things worse with management by bringing up the Women's Protection Bill and insisting that it was unreasonable to ask the crew to shave. Union member Saleem therefore acted to broker the affair on her behalf. First, he talked Razia down, telling her to cool down and rein in her anger, then he went along with her to the management office to smooth things over with the bosses there. Razia returned to the union office considerably pacified. "Now, it's all settled," Saleem told her. "There's nothing to do or worry about," he said. "All you need to do now is write a letter presenting your version of events, and that's it." "But I can't write a letter!" Razia exclaimed. "In English? How can I write in English?" Saleem sighed and shook his head. He then asked me to write the letter on Razia's behalf. Together Razia and I spent an hour drafting a letter by hand, which she then took to Saleem for comments and changes before asking another male colleague to get it typed up for her.

Razia was not alone in seeking men's help in dealing with management. I met Sameena in the midst of her attempt to get help manipulating a roster.

She had come to the union office to ask for help getting out of a scheduled training session and struck up a conversation with me while she waited for the union staff to get done with their other errands. Every few years, she told me, airline attendants are required to undergo supplementary training, which equips them to serve on additional kinds of aircraft than the ones for which they had initially trained. In this way, the crew's ability to handle different kinds of equipment advances with time. But Sameena did not want to take on the added competence the training would provide her. She feared that the training would qualify her to get assigned to work on longer journeys, which would mean she would have to spend more time away from home. "I prefer doing up-down flights," she explained to me, referring to the primarily domestic routes that took attendants "up" on early morning flights out of the city and brought them back "down" in the evening of the same day. Sameena said these flights allowed her to balance work and domestic responsibilities. Her husband, she said, was an unusually fussy person: 'He likes his food to be cooked fresh, daily, and at home,' which she would not be able to do if her schedule took her on overnight flights. 'I would have to quit if that happened,' she said. 'But I don't want to quit my job because the money allows me to send my children to good schools and to pay for after-school tuition programs.'

To maintain this uneasy balance between a taxing job and a demanding husband, Sameena was forced to turn to Faisal, the union boss, even though she said she found it distasteful to ask for help like this, 'on a personal basis.' 'My husband doesn't like it when I get too buddy-buddy with the men at work,' she said bitterly, 'but here [in this job], you have to hold someone's hand like a child learning to walk. If you want to get out of training or get a preferred route assignment, you have to seek patronage.'" She said, 'You can't go speak directly to the GM [general manager] or DGM [deputy general manager]. The monsters won't do anything without their [the union's] say-so.' She said that the union representatives 'These guys bring the clout of PPP, PML(N) [local political parties]. Nothing can happen unless it goes through them."

As she wound up this speech, Faisal the union boss suddenly burst in through the door, three women forming a train behind him. He came in and said, laughing, 'Today there are lots of women chasing after me.' His entourage didn't seem to find this funny. Faisal came up to Sameena and asked her roughly, 'You already did *sifaarish* [sought assistance from a high-ranking person], so then why did you ask me?' 'No, no!' she replied in alarm. 'I have no connection, who would I use?' Faisal eventually got Sameena out of the training.

These gendered dynamics of women seeking and men tendering assistance were especially amplified during training sessions. In each module of training, I observed that trainers would get more and more irritated as women continued to hang back looking nervous and irresolute. Meanwhile men would attempt to leap into the breach, making lighthearted excuses for the women, coaxing their colleagues with jokes, and deflating the tension with ribald humor. During a fire-fighting module, for instance, the trainer, a well-dressed woman in heels, had to repeat her barked orders multiple times before Shehnaz, trembling, complied. "Shehnaz, forward! Forward! Forward!" the trainer said. Shehnaz tottered up to the fire in her heels, ducking and cringing. With her face turned toward her shoulder, she called out "Fire!" in a faint voice, lifted the extinguisher and pressed the nozzle but forgot to sweep the fire. The trainer scolded her and told her to do it again. When it was Ahsan's turn, he leapt forward with a cinematic flourish, crying out, "Fire on the deck! Fire! Fire!" in such a melodramatic fashion that his colleagues burst into laughter.

The relentless comedy irritated the trainer, Hira, who said, 'I'm fed up with your unserious attitude!' Some of the women appeared irritated too, snapping at the men to 'stop it,' but others seemed to appreciate the humor, which helped make a long grueling day pass more quickly. Training was exhausting. The exercises were long and had to be repeated again and again. The equipment was not always in order. Some of the exercises, like sliding down the emergency chute, caused bruises. Women were in a rush to get home and see to their children. But they were frequently unable to complete tasks and were told to keep practicing till they got them right. All this made the session an emotionally fraught affair, producing stress and fatigue.

Men tried to manage the emotional tension by cracking jokes and by pushing forward to complete tasks the trainer demanded they perform. Women, by contrast, responded to the strain by holding back, apparently hoping that they would somehow escape some aspects of the practice.

During the emergency simulations, for instance, men would volunteer to play the lead parts, while women hung back, staring into their phones or huddling with other women. During the crash landing simulations, none of the initial rounds, which were all led by men, were smoothly executed. The training was conducted in both English and Urdu and while trainees managed to get through the Urdu rounds with fewer slip-ups, they appeared to find the English rounds impossible to get through. After several rounds of practice, the trainer insisted that one of the women take the lead for the final round. Roshanay, a middle-aged attendant, gamely put her hand up, volunteering to lead. The others clapped and cheered for her. Roshanay made very few mistakes and wound up doing a better job than her male colleagues. As everyone broke for lunch, Roshanay strutted around proudly. The others gave her high fives and clapped her on the back.

After lunch, the trainees assembled at the swimming pool for a water landing simulation. Roshanay had lost all her swagger. She grabbed my arm on the way to the pool, urgently whispering, 'I don't know how to swim!' When we got closer to the pool, I saw the women huddled in the back, near the changing rooms, many already in life vests. One of the women came up to me, saying, 'Listen, some of the girls are having their menses. You go and speak to ma'am. Tell her they should not make them go in the water.' This demand came as a surprise to me, given women's usual cosmopolitan performances. I had assumed they would have the forethought and resources to manage such eventualities, especially since none of the trainees on this occasion were fresh recruits and therefore would have known that the day would end with a dip in the pool. I was very reluctant to take what felt to me like a banal schoolgirl excuse up to Hira, who was now looking quite belligerent, shouting commands into her bullhorn. But I felt like I had no choice. Hira stared at me in shock! Then she yelled into her bullhorn, 'Anyone who doesn't go in the pool doesn't pass the course!' A former flight attendant, Hira was among those who felt that standards at PIA had fallen drastically in recent years. Her own batchmates, she told me, had been thorough professionals. They put work before everything else and never made excuses. Hira had never married; she said that she was married to PIA. She had no patience, she said, for the excuses the new generation of women attendants made to get out of training.

After a great deal of yelling on Hira's part—and flailing on the part of the airline women—eventually Hira got everyone into the pool. They all huddled together in the shallow end, clinging to a bar on the side and to each other. Hira yelled at them to form clusters of six around each of the several life-tubes floating in the deep end. Thirty minutes later, a few small clusters made up of three or four people had begun to form, but none of these had reached the target, which was a cluster of six. Many of the women were holding onto the bar at the edge of the pool, grimacing, apparently distrustful of their life vests. Roshanay was among those clinging to the bar, looking distressed. Hira tried to pry her hands loose but failed.

The rest of the crew was scattered around the shallow end of the pool, trying to figure out how to move across in their vests. It seemed to me that few of them knew how to swim. A few more clusters got formed. Hira kept shouting that no one was going home until she had all her clusters. A few more clusters came into being. Finally, with two clusters remaining, Naushaba, the head trainer, showed up. She was frowning and shaking her head in apparent dismay. She commanded, "Everyone out of the pool!" It took several minutes for everyone to comply.

Naushaba got the crew to form a line, telling them that they had to jump in, swim up to a raft at the far end of the pool, jump onto it, secure the lines, steady the raft, and then help their team members up. Some of the younger men took the lead, volunteering to go first. Two men who looked to be in their twenties dove in neatly, swam over, yanked themselves up, and secured the lines. Two other young men followed them and clambered up, holding their hands out for their colleagues to grab.

Gradually the crew made its way to the raft and got on board. Everyone did it but Roshanay, who was still holding on to the bar for dear life. 'I can't do it,' Roshanay said. 'I've just had eye surgery.' 'I will fail you!' Naushaba said in response. Roshanay looked at the raft in dismay. 'Come on! We got you!' Mustafa called out to her. He held his arm out. Roshanay flailed off toward the raft, her eyes narrowed, panting hard. She paddled over in her life vest grabbing desperately for Mustafa's hand. Mustafa grabbed her outstretched hand and hauled her up on the raft.

This desperate tableau reminded me of my conversation with Sameena, who had remarked that to get ahead in PIA, women had to 'hold someone's hand, like a child learning to walk.' The training sessions amplified the more quotidian gendered dynamics of dependence and deference encapsulated in this pithy comment. Both men and women, through their different approaches to training, reaffirmed the gendered hierarchies that underpinned the relational dynamics of airline work. Men, pushing forward, took charge and tendered support. Women, hanging back, vacillated and held their hands out for assistance.

In part, I understood these gendered dynamics of deference and dependence as a strategy for coping with the stress of a risky job, the dangers of which were never far from people's minds. During my fieldwork, a PIA plane crashed en route to the capital city of Islamabad, killing everyone on board. Crew members frequently brought up the risk associated with their jobs in interviews and casual conversations with me.

Men managed this stress not only through comedy but also by enacting the role of protector and benefactor. Women managed the stress by leaning on men. Each group relied on conventional gender scripts and performances in order to manage the fear and anxiety brought on by the risk of their work.

But women's departure from the cosmopolitan autonomy they otherwise proudly asserted was only partially related to the risk and uncertainty of their jobs. Training sessions, after all, were uniquely taxing arenas of professional activity. Women did not perform deference and dependence only in these demanding settings. They also did so during casual interactions, like when they were socializing at work with their colleagues. They asked men whether they should join a gym and for help picking out a cell phone. They asked for advice about car problems and about places to visit in China. They made tea for their male colleagues and set out the plates for them at mealtimes. They tidied up shared office spaces and cleaned up after meals. Why in these mundane moments did women suspend the cosmopolitan performances that they relied on as shields against stigma?

Stigma, as I have argued throughout this book, is made up out of a complex of intersecting local and global structures, practices, and processes. The processes of stigma and destigmatization, I have suggested, flow through a multiscalar network of macro- and micro-level structures, including the matrices of class as well as gender—two sets of structure that not only pattern the meanings of various symbols, such as lipstick and high heels, but in doing so also shape the relational possibilities and affordances these symbols yield.

The cosmopolitanism that airline women are able to access and enact turns on gendered symbols, like designer purses, that disrupt some of the classed dimensions of women's stigma. The travel their work requires, which society sees as a source of sexual threat and pollution, is transformed through their cosmopolitan performances into a source of dignity. Transnational journeys do not pose a threat to women's chastity, the women argue; rather, global mobility is a luxury that provides women with money, safety, and freedom. By relying on the money and spatial mobility provided by their work, airline women are able to cultivate tastes and embody sensibilities that are usually associated with wealth. By learning the difference between Medora and MAC, touring the pyramids, sampling bagels in New York and crepes in Paris, women acquire cultural competencies that help them transcend their working-class origins. They learn how to order meals at restaurants, how to fashion their hair and accessorize their clothes, and how to skillfully shut down unwanted flirtations. The classed skills they acquire baffle their working-class friends and relatives. Brothers and partners are taken aback when women take charge at restaurants, speak to strangers, or display the expensive items they have purchased.

Yet, focused on aesthetics, consumption, and personal responsibility, the cosmopolitanism airline women enact reflects a gendered neoliberal sensibility—an individualized, depoliticized, self-help kind of sensibility that scholars call postfeminism. Postfeminism connects women's freedom with the choices they make around consumption. Addressing women as paragons of potential agency who are pregnant with the power to make over their own lives, postfeminist discourses link liberation with the freedom to pursue feminine fashion and style. Similarly, postfeminist cosmopolitanism equates gendered symbols of wealth and taste, like makeup, sunglasses, purses, and shoes with modernity and gendered emancipation. To perform their classed distinction from ordinary Pakistanis, airline women describe their willingness to break customs around cooking, cleaning, and shyness. In contrast with the "ordinary" women who spend hours cooking curries and cleaning their homes, airline women enact freedom by purchasing chicken nuggets and paper plates, Swiffer cleaners and lipstick. In place of the "traditional" gendered patterns that dominate the lives of working-class women, airline women enact a postfeminist liberation involving consumption, dazzling appearance, and extroversion.

Symbols, however, aren't just tools actors use to tell new stories about their social situations; they are also keys that help actors to unlock various relational possibilities. Symbols can generate cooperation and connection, as sports jerseys do when they demonstrate affiliation between fans and teams. And they can also foster distinction and disconnection, as motorcades and bodyguards do when they signal the unapproachability of VIPs. The relational affordances that symbols yield are patterned not just by class but also by gender. Expensive makeup is not only a sign associated with elite consumption and distinction, but it is also a gendered sign that connotes specific gendered sensibilities. The relational affordances generated by classed and gendered symbols, therefore, reaffirm certain hierarchies even as they unsettle others. Postfeminist cosmopolitanism might unsettle some of the classed inequalities that underpin airline women's stigma, but it also strengthens other, gendered hierarchies that also sustain their devaluation within their field of work.

By tapping into the classed meanings of global products and consumption practices, airline women are able to secure one kind of relational objective. The association of these symbols with wealth and elite status allows women to distance themselves from those who stigmatize them for their work. But since the symbols they invoke are also associated with a specific kind of gendered sensibility, one that emphasizes heightened forms of femininity, women's performances unlock a gendered pattern of relationality, one that deploys dependence and deference in exchange for gallantry and patronage, signs of weakness and incompetence in exchange for aid and support.

Men recruited via gendered enactments of deference and dependence act as agents for women. They help women smooth things over with management, they root around for a contact willing to provide unofficial access to the datasets that women need for an assignment, and they help women get out of training when they do not wish to take it. This cooperation is crucial because women are unable to gain the same kind of access to the informal networks of patronage, such as political parties, that men enjoy. Unrestricted by the rules of purdah, men in this context are endowed with greater spatial and temporal privilege than women and are therefore able to cultivate deeper relationships with political actors, who can pull strings and move resources within PIA. Thus, by tapping into the classed and gendered meanings of postfeminist cosmopolitanism, women are able to accomplish two different relational objectives. They are able to disconnect from those who would vilify them for their work and yet also recruit men colleagues as allies they can use to tap into informal networks of power. At the same time, however, postfeminist cosmopolitanism reaffirms men's dominance in PIA and Pakistan's backwardness globally.

## THEORETICAL IMPLICATIONS

In chapters 3–5 we have seen how policewomen, health workers, and airline attendants draw on classed and gendered symbols, like their veils or their makeup, to construct a set of destigmatization performances. By styling themselves as martial mothers, delicately veiled women, or postfeminist cosmopolitans, they work to negotiate the stigma surrounding their work, which is considered too rough, too indecent, or too brutal for respectable women. Using classed and gendered resources, like veils, handbags, and kinship language, the women craft destigmatization performances that make claims about their delicacy, their bravery, or their distinction from crass stigmatizers. These performances sometimes draw on local symbols and sometimes on transnational ones. Women's agency may be embedded, but since people, symbols, and discourses all travel, it is not restricted to local contexts for meaning making. Whether local or global, the women's destigmatization performances do offer them some success in mitigating stigma, but both local and global symbols also work to reinforce some of the mechanisms of inequality that uphold the stigma matrix.

When they reinforce localized gender norms in service to classed respectability, as in the case of policewomen, frontline women wind up reinforcing the idea that policing is an occupation unsuited to women's essential nature. When frontline women combine the gendered scripts associated with holy war and those associated with veiling, as health workers do, they are able to connect with working-class clients but are unable to recruit elite bosses, who are unwilling to recognize LHWs as legitimate agents of the state deserving to benefit from the honors it can bestow on its officers. And when, like airline women, they are able to mobilize global signs associated with cosmopolitan elites, they wind up strengthening the gendered relationships that limit women's autonomy and authority at work.

Chapters 3–5 have highlighted the structural limits of women's destigmatization strategies. In each case, the stigma matrix obstructs women's efforts because it is composed of multiple structures (class as well as gender, local inequalities as well as global ones) that shape women's experiences and encounters at the micro level of interaction. In the next chapter, I examine one additional strategy that women across all three field sites use to manage stigma at the interpersonal level—spectacular agency, a particular kind of performance that is intently and intentionally focused on recruitment, which women attempt to secure via publicity.

# 6 | SPECTACULAR AGENCY: STUNNING DRAMAS OF RECRUITMENT

**ON A SULTRY AND OVERCAST** morning, I made my way to the women's *thana* (station house) for a scheduled interview with Constable Sheila, but she wasn't there. None of the usual gang was there. Hina, the radio operator was holding down the fort, along with an elderly woman everyone called Aunty, who usually did the night shift, as she was, or so she explained to me, "too old for regular duty." The morning shift posse arrived a little after noon. Sheila, large and cheerful, led them in. For once she was in uniform. Twirling a rose wrapped in a cellophane cone, she was singing cheerfully, *"Aaj mausam bara beiman hai"* (today the weather is truly insincere). The weather was overcast, and it looked like it might rain. Since Karachi doesn't usually get a lot of rain, such weather tends to cheer people up, and Sheila looked to be in a festive mood. All the ladies, in uniform and wearing a great deal more makeup than usual, were smiling and singing along with Sheila. Like Sheila, each of them carried a cellophane wrapped rose in her hand. 'We have been on TV!' Sheila told me gleefully. The women crowded around the tiny hallway that served as their sitting room. A few had their cell phones out; others were peering into their screens at text messages from colleagues at other stations. 'When will we get to see the show?' a tall woman asked. 'It was live!' Sheila replied. The tall woman looked disappointed. 'You mean we won't get to see it?' Sheila ignored her and turned to me, saying again, 'Did you hear? We were on TV!' she said. 'The host was amazed with us. He couldn't believe how educated our police people are,' she said. 'Can you believe one of us has an MBA?' she asked me. 'The host was very impressed.'

Over the next few days Sheila kept asking me over and over again if I had searched for the show online. She was eager for me to watch it. I kept looking for it and finally found it on YouTube a week later. It was a special episode of a weekly talk show hosted by a well-known actor. This particular episode featured three police officers, two men and one woman, seated on a stage alongside the presenter. A large group of uniformed policemen and women made up the studio audience. Sheila, seated among these spectators, was handed the microphone for just under two minutes to answer a question about the family pressures women police face in taking on this challenging occupation. The host kept interrupting her as she spoke, teasing her with questions about her domestic affairs. He asked her if her husband, a civilian, ever complained that her job had made her too bossy at home. She replied that since her husband also worked long hours, their time at home rarely overlapped and so they didn't often get a chance to talk. The host pressed the point, however. "But if you happen to put too much salt in the food," he asked, "does your husband scold you?" Sheila's response was lost in the laughter that ensued. The two policemen seated on stage interjected humorous remarks into the host's speech: wives are bossy even when they're not in the force, one said. The other joked that Sheila's husband probably stayed out late on purpose in order to avoid interfacing with his wife.

This all-too-brief and slighting treatment combined with Sheila's excitement and her insistence that I watch the show suggest both women's keenness for visibility and recognition as well as the challenges they face in securing it. Indeed, Sheila, like many of the other women in my field sites, saw such opportunities for visibility as marks of a signal honor. Access to public platforms, and to publicity, was for these women an important indicator of distinction, a sign of their having arrived, of having "become somebody." For these women, public appearance, whether on television or at a traffic signal, was a sign of their acquisition of personhood.

Yet, as Sheila's two-minute interview shows, the spotlight doesn't just make women somebody, it makes them a marked somebody, a gendered and classed somebody, who can neither escape nor elucidate her social situation. The host of the TV show did not ask any of the policemen if their wives felt that they had become too bossy as a consequence of their jobs. Nor would it be thinkable for him to ask one of the men how their families would react if they were to put too much salt in the food. Lost in the short but disorderly exchange between host and policewoman was Sheila's working-class lament about the lack of personal, intimate time for conversation with her husband. Her quest, shared by her husband, for class mobility was obscured in the general laughter and clichéd banalities about over-salted food and henpecked husbands.

As I came to know from my interview with her, Sheila is married to a much younger man, a country cousin some fourteen years her junior whose father picked Sheila for his son not only because she was possessed of a secure government job but also because he hoped that she would be able to help and guide her husband to adjust to life in the big city. Sheila told me that the early years of her marriage were taken up with helping her bewildered and disoriented husband learn how to navigate Karachi's roads. Subsequently, she said, she had helped him find a job as a shop assistant in a fabric shop, but despite the supplementary income this job brought into the household, the couple had recently had to move from what she referred to as a "posh" neighborhood to a more depressed one. But these inconveniences were mitigated, Sheila said, by her husband's mild-mannered and gentle disposition. "He never questions or challenges me," she said. "He is the one who does the cooking, also—although I do the cleaning."

It should go without saying that precisely none of these complicated gender and class dynamics came to light in the TV interview. We never heard of the understanding and support this working-class husband contributed to his wife's public job. We learned nothing of the class project that may have shaped his willingness to do so. Instead, the host chose to reduce Sheila to the gendered stereotypes that attach to women in domestic roles, and he did this even though he had invited her on the show that day with the explicit purpose of celebrating the sacrifices she made in service to her public role. By entering a "male" occupation, he appeared to imagine, Sheila risked emasculating her husband. Thus, in the short exchange with the host, Sheila came across as neither a competent woman nor a capable police officer.

And yet, despite the unflattering representation, the two minutes of fame were precious to Sheila. The episode not only illustrates women's desire for visibility but also underscores the paucity of scripts available to them for navigating this visibility with dignity. Even when the actual arrangements of their lives disrupt the social norms surrounding gender, women are unable to mobilize their familial achievements to challenge the stereotypes that mar their public appearances. Nor are they able to avoid such typecasting questions altogether. Their official status, underscored in Sheila's mediated moment by her uniform, can't protect them from having to acknowledge and address aspects of their identity that mark them as strangers to their public roles.

While they may not be as brutal or violent as the encounters I described in the beginning of this book, interactions like the one between Sheila and the TV host serve a similar social purpose. Just like the stones pelted at Sharafat Khan, the police inspector, and the cynical cartoons targeting Assistant Superintendent of Police Sohai Ali Talpur, such encounters mark women agents of the state as outsiders, as aberrant and anomalous to their public roles. They not only take aim at women's official personas but target their identity as women. Sheila is assumed to be guilty of over-salting food, a sign of her domestic incompetence. Sharafat Khan was stoned for her use of abusive language, an intolerable sign of disrespect for a woman to exhibit. And Talpur was censured for her purported lack of concern for her slain colleagues, a sign of an unwomanly lack of care.

When they occur in public arenas, like on TV shows, such stigmatizing gestures, interactions, and encounters aren't merely punitive; they are also disciplinary and instructive. They don't just rebuke women for troubling gender norms; they rehearse and reestablish these norms for both the women and for those observing the drama. These dramas play out at the micro level of interaction, but when they circulate on the media, whether as memes or viral videos, they can travel up the stigma matrix, toward the structural levels, where stigmas are encoded, like tracks in a well-worn path. For women agents of the state, these ritualized rehearsals of the gendered social order constitute what I call *gendered authority threats*. Gendered authority threats are quotidian stigma rituals that mark women as strangers to authority and women's authority as strange.

### GENDERED AUTHORITY THREATS AND SPECTACULAR AGENCY

Gendered authority threats are disruptive dramas of repudiation, which work to physically or symbolically mark women's bodies and their identities as aberrant or unsuited to their public, authoritative roles. These dramas, which run the gamut of repudiating responses to women's public authority, from humor to physical violence, seek to stamp women's bodies and their personalities with a particular and an exclusionary vision of the public sphere. By laughing at, attacking, heckling, or ignoring facets of a woman's public authority, these quotidian refusals transform human interaction into a drama for the reproduction and reenactment of unequal gender relations.

Since daily life has become saturated by recording devices, such as camera-fitted cell phones and distributary social media platforms, even the most intimate and private dramas of repudiation can become public spectacles of stigma and humiliation, circulated on various media to entertain, instruct, and usher broader audiences into a particular, gendered, social order, as in the case of the mediated critiques of Talpur (see Handelman 1997). But if gendered authority threats can escalate and become spectacles of humiliation, women's responses too can sometimes be spectacular. When they harness the publicity potential of these stigmatizing dramas for their own ends, women engage in what I call *spectacular agency*.

The possibility of publicity does not just make dramas of repudiation more corrosive; it also provides women with opportunities for redress. Spectacles, as scholars have noted, are not just elite instruments of exclusion. Marginalized people can also harness the power of spectacle, for instance, to demand inclusion by seizing control of public space (Goldstein 2004; Rosenthal 2000). To manage the authority threatening dramas of repudiation they face in the course of their public work, frontline women also sometimes harness the arresting power of spectacle to enact spectacular agency, a form of agency that uses spectacle as an instrument for contesting exclusion. Frontline women draw on the various affordances of their state jobs to orchestrate stunning displays, such as beatings, arrests, and collective rituals of mourning in order to call out, discipline, and punish their harassers. They use the discretion, the authority, and the sacred symbols associated with their offices to make visible abuse, win over allies, humiliate abusers, and protect their dignity.

Just as fences, walls, guard towers, drones, and state agents of various kinds seed the spectacles that states use to signalize and project their sovereignty, uniforms, gates, violence and confinement help compose the spectacles frontline women use to protect and project their dignity (see Mainwaring and Silverman 2017). Women sometimes stage contained, miniature spectacles aimed at punishing, disciplining, and educating specific individuals, and they sometimes stage sprawling, seething, impassioned spectacles to take on the state itself. Their spectacular agency is at times aimed at preserving their own dignity and at others at reclaiming it for others. Spectacular agency is not only a mode of punishing and protecting but is also a mode of protest and critique. Women use it not only to squash or deflect humiliation; they use it also to protest and renegotiate the subordinate status of women in society.

In what follows, I describe the various ways frontline women enact spectacular agency—to make visible abuse, to punish abusers, to critique the gendered order, and to take on powerful opponents. But, as I show, the attention that spectacular agency supplies comes at a cost. In exchange for the tenuous and limited protection and redress it provides, spectacular agency extracts financial, physical, relational, and emotional costs from women. To cultivate inclusion via spectacle, women have borne various financial expenses, they have sustained injuries to their bodies, they have foregone time with their children, and they have embraced the humiliation that sometimes comes from transforming oneself into a spectacular object.

Frontline women have also made gains from their use of spectacular agency. Even in cases where spectacular agency failed to meet women's expectations, as in the case of spectacular protest outlined toward the end of this chapter, this kind of agency provided women with something else they valued—a sense of capacity and accomplishment and a belief that they have discharged their obligations to future generations of women. As Rehana, an LHW on the brink of retirement put it, "I don't feel sad that I derived little benefit from that effort [the protest]," she told me. "I feel that you should do whatever you can do. Whatever we can do for the next generation, we do it," she said. "You can't control the outcome, but you can say: 'O Allah, I have fulfilled my obligations. I spared no effort to create a better world for the next people who will take my place. Now it's up to them and you.'"

This chapter focuses on spectacular agency, a strategy women use to negotiate stigma, recover dignity, and also to punish abusers and critique an unjust system. Unlike the destigmatization performances that I described in chapters 3–5 (i.e., veiled delicacy, martial motherhood, and postfeminist cosmopolitanism), which wind up reconfirming some of the inequalities that hold the stigma matrix together, spectacular agency can be critical and transformative. It aims to make visible and question the inequalities and injustices women face in the course of their public service. Like destigmatization performances, spectacular agency is also concerned with recruitment, but in this case, recruitment is a more explicit and crucial aim. Moreover, as I show in this chapter, actors sometimes use spectacular agency to recruit not only those within their immediate orbit, such as witnessing colleagues, but also more distant allies, such as social media users. This attempt at broader recruitment suggests ways that agency can be global, concerned not only with recruitment and relations in an actor's immediate environment, but at times, concerned with more distant ones.

In the previous three chapters, I have been arguing that agency runs on two motors, that it works not only to make meaning but also to recruit others to buy into an actor's performance and aid her in extending the meaning of her performance over time and space. Policewomen in positions of leadership, for instance, need their subordinates to reinforce their authority performances even, or quite possibly especially, in situations of the boss' absence. The connection between agency and recruitment comes into sharper focus in this chapter, through the case of spectacular agency. Since it relies so heavily on publicity, this kind of agency is intentionally and clearly focused on recruitment. Women work to negotiate stigma by calling on spectators to witness the injustice of their situations. Since it is dependent on spectator engagement, spectacular agency is used less frequently than destigmatization performance and is deployed primarily in public settings. Unlike destigmatization performances, spectacular agency involves short, sharp bursts of display work. Since it involves a form of theater, it is relatively bound in space and time. However, as I show toward the end of this chapter, women can use spectacular agency in a sustained way, as LHWs have done, by organizing repeated spectacles.

In what follows, I outline the various ways women use spectacular agency: for making abuse visible, punishing harassers, critiquing the system, and to mount longer and more sustained protests against the state. I then describe the sources of spectacular agency, the symbols, allies and discretion it mobilizes. And finally, I lay out the costs of this kind of agency, which can be painful and expensive to enact.

### THE USES OF SPECTACULAR AGENCY
#### Making Abuse Visible

'What does he want?' LHW Rida called out. 'What is it this time?' she said, as she made her way down the crowded hospital corridor. One of her colleagues had told her that the doctor, her supervisor, wanted a word, and Rida was heading to his office, loudly demanding to know what it was he wanted. She shoved open his door and entered, saying loudly, 'Yes, sir. You called me. Did you have some work?' Later, she told me that she did this to disarm him. 'If you're worried that someone is going to harass you,' she said, 'you make sure that everyone knows where you're going and what is happening in that encounter.' By transforming an ordinary interaction into a miniature spectacle, women draw the attention of bystanders in an effort to neutralize potential harassers. 'It's like you are waving a flag and everyone is looking, so that makes them [the potential harasser] cautious, that "everyone is looking at me, I better be careful,"' she explained.

Constable Razia Khan also deployed similar tactics to deal with the harassment she experienced at a police headquarters, where she was posted as a new recruit. "When I was posted there I was new in the force, so I used to wear capris and short trousers," she told me. "So, *nah*, some of the policemen would stare at me and look and make comments." Tired of this harassment, Razia decided to "make a racket." At a meeting, she decided to complain to her boss about the harassment. "I said, 'Sir, I didn't join the force so that I would have to face this kind of thing or talk to such people,'" she recounts. "I said, 'If I had wanted this kind of thing, I was fine outside [the force].'" The boss scolded the other men and threatened to dismiss them from service. "So, after that," Razia tells me, her colleagues "all got to know that 'this is what she is like, she is the type who will create a scene, so stay far away from her.'" Like dramas of repudiation, spectacular agency is also disciplinary and instructive. Razia's aim was not only to make visible the harassment she was facing, drawing her boss' attention to it, but also to teach her colleagues that she was the kind of person who would make trouble for them. "The men were not used to women like me," she explained. The office she was posted at was staffed primarily by men, and they had not worked with someone like Razia before, who dressed in ankle-exposing pants, "so it was important to give them this demo, to teach them how to behave around a woman like me," she said.

Spectacular agency is instructive not only for harassers but also for others who are called upon as witnesses to the drama. When I asked Shazia, an airline attendant in her mid-twenties, how she managed unwanted flirtations during her flights, she said, "Make a noise. Raise a ruckus." Such a miniature spectacle, she said, draws the attention of other passengers and frightens the harasser, who then "doesn't have the courage to do it again." Seema, another airline attendant referred to this tactic as a "shut-up call." "Get a load of our girls, okay," she said. "We have literally become so impudent in this matter [of harassment] that if someone flirts with us, so on the spot we give him a shut-up call." I asked her what a shut-up call is. She said, "Just you know, like openly be rude, like saying loudly, 'Shut up!'" A shut-up call, she explained, not only shuts down the harassment but also serves as a warning to other passengers: "Be careful how you behave with her, she's one to deliver a slap to the face."

In addition to making visible abuse, educating harassers, and alerting bystanders, spectacular agency also enables women to reverse the affective registers of quotidian stigma rituals for their own ends. Laila, an airline attendant, said that she had recently become fed up with the security guard posted outside the briefing room, a kind of waiting room where airline staff gather prior to takeoff. "He knows who I am. I am in uniform. I have my

ID. I come almost every day to the airport. But still, every day, he stops me and demands to look inside my bag," she complained. "The thing is," she explains, "I smoke, and he knows there's a packet of Marlboro in my purse, so he likes to pull it out and look at it and then he goes, 'tsk, tsk,' every time, just to humiliate me, because you know in our culture decent women don't smoke." So, one day, Laila says, she decided to stage a little drama. "I had pads in my purse, so when he again said that he needs to search my bag, I said, 'What do you want to see? You like looking at ladies' purses? Okay, I will show you,' and I began unpacking all the things on the counter. I pulled out my cigarettes, then I pulled out a large packet of Always pads, and I said, 'Here, look, are you happy? Do you need to see more?' All the people around us were lowering their eyes in shame. His face went red with embarrassment. He never bothered me again." By revealing and making visible an offending actor's clandestine gestures, women use spectacular agency to mark challengers as creeps. By using spectacle to call attention to the guard's humiliating daily rituals, Laila lobbed humiliation back at him, thus effectively reversing the affective registers of his stigmatizing ritual.

## Punishing Abusers

While women respond to some stigmatizing dramas by engineering relatively benign miniature spectacles, such as the shut-up call, in order to publicize, instruct, and humiliate harassers, they respond to other dramas of repudiation with a more pronounced and dazzling kind of spectacle, one aimed not only at calling attention to the harasser but also at punishing him. Sabiha, a 26-year-old flight attendant described one such punitive spectacle. "It happened on one of my own flights," she told me. "We called the UK police out." I asked her what the passenger had done to warrant such an action and she said, "The guy had used abusive language, had tried to hit her [another airline attendant]. He tried to push her like this [she mimes pushing], and so we confiscated his passport, and when we got on the ground, we called the UK police." I asked her what happened next. "The UK police gave us two options," she said. "We had all been ladies on the flight [i.e., the airline attendants were all women]. [The police said], 'You can either have this man properly arrested, but then you will have to make circuits of the courts, in the UK, all of you.' Meaning, all of us would have to go to the courts over and over again" as witnesses and accusers. If the women were willing to take this option, Sabiha explained, then the UK police were willing to follow all their procedures and lock the man up. "They have very strict procedures," she remarked. The second option the UK police gave the women, Sabiha said, was that "the guy will ask you for forgiveness, and you forgive him, and we will give him a warning, that if he does something like this again, he will not be permitted to travel on your airline again."

According to Sabiha, the women discussed the two options among themselves and decided "that the second option is a better one. Otherwise, they [the police] were trapping us, in a way," she said, "[telling us] that you will have to give evidence, give testimony etc., so we said, 'The second option is best.'" I asked her if she thought the second option had been effective. And she said that it had. "He got scared, and later we came to hear, the next time I flew to the UK, my station manager told me that the police are still after him. The guy has not been able to relax," she said, because "they keep questioning him from time to time, the UK ones, so he is fearful, scared, and he does think to himself, 'Why did I do that?'"

To protect their dignity, Sabiha and her colleagues called upon the highly visible apparatus of a foreign state, drawing a large group of uniformed cops to their aid, who publicly apprehended the harasser, took him to the side, in full view of the other passengers, patted him down, questioned him, rebuked him, and forced him to apologize in a public way. In Sabiha's view, the drama of apprehension and apology was sufficiently instructive and punitive. There was no need to pursue the case further in courts, a line of action that would raise the cost of complaint for the women. Simply calling upon the arresting apparatus of a foreign state to create a spectacle by publicly disciplining the harasser was sufficient. By doing so, Sabiha and her colleagues had not only displayed their own capacity for retribution and self-protection, but they had also marked the man as a problem in front of the other passengers as well as for the police, who subsequently kept an eye on him.

Airline women were not alone in calling upon the highly visible apparatus of the state, such as uniformed men, in punitive ways. Policewomen also used state symbols and resources to humiliate and punish abusers. Huda told me that early in her time on the police force, she was on her way to the station in uniform when she noticed a rickshaw driver ogling her. "One is used to men staring," she said, "but he was just not stopping." After a while, she said, she noticed that he was making obscene gestures. "He was doing something there," she said, indicating the pelvic region. "I just couldn't take it anymore, so I went and picked up two men [i.e., cops] from the station and grabbed the driver, 'arre bharway' [you pimp], and I beat him and beat him, and I punched him and punched him, and then we took him to the station, where I beat him some more." At the station, she said, her male colleagues asked her, "What happened, madam?" and she replied, "This man was harassing your madam." She commented incredulously, "I am in uniform, and this is how he is behaving!" I asked her what happened next, and she said, "Then we confiscated his rickshaw. I said, 'I can be complainant; we can file a case. So we kept him all day in the lockup. In the evening, his family came and begged us to release him, and I told them what he had done. He was crying and saying, 'You are my sister,' and I said, 'Really? Do you make such gestures in front of your sisters? Do they too have to see you making these kinds of motions?' She said the man's family "was also flashing curses at him"—holding their palm up in front of him, a gesture implying a curse. "And he cried some more, and I said, 'Why are you crying?' and he said, 'Because a woman has beaten me.'" Huda replied, "I'm not a woman. I am a police!" Huda did not press charges against the rickshaw driver and released him from the lockup later that evening. She said she felt that the humiliation the man had faced in getting a beating from a woman in public and then later in front of his family was sufficient as a warning and a punishment.

Frontline women use spectacular agency not only to punish their own harassers but also to punish men on behalf of other women. Three different policewomen independently recounted one such instance of spectacular punishment to me. In separate interviews, I had asked each of these women to tell me about a situation when they had come to the aid of a woman citizen. Razia, Hina, and Seemi separately brought up a particular case of domestic abuse that was handled by their station. A woman came to the station one day, they told me, her clothes drenched and smelling foul. She complained that her husband, apparently not satisfied with just beating and cursing at her, had urinated on her. All three policewomen said her story had enraged them. Immediately, they said, their station head had sent out a police van full of men and women to go pick up the offending husband. He was brought to the station and kept there all day; the women said they took turns beating him. Hina explained, "We, not the men, beat him ourselves, as it was a woman he humiliated, so it was us women who punished him." "He was crying and begging for forgiveness," Seemi told me, "but we said, 'Don't apologize to us! Apologize to your wife!' And we made him get down on his knees and say sorry to her." The policewomen also called the couple's family to the station, telling them what he had done and demanding that he apologize to each of them. "You see," Razia explained to me, "in most cases the wife is not willing or able to pursue separation or divorce. Even if she does decide to go for separation, then later, out of poverty, she will decide to go back to him, and it will be even worse for her." Since women rarely wish to take their domestic abuse cases to court, policewomen say, they try to "put the fear of God" in the husbands. It is important for them to make an example of an errant husband. They beat him and taunt him and "show him the might of the police" to scare him, "so that that fear comes into him that, 'Never mind my wife, this police-madam will not leave me,' so then he will behave more decently at home."

In each of these cases, frontline women drew on the signs and resources of the state—police officers, detention, violence—to stigmatize and humiliate their harassers. The coerced apology, the apprehension and beating, and the exhibition of the harassers before others served to not only debase harassers and mark them with stigma but also demonstrated women's capacities, their authority and their willingness to protect their own dignity and the dignity of other women.

### Critique

Frontline women deploy spectacular agency not only to visibilize abuse and to mark and punish harassers but also to critique and renegotiate the status of women in society. A particularly compelling instance of this mode of spectacular agency was narrated by Constable Shahbano. Shahbano had been a constable for fifteen years when I met her at the police academy, where she was undergoing training for promotion to the rank of head constable. Shahbano had grown up in Karachi, she said, but as a child she frequently went with her father to visit her ancestral village in central Sindh, the province that contains Karachi. These visits made her feel very angry, she said. "My village runs according to the *wadera-shahi* system" (feudal landlordship system), she told me, explaining that in this system, "ladies are considered absolutely nothing, less than nothing." The poor status of women in the village enraged Shahbano, "so, when we went to the village, we were told to segregate from men," she said. "When we were in Karachi, we [she and her sisters] did as we wished, like we would wear a *dupatta* [a simple stole or wrap], no one said anything. But when we were heading to visit the village, our father would stop us at the bus stop, particularly, and tell us to put on a *burqa* [a full-body veil]. He would say, 'Your personal will comes to an end here. Here it is our *biradari* [tribal] system that holds sway, and you have to put on the burqa and follow tradition.'" These prescriptions angered Shahbano, who felt that the gender arrangements in her village were unfair. "The way it was in the village," she said, "gents would sit in front, ladies were sent to sit in the back. I used to feel that why don't they let us come forward?" Women weren't just told to retreat to the background, they were also forbidden from taking on jobs outside the home, "and as for jobs," Shahbano says, "there was no such thing as a good post [i.e., job opportunity] for women. So, I used to say to myself that I want to do some such job where I too can sit or stand in front of [confront] these *waderas* [local landlords] as an equal, and I should show them that if they have money, that's fine, whatever, if we don't have money, so we should stay forever in the background? We also have aspirations. Our heart also wants that we also should sit and stand like you. So this is why I always wished I had the power, so that I could show them." I asked Shahbano if her job had provided her with this desired capacity, and she recounted an episode involving the headman of her village, who was also an elected member of the provincial assembly.

One day the headman came to the Sindh (provincial) Assembly building (located in Karachi), where Shahbano was posted as a sentry at the gate. "He didn't have a pass," she said. "No one was allowed to go in without a pass." Shahbano decided to use this opportunity to engineer a spectacle in order to demonstrate her newly acquired wherewithal to her village headman. "I deliberately said to them [her male colleagues], 'Let him cool his heels for a while. He is from my village, and I want to teach him a lesson.'"

She explained, "Just like he would make people from my village wait when they came to speak to him, his sentries would say, '*sahib* [sir] is relaxing right now, or he is busy, or he has guests right now.' So I said, 'Make him cool his heels, so that he also gets to realize what it is like to be made to wait.'" Her colleagues willingly acceded to her wishes; Shahbano said that since security is kept tight at the assembly building it was not difficult to deny the headman entry since he had failed to bring along his pass.

Shahbano then intervened in the situation she had engineered. "So then I said [to the men], 'Ask him his caste.' Then I said, 'Tell him that the madam who is from your tribe, she is saying, that on *her* behalf, you will be allowed to go through.'" This revelation astonished the headman. Shahbano said that he couldn't believe it. "So he says, 'Who is that? There is no lady in the police from our tribe, who is she that I don't know?'" At this point Shahbano revealed herself. "So then I told him, 'I am the daughter of so and so,' and he said, 'Really?'" Surprised at encountering Shahbano in the role of gatekeeper, the headman interacted with her in a whole new way. "Then, our village culture got tossed aside. He met me Karachi style, in a friendly way. No one would know from looking at us that he is the leader in our village and that I am a poor kind of person," Shahbano told me. "Forget about those distinctions. He was giving me his [phone] number. He was saying, 'Daughter, these men of mine will come, so do let them through too.' I said, 'No! I am not your servant. I am a servant of the *sarkar* [the state]! And the same system that is in place for everyone will apply also to you. It's just that I wanted to show you a *demo* [demonstration] of how things stand, buddy." Proudly, Shahbano told me, "Now, because of my job, I am out of the clutches of our tribal system!'"

Shahbano's experience with her village headman at the gates of an assembly building illustrates how women use spectacular agency to critique and renegotiate the status of women in society. Shahbano, who had long been "irritated" by the status of women in her community, orchestrated a simple spectacle to demonstrate to her village headman that low-caste and poor women too can hold positions of power and authority. By using her official position to first bar and later permit the headman to enter the building, Shahbano sought to instruct the headman about the capacities of women from her status group. Describing herself as "not your servant" but a servant of the state, Shahbano didn't just revenge herself for past indignities, but by jettisoning the localized gender and class hierarchies that had irked her, critiqued them.

A similar use of spectacular agency as critique was also narrated by airline women. Hanna, a 37-year-old airline attendant recalled how her fiftysomething colleague relied on spectacle both to defend her own dignity and also to critique the system and culture that allowed others to threaten it. "My colleague, Sabira, had an early morning flight," Hanna told me.[1] "Sometimes, the shifts are arranged so that you have had no rest, and for the early morning flight, we were getting to the airport at 3:00, 3:30 a.m., so she had not had enough sleep, and of course, there were the usual stresses. So, one of the passengers, they took a photograph of her, that she has a bad expression on her face, and they posted it online," Hanna said. Such crude invasions of frontline women's privacy are, unfortunately, not uncommon. Airline women say, they frequently notice passengers snapping photographs of them without their permission. In Sabira's case, however, the image, which was eventually posted on Twitter by a media personality with the caption, "World's most senior air hostess welcomes the passengers on board with this face," soon went viral.

In the image, an unsmiling Sabira is pictured standing with her arms folded on the back of a seat in the plane. She is in her early fifties and actually looks younger, but some social media users responded to the image with critical comments about her appearance. "Nani" (grandmother), one user commented. "What a Dracula they have picked and kept," another user said. "I think madam shd be given double sallery (*sic*) to sit at home rather than welcoming anyone," a third suggested.

According to Hanna, Sabira was very distressed by these social media posts. "She was worried that the airline would blame her, that PIA would maybe take some action against her because of it." While some of her colleagues thought Sabira should stay silent and let the whole thing blow over, Sabira decided to post a picture of her own on social media. Hanna says, she posted "a photo of herself, nicely with makeup, smiling, and with a caption saying that yes, sometimes, we have to get up very early, and we are having a bad day, but that does not mean that we do not care about our jobs or our passengers. We are working very hard for the airline." Sabira's smiling picture, which was also posted to PIA's social media account, circulated widely on social media and was picked up by various blogs and newspapers, who praised the airline for its response. A local journalist then interviewed Sabira to get her take on the issue. In a feature article, Sabira got a chance to respond to the ageism evident in the original disparaging tweet. She pointed out that she had served PIA for over thirty years and that her lengthy service had allowed her to hone her skills and gain valuable experience, but "passengers do not respect air safety. They only think of cabin crew as eye candy," an objectification that overlooks that "we are trained professionals and deserve respect."

Although Sabira did not stage the original spectacle, which had drawn attention to her appearance, she responded to it with a spectacle of her own. By posting a smiling photograph of herself online, and through it attracting the attention of journalists and supportive social media users, Sabira was able to intervene in the ongoing conversation about her age and her unsmiling appearance with a critique that showcased her perspective. The backlash she faced was fueled by sexism and ageism, she pointed out, and the focus on appearance missed the point of airline attendants' service. Airline work is not just aesthetic, and air hostessing is not simply about smiling and serving passengers, she argued. Airline attendants work hard to ensure passengers remain safe while on board their flights and should not therefore be reduced to sexualized objects to be evaluated for their youthful looks and their congeniality.

Like cops and airline attendants, LHWs also drew on spectacular agency to critique existing arrangements and abuses. Nida, a 43-year-old health worker and single mother, recounted her attempt to level criticism against her unrelenting boss. "Polio work is not part of our official job," she explained, "and over and over again, I told him that I am not going to do it anymore, [he should] find someone else." When it was time for yet another vaccination round, however, Nida's boss again disregarded her unwillingness to do polio work. This time, however, Nida was past endurance. "My son was in hospital. He had had an accident," she said, "and I was in a very desperate state. There was no one I could turn to for help, my son was lying there alone." Her boss, however, did not see her son's illness as a sufficient reason for Nida to beg off polio work. "He said, "If you can't do it, then I will replace you. I will suspend you from your LHW work. You will not have this job anymore," she said. "Believe me, I was pressed so hard. I couldn't breathe. I couldn't go on, so I stood on the veranda outside his office, and I cursed him, I said, 'God will see to you for this,'" she said. "Lots of people collected to see what was going on," Nida said, and she took the opportunity to vent her feelings about the system. "'We are women. We are poor. We are powerless, so you think you can push us around,' I said, and I said I send *lanaat* [a curse] on you. God will fix you.'" Nida says the curse shook her boss. "He came to me later and said, 'I won't give you polio assignments anymore. You give *bud-duas* [negative prayers], and others came to me and said the boss is very upset that you cursed him. He is saying, 'Don't push Nida. She gives curses.'"

Like Shahbano and Sabira, Nida used spectacle to call attention to what she saw as an abusive and unjust system. Just as Shahbano used her gatekeeping role to critique the gender and class relations in her village, which constructed women like Shahbano as "less than nothing," and Sabira used social media to critique the ageism and sexism that demean women airline workers for failing to smile or look young, Nida used the medium of curses to critique the exploitative arrangements within her health job. By yelling curses at her boss, Nida also criticized the system he represented, which, according to her, was leveraging women's poverty by forcing them to do "voluntary" work they did not wish to do. In Nida's view, this exploitation was rooted in both class and gendered oppression, so when she was pushed beyond her endurance, she orchestrated a spectacle invoking God in order to air her critiques in front of a broader audience.

### THE SOURCES OF SPECTACULAR AGENCY

Thus far I have outlined the various ways women employ spectacular agency and the various ends they put it to. I have shown how women draw on spectacle to make abuse visible, punish abusers, critique and renegotiate the status of women in society. For some of these women, the ability to orchestrate these kinds of spectacles rests on their access to official resources—the discretionary authority they can call upon to engineer their spectacles, as well as the signs, symbols, and relationships they can mobilize to animate them. For others, spectacular agency requires the disbursement of considerable personal resources—money, time, courage, and the willingness to endure the embarrassment that spectacular attention sometimes involves. In this section I examine the resources spectacular agency requires and discuss ways that states, agencies, and activists can work to amplify women's access to these resources.

### Discretion

Women's ability to mount protective, punitive, or critical spectacles sometimes turns on their ability to exercise discretion. Discretion, which refers to the wiggle room left over between formal rules and their real-world application, is the often-unacknowledged capacity bureaucrats and other agents of the state possess to go beyond the letter of the law. Since policy prescriptions can sometimes be too abstract or incomplete to cover complex real-world situations, frontline workers have to be provided with discretion, an ability to interpret rules and also to plug gaps in protocol. On the front lines, where service work occurs in face-to-face encounters with clients, individual needs and circumstances are often too complicated to be reduced to programmatic responses. When workers use discretion, their organizations don't just acquire flexibility and responsiveness, speed, and agility; they also obtain benefits from the meaning and feeling that discretion allows workers to inject into service in order to make it more personal and more human. This kind of meaning-injecting discretion was seen for instance, in chapter four, where lady health workers went off the official script by offering women herbs or breastfeeding advice. These homespun remedies departed from official protocols of care but allowed health workers to connect with their clients. This connection, in turn, helped them cajole clients to abide by policy requirements.

Discretion does not just make service-work faster, more flexible, and more meaningful; it also provides workers with the ability to preserve or enhance their status and to protect their dignity. They can, for instance, use discretion to stall or withhold service from abusive or uncooperative clients, as lady health workers do when they refuse to provide supplements to abusive clients. Workers can also use discretion to provide more or better service than they are officially required to do, as flight attendants, do, for instance, when they reward cooperative or friendly passengers with better seats or meals.

Discretion doesn't just enhance worker status; it can also nourish their capacity to engineer spectacle. Shahbano's spectacular agency, for instance, drew upon the discretion she enjoyed as a constable assigned to guard the gates of the legislative building. To give her village headman a "demo" of women's capacities, Shahbano drew on the discretion that allowed her to choose whether to rigidly apply or suspend or overlook official rules for entry. This discretionary capacity is what allowed her to engineer a spectacle by first barring and later allowing the village headman to enter the building.

Similarly, Huda's spectacular agency also relied on discretion. To punish and humiliate the rickshaw driver who harassed her, Huda drew on the discretion that allows cops to operate in the shadows beyond official procedure and protocols. When she told me this story, what struck me was the pride Huda seemed to feel around her ability to exercise violence and verbal abuse. She appeared not to realize that she was describing an episode that might be seen as an example of police excess, of their propensity to overrun the legal authority vested in the force by the state. Indeed, violence and humiliation were so endemic to their jobs that the policemen and women I spoke with rarely exhibited any self-consciousness in recounting incidents exemplifying legal excess. Instead, they appeared to consider these accounts as evidence of their competence and efficiency. In her study of police violence in India, Rachel Wahl (2014) notes that far from feeling shame for their violation of human rights principles, police officers see violence as a necessary part of their jobs. Similarly, my research participants produced descriptions of violence as proof of their commitment to social justice, which they seemed to feel was often thwarted by official procedures and processes. Although Huda could have filed charges to make the rickshaw driver case an official one, she chose instead to use her informal discretionary capacities to impound the man and his vehicle, to beat him, and to have this beating witnessed by his family.

## Signs and Symbols

Besides discretion, spectacular agency turns also on various cultural signs and symbols that give meaning and direction to the spectacular drama. Airline attendant Laila used sanitary napkins as a sign of the gendered privacy that was under attack from the guard's daily intrusion. As a loud and obtrusive disruption, Seema's "shut-up call" is also a sign. Like an alarm, it lets others know that something is amiss. And it informs bystanders about the lengths a woman is willing to go to in order to protect her dignity. Lady health worker Nida's use of curses was also a sign, one that showcased her utter helplessness. A weapon of the oppressed and defenseless, her curses marked her boss as an archetypal oppressor, a characterization that apparently alarmed him.

Signs and symbols don't just invoke privacy, oppression, and a readiness to self-defend, they also call on bystanders for whom the symbol may hold meaning to add their weight to women's spectacular projects. One example of this recruitment capacity of symbols may be seen in the work that Huda's uniform did to activate her male colleagues to come to her aid. Even though she was in uniform, Huda did not approach the rickshaw driver alone but instead brought male colleagues to help her round him up. In recounting the story to me, she said that like her, her male colleagues had been enraged at the insult to the police uniform the rickshaw driver's behavior implied and therefore keenly assisted her in punishing him. Her spectacular agency turned therefore not just on the discretion she enjoyed as an agent of the police but also on a set of signs that her male colleagues, like her, held to be sacred. For both male cops as well as women police, the police uniform was a hallowed and therefore inviolable symbol of their service and their authority.

Both men and women police, including those at the lowly rank of constable, would describe their uniforms to me as a "lion skin." Laila, a 25-year-old constable, for instance, said that she had joined the force in emulation of her father, who had served as a police officer for forty years. In the beginning, she said, she had not felt very enthusiastic about her new job. "I was not that excited to join [the police]. I already knew what to expect. For me it was just a normal job, not something special," she said. "But then my father said to me that 'an ordinary person thinks like an ordinary person, but when you put a uniform on your body, it is a lion skin, it changes your thinking, you get a power inside you.'" She said that she had come to agree with her father's belief that the uniform possessed magical transformative qualities. "Right now," she explained, "I am speaking to you normally because I am in civilian clothes, but when I put on my uniform then it will be something else, it feels different, you feel changed. This is the truth." I asked her in what way it felt different, and she explained, "When my father used to come home in his uniform it felt like ten people have entered the house and when he took the uniform off, then everything became relaxed, he felt like himself again," she said, laughing.

Like Laila, many of the women I spoke to took tremendous pride in their uniforms, saying that putting these on had transformed them, imbuing them with an almost magical power. For instance, when I asked Hina, a constable, to tell me about a time when she had felt pride through her job, she said, "When I first put on my uniform." When she had first received her uniform, Hina said, she had put it on and gone right away to visit her father's grave. "He would have been proud," she said. "He was a bus driver, and as such, he was a person who had to follow police commands. I wish he could have known that today his daughter is the one who gives the commands." Women's claim that their uniform is a lion skin, an enchanted talisman of power and an emblem of their connection with the state, motivated Huda's male colleagues to support her spectacular punishment of the rickshaw driver.

## Supporting Actors

As Huda's reliance on her colleagues suggests, spectacular agency hinges not only on discretion and symbols but also on the willing cooperation of observers and supporting actors. Shahbano's ability to critique the gender arrangements in her village required the cooperation of her male colleagues. Since police work is often gender-segregated, gatekeeping tasks are organized according to gender. As a woman, Shahbano was tasked with handling women citizens seeking entry into the legislative building, while the village headman, a man, was processed for entry by the policemen posted at the gate. This is why Shahbano initially communicated with the headman via her male colleagues, only revealing herself to him later. She said her colleagues had cooperated with her because it amused them also to watch this schooling of an elite actor. "VIPs" like the village headman "usually don't have any time for the police," they "throw their weight around, drop names, and treat us like servants," she said. The opportunity to put such a VIP "in his place" was therefore attractive also for Shahbano's male colleagues.

Similarly, to punish the harassment of an airline attendant, Sabiha and her colleagues required the support and cooperation of the UK police. By compelling the passenger to apologize, these officers provided the women with a low-cost means of redress for their harassment. They enabled the women to punish the harasser without having to approach the courts.

Even smaller gestures like the shut-up call or the display of sanitary napkins to punish the guard at the airline briefing room gate require the cooperation of others. Such mini-spectacles also require observers, who are called upon to take the role of witnesses, which involves acting in ways that extend the meaning women are attempting through their spectacles to convey. The spectators who observed Laila's display of sanitary napkins signaled their agreement that the guard had violated Laila's privacy by hanging their heads in shame. Airline attendant Sabira, who responded to critiques about her appearance by posting a smiling photograph of herself on social media, also needed others to support her critique of the ageism and sexism implicit in her harassment. Her efforts to use spectacle for repair were successful because PIA's social media accounts amplified her response and because social media users praised PIA for its defense of an employee and because journalists picked up the story and projected Sabira's interpretation of events before a broader public. Thus, spectacular agency sometimes requires others to reflect and project the meanings that women attempt through spectacle to advance.

This reliance on others makes spectacular agency tenuous. When they set out to create a scene, women have no way of knowing whether and how those witnessing the drama will respond. Sabiha and her colleagues had never dealt with a foreign police force and did not know what kinds of events would be set off when they called upon the UK police. Razia, the constable who complained about her colleagues' staring at her ankles, didn't know whether her boss would take her side or instead tell her to dress more modestly. When she put her sanitary napkins on display, Laila did not know whether others observing would tell her to hurry up and stop holding up the line or join with the guard in commenting on her possession of cigarettes. And when she posted her own photograph online, Sabira did not know if this, too, would generate critical comments about her age or indeed if it would get lost amidst a crowded social media landscape.

## THE COSTS OF SPECTACULAR AGENCY

The benefits that spectacular agency provides by highlighting women's problems, punishing their abusers, and critiquing the system often come at a cost. To punish the guard who would humiliate her by expressing judgment over her cigarettes, Laila had to embrace a certain amount of embarrassment by putting her personal hygiene products on display. To rebuke the abusive passenger, Sabiha and her flight mates had to brave approaching a foreign police force in a foreign country. To take action against the rickshaw driver, Huda had to share details about the episode with her male colleagues. In each case, women took a risk and paid a price by giving up some of their privacy. To draw attention to their situations, they had to step into public view, put their sanitary products, their smiling face, or their abuse on display. To enact spectacular agency, women sometimes have to give up some of their privacy and put their dignity at risk of further damage.

More sustained spectacular agency can involve much larger costs. While the short-lived events recounted above cost women comparatively modest disbursements of time, energy, and relational resources, more sustained efforts at spectacular agency require much larger expenditures of time, energy, and personal resources, including money. These more onerous expenditures are most clearly evident in the context of a particular and sustained case of spectacular agency enacted by frontline women—the spectacular protests of lady health workers. These protests, which have been ongoing since 2010, are remarkable in a number of ways—the spectacles they mount, the relationships they require, and the sheer cost of enacting them. In this final section, I expend space to describing these protests, which are deserving of scholarly attention for the sheer grit, energy, and sacrifice they exemplify. This final section illustrates spectacular agency and its heavy cost. In the conclusion, I offer a few suggestions about what scholars and policy makers can glean from the findings presented in this chapter.

### Spectacle and Expenditure

The National Health Program began inducting women into the lady health worker force in 1994. In chapter four I describe in detail how the work of the LHWs changed over time and how it came to expand and become simultaneously devalued.

By 2010, lady health workers were so fed up with the poor conditions and informality of their jobs that they banded together to form the All-Pakistan Lady Health Workers Association (APLHWA), a nationwide union, and through the union, they began agitating to have the state regularize health worker jobs and to provide health workers with fairer work conditions. These efforts were spearheaded by Bushra Arain, a health worker from Larkana, in Sindh province, who used her own personal resources to travel from district to district recruiting other women to a spectacular project for redress. She managed to gather a large and dazzling force of women who congregated in various large and small cities to protest against their poor working conditions. Health workers who were not able to join in the protests contributed money and other resources to the protesters.

"What we wanted," Shehnaz explained to me, "was for them to regularize our work, to make us official workers of the state." This demand for regularization was a demand for the state to recognize the time and effort that workers put into their jobs. Despite their informal status, health workers said, they were required to put in long hours of backbreaking work. "They forced us to do polio work. Even if I said, 'I don't want to do it,' they said, 'Okay, we will fire you.'" Hira says. "It's not just polio or the work we do in people's homes," Shazia complained. "One day it is measles, so LHWs have to arrange an event, gather women, provide juice for the children [who are also present], arrange a function for the community, like an awareness campaign. Then next month it is another function. The doctor will come and talk to women about condoms. I have to arrange the event, gather the people, organize everything." Their designation as informal workers obscured the excruciating hardship of their jobs. Women reported passing out from exhaustion and dehydration in the course of their work. Some said they had been pelted by stones during polio vaccination rounds; others said they had received death threats from armed men.

The demand for regularization was not just about getting the government to acknowledge the time, effort, and suffering health workers endured while doing their work; it was also a demand for official recognition that LHWs were a valued and respected part of the health care edifice of the state. "We have no badge or reference slip," Salma complained. "When any of us refers someone to a hospital," she explained, "for any situation, be it gynecology or TB or for family planning, the doctors do not recognize us. They have no idea who we are." Because of this lack of recognition, Salma says, lady health workers lose status in the eyes of their clients, who wonder why the LHW gets treated like any other poor or working-class woman. "So the next time I tell my client, 'I think you need to get a TB test,' or if I recommend that she come with me to the doctor for an injection or a test, she will say, 'Forget it. They don't even know you there.'" Frustrated by her inability to help her clients more easily navigate the health care system, Salma bemoaned LHWs' lack of official status. If only the state were to provide LHWs with an official rank, she felt, she would have more authority with her clients.[2] An official rank, she said, would come with "service books, office space, transport and fuel allowances"—official scaffoldings of authority that would boost health workers' status in the eyes of the public and help make the LHWs more credible as agents of health in the eyes of their clients.

Nuzhat, an LHW nearing retirement, echoed Salma's views. "A sign of our low status is this. We don't get our salaries, sometimes, for six or seven months," she told me. "Then I have to borrow money from people, take credit from the grocery shops. I owe money all over the place. So then, how can I retain the respect that I had in my community?" she asks. "When I can't even give them back their money because for months and months, I have not received my salary, how will they respect my authority as a state official?"

In search of redress against the informality of their jobs, the delays in the payment of their salaries, their routine and arbitrary dismissal from service, and their harassment at the hands of health officials, the LHW's union spent two years traveling and protesting all over Pakistan. Lady health workers, their supervisors, their drivers, and even their children staged exhausting demonstrations, sit-ins, walks, and hunger strikes in big cities and small, outside press clubs and parliamentary buildings, outside Governor's Houses and health ministry offices, at the mausoleum of slain prime minister Benazir Bhutto (also the founder of the LHW program) in Larkana, and outside the Supreme Court of Pakistan.

For two years, the protesting workers were subjected to police batons, water cannons, and tear gas. They braved hot weather and cold; they endured hunger and thirst. They were locked inside Lawrence Gardens, a park in Lahore, and they were pushed and pummeled by irate motorists enraged by the disruption of their traffic. They were injured and brutalized; some of them passed out from the heat. Laila broke her arm.

"We ate jail, batons, torture, stones, tear gas, going blind, falling upon bars," Laila told me. "We saw such things and yet, the next month, again we were ready for *dharna* [sit-in]," she said, proudly, "[they poured] hot water on us. We were near the Chief Minister's house. Hot water was thrown on us. I broke my elbow [pointing to her left elbow], this one, I was shielding one of my girls. I got hit with a baton by a lady police. They [the police] pulled my hair and dragged me so hard; my shoes broke. When she released my hair, there was a handful left in her [the policewoman's] hand," she recalled. "All kinds of violence and brutality, we faced. They did everything, and yet they [government officials] did nothing [to improve the situation of LHWs]."

Laila's experience was caught on camera. In a video recorded by a local TV channel, her shoe appears briefly on the screen, lying forlorn and broken on the ground, while around it women flee squealing from the baton-wielding police. Other images of the workers' prolonged and exhausting protests were also caught on film by the Pakistani media, which broadcast a large collection of protest scenes—women dressed in colorful clothes and veils, sitting stoic under banners. Women seated on rugs and carpets they brought from their homes. Women carrying children in their arms. Women swaying; women chanting, "Shame! Shame!"; women shouting, "The daughter of the nation is out on the road. The leaders of the nation are sitting on a throne" (*qaum ki beti sarak per, hukmaran takht pr*). Women ducking under umbrellas, reclining beside plastic bags full of their belongings. Women with thermoses and lunch boxes settling in for a prolonged sit-in. Women shivering under blankets or fanning themselves in the heat. Women wearing lipstick and veils and holding their fingers up in a "V for victory" gesture. Women breaking the lock on a gate with a brick; women swooning, beating their chests, crying. Women squealing as they run from the police, who are charging at them with batons; women falling down on the ground; women lifting each other up; women sobbing and shrieking; women grappling with the public; women being carried off on stretchers into ambulances; women lying in a hospital bed hooked to an IV. Women who have transformed their pillows into effigies that bear the names of their various bosses; women setting these effigies on fire and then kicking them with their heeled sandals. Women chanting mournfully, "Whether we live or whether we die, the dharna [sit-in] will go on, the dharna will go on" (*jeena ho ga, marna ho ga, dharna ho ga, dharna ho ga*). Women staging a variety of spectacles in their quest for redress.

"Imagine, if you have not eaten anything," Hajra, a 53-year-old health worker, said when I asked her to tell me what the protests had been like. "There's hunger, and the storms are raging. There is thick darkness around you, women police, gents police are surrounding you, and there are a lot of people from the government," she said, drawing a vivid image of her experience, "and tear gas and these big, big, water [cannons]. Water is thrown at you with pressure. All these things are there, and when it feels like even God has abandoned you, and you are panting and panting, and all of us females are sitting in the middle of the road, poor things, for so many hours, sitting." I asked her how she had found the courage to go on, and she replied, "The more they oppressed us, the firmer our feet became."

On April 18, 2012, a group of lady health workers and their supervisors, drivers, and affiliates gathered outside the Press Club in Pakistan's capital city, Islamabad. They had come to the capital from all over Pakistan. They had been traveling and protesting all over the country for more than two years and were now at the end of their tether. Frustrated with the false promises and fake assurances they had received from various officials, they issued the government with an ultimatum: if their demands were not met by 3 p.m., they said, they would commit mass suicide. Outside the press club, they waited and waited. 3 p.m. came and went, but there was no response from the government. Finally, twenty-five of the demonstrators doused themselves with gasoline and tried to set themselves ablaze. Onlookers banded with the police and managed to stop most of them, but one man—my participants say he was a driver employed by the head of their union, set himself on fire. He was rushed to a nearby hospital for treatment.

In video recordings from this day, the workers look grim and upset. One woman, dressed in black, the color of mourning, is pictured swaying on her knees, beside herself with grief. She is hitting herself repeatedly on the head, in an emotionally charged ritual of grief and mourning. Another woman holds her up, trying to lift her to her feet but the woman in black falls down on the ground. Curling up in the fetal position, she continues to hit herself. The women around her embrace her; one pats her hand and strokes her hair. The woman in black continues to cry. The camera pans to another woman; this one is pictured sitting on the ground and wailing. A small child leans on her shoulder and is also sobbing.

Finally, these spectacular displays of protest drew the attention of the Supreme Court. Chief Justice Iftikhar Chowdhury took Suo Moto notice of the women's plight and ultimately directed the government to regularize LHW jobs. The government has been dragging its heels, however; at the time of this writing, nearly a decade later, lady health workers are still protesting various abuses and injustices.

Although their spectacular protests were successful at generating media attention, their efforts have brought mixed results. The spectacular protest LHWs staged, their use of mourning rituals such as self-flagellation, their threats of suicide and self-immolation, their catchy chants and slogans and the images of their grief did make visible and draw attention to their suffering. Their displays have repeatedly drawn the media and even the courts to take notice of their situation. But these attention-grabbing spectacles did not bring women an unalloyed success.

When the government did finally begin the regularization process during my fieldwork, some five years after the Supreme Court's directive, officials worked to weed out those workers who were unable to meet the bureaucratic paperwork requirements. Mehreen, for instance, said that she had lost her educational credentials during her divorce. Her husband had held on to her possessions and had refused to let her have anything, including important papers. Without documents to support her claims of schooling, Mehreen would not be able to join the ranks of regularized workers.

Other LHWs were locked out of the benefits regularization would provide because of their age. Those who had retired or would soon retire would not receive benefits such as pensions. Nuzhat was one such LHS. She had retired before the program was regularized and would therefore not reap the benefits she had struggled so hard to secure. "The first protest was in June 2010," she told me. "I went too. I used my own money. I spent around 6,000 rupees for travel and other expenses," she said. "When it came to the struggle [for regularization] I never lagged behind, but I will not receive the fruit," she said, sadly. "How does that make you feel?" I asked her. "It doesn't matter. The next generation will get it. One person grows a tree so that the next generation can sit in its shade," she said. "What is important is that you plant it."

## Costly Agency

To bring their plight to the public's attention, LHWs paid out of their own pocket for the establishment of their union. They paid for train and bus tickets; they paid for their accommodation when they traveled to Islamabad; they paid for lawyers to represent them in court; and they paid for the treatment of their injuries. The payments they had to make in service to spectacle included personal time and physical effort. To participate in protests, women had to leave behind (or bring along) small children; they had to suspend their domestic chores and overlook the needs of ailing relatives. They had to endure broken limbs and painful wounds, and they had to brave the rain, the heat, and the cold. They were thrashed by the police; some of them were rounded up and taken to jail. They sustained injuries, weathered the elements, and endured sometimes severe privation to mount their prolonged and sustained spectacles. They suffered financial, physical, and psychological injuries. And yet, as noted, many will never see the fruits of their spectacular efforts.

Spectacular agency, in short, sometimes comes at a considerable cost. To make their suffering, their harassment, and their abuse public, women have to endure not only a loss of privacy and shelter but also the financial, emotional, physical, and familial cost of publicity. They have to brave the potential shame of publicizing abuse, and they have to suffer the physical, relational, and temporal cost of engaging in protest and the pain of reprisal, when it comes from actors, like state officials, who punish spectacular agents with water cannons and jail for publicizing the injustice and inequality encoded into state institutions.

## Conclusion: Theoretical and Policy Implications

In this chapter I have documented how frontline women negotiate the authority-threatening dramas of repudiation they face in the course of their public service work by enacting what I call spectacular agency. Spectacular agency uses the arresting power of spectacle to call out, discipline, and punish harassers and to critique and renegotiate the subordinate status of women in society. To mount these spectacles, frontline women draw on both the official affordances of their state jobs as well as on personal resources, including monetary, temporal, and emotional outlays. The spectacles they engineer are sometimes as small as a momentary "shut-up call" and sometimes as large and prolonged as public protest.

These efforts bring a range of results. In some cases, like that of police constable Shahbano and airline attendant Sabira, such spectacles can provide onlookers with instruction about the capacity and dignity of frontline women. In other cases, like that of the health workers' protests, spectacular agency can bring mixed results, on the one hand failing to meaningfully change women's status in their fields of work but, on the other, providing women with a sense of achievement for having discharged their duties to the future generation.

By describing these various instances of women's spectacular agency, this chapter has showcased the multifaceted agency of Muslim women from the Global South, who negotiate stigma in multiple ways. As I have shown in this chapter, stigma management can at times involve recruitment via spectacle. By mounting a spectacle, women sometimes seek to recruit actors within their immediate orbit, as Rida, the LHW, did when she entered her boss's office in a loud and confrontational manner. And they sometimes try to recruit more distant allies, as flight attendant Sabira did when she used social media to challenge the ageism directed against her by a passenger. These findings suggest that Muslim women's agency is not limited to localized contexts. Both wings of agency, symbolic as well as relational, can draw on broader contexts, including global ones. These findings can help extend feminist models of agency and can help scholars get past problematic binaries, such as the ones that pit Islam against the West by suggesting that Muslim women's agency is contained within the localized context that embeds it. In contrast, this book has suggested that agency, which takes many forms, can draw on multiple contexts, from local to global, and micro to macro.

The instances of women's agency described in this chapter also have important policy implications. These findings suggest that it is not enough for organizations, such as those connected with the state, to pursue gender mainstreaming via quotas or recruitment drives. Gender-mainstreaming policies must also include provisions for managing the dramas of repudiation that erode and threaten women's authority once they are inducted into frontline work. This means providing women not only with the training and the tools (e.g., law and policy) for taking action against those who threaten their dignity but also with other kinds of resources (such as signs, symbols, and supportive colleagues) that they can use to fend off such attacks. To be clear, the Pakistani legislature has passed anti-harassment laws, and women are aware of these laws, but my participants rarely turned to them. Instead, as I describe here, they opted to rely on their own ingenuity to manage the dramas of repudiation that come their way.

Rather than filing cases, which would require time and effort, they relied on the informal support and cooperation of their colleagues and of sympathetic audiences. These colleagues and bystanders could be more formally tasked with supporting women in public space, and they could be trained via simulations to support women's dignity projects. States should perhaps also undertake public education programs to raise awareness about the dignity dilemmas and gendered authority threats frontline women face and to provide the public with repertoires for contesting these threats and supporting frontline women.

# CONCLUSION
## MOVING FORWARD WITH THE STIGMA MATRIX

**IN THE 1940S MY GREAT-GRANDFATHER**, an OBE,[1] worked as a bureaucrat in the Indian Civil Service in Sindh province, then a part of the British Empire in India. One night at a party he was hosting, his teenage daughter came down to socialize with guests wearing a stole, locally referred to as a *dupatta*, draped around her shoulders. 'What is this?' one of the white British men in attendance asked her. 'It's a dupatta,' she told him and began to explain the conventions of its usage. 'Hmph, *dekhawa*,' he commented, using an Urdu word meaning "sham" or "facade." My mother told me this story while I was writing this book. She had heard it from her mother. Neither of them was sure what the white man could have meant, but when she heard some of the arguments I make in this book, my mother was reminded of this strange episode.

Those of us reared in the contemporary context of niqab bans and headscarf debates are accustomed to hearing Westerners describe Muslim sexual practices as regressive, oppressive, and overly regulatory. For contemporary Muslims, anecdotes like the one involving my grand-aunt can therefore be inexplicable. We are hard pressed to understand such interactions because they enshrine a different kind of narrative, one that imagines Muslim women's veils as camouflage and understands their attempts to convey modesty as a sham. Yet, accounts from history suggest that the sexuality of indigenous peoples, including colonized Muslims, was viewed and discussed very differently during the colonial period. Take for instance the stories that are told about British attitudes toward Ruttie, the wife of Pakistan's founder, Mohammad Ali Jinnah.

In a book focused on the life of Ruttie Jinnah, Pakistani journalist Khwaja Razi Haider describes a scene from a dinner party hosted by British officials at Government House, the official residence of the Viceroy of India. Mrs. Jinnah accompanied her husband to this party in a low-cut Parisian dress, he tells us. Apparently shocked by Ruttie's revealing outfit, Lady Willingdon, one of the British women in attendance, asked an aide-de-camp to fetch a wrap for Mrs. Jinnah, in case she felt cold. Angered by this slight against his wife, Jinnah rose from the table and declared, "When Mrs. Jinnah feels cold, she will say so, and ask for a wrap herself" (see also Wolpert 1984).

The encounter is remembered in Pakistan today as an instance of Mr. Jinnah's quick wit and his ability to parry British insults. Yet Lady Willingdon's remark also reveals something about British attitudes toward indigenous women. Ruttie's lowcut outfit, Lady Willingdon seems to have suggested, was inappropriate for a dinner party. Her excessive sexuality required intervention from her British hosts, who would provide the wrap needed to contain and moderate this excess. Again, like the anecdote involving my relative, this one suggests a very different western perspective about indigenous women than the one we are familiar with today. Where today, brown women may be stigmatized for their pathological modesty, these anecdotes suggest that they were once stigmatized for their sexual excess.

Lady Willingdon's feigned solicitude for Mrs. Jinnah's modesty is grotesquely reflected in the sexualized stigmas that Pakistani women have been subjected to in various public spaces since the 1980s. At universities and colleges, on the streets and in bazaars, many women have reported receiving instruction from strangers to 'fix their dupatta' (Jafar 2005). At first blush, such stigmatizing encounters may appear to be singularly local. They might look like the unique products of a particularistic religious ideology (i.e., Islamic fundamentalism) and a specific, South Asian version of patriarchy (see Kandiyoti 1988). Yet the historical record suggests that these stigmas were also, at least in part, seeded by the nineteenth century global process of colonialism. Cultures, after all, are the product of both local and global, intercultural as well as intracultural struggles and negotiations over difference. These local/global struggles, which often involve women's bodies, are not just relics of a bygone past but are active and ongoing (Baumann 2017). And as we know, encounters between local practices and global values can, as in the case of Muslim women's veils, widen not just intercultural chasms but intra-cultural ones as well (Shahin et al. 2021). The sexual stigmas that shape women's experiences in public space, therefore, are not merely local; they are also transnational—shaped by colonial-era encounters and then nourished in subsequent years by a more recent set of global processes, like neoliberalism, securitization, and Islamization, which have worked to amplify various class and gender-based inequalities and in doing so have exacerbated women's experiences of stigma.

It was to capture these often-obscured global dimensions of local gender-based stigmas that I developed the framework of the stigma matrix. This framework encourages us to step back from the micro-contexts of stigma and apprehend the broader forces and structures that shape them. It urges us to move beyond the interpersonal arena where stigma is instrumentalized and to focus also on the organizational, the global, and the historical-colonial arenas that help to establish and reinforce stigma.

By adopting a multiscalar approach to understanding stigma, this book sidesteps some of the problems that plague social theory and globalization scholarship. Critics have noted that both these bodies of work suffer from metrocentrism, cultural relativism, imperial bifurcation, and a tendency toward orientalism. These issues can be avoided, I have shown, by deploying a framework that allows us to seek out the interconnections between North and South—the history of Pakistan's entanglements with countries like the United Kingdom and the United States as well as the dynamics of its continued involvement in ongoing global processes that wed forces like neoliberalism with Islam and in doing so, have the effect of complicating women's experiences of stigma in public space.

I examine the interplay of local and global, historic, and contemporary dynamics of stigma in the context of frontline women for several reasons.

(1) Frontline women occupy a unique social space, a frontier where local meets global, state meets citizen, public and official meet private and personal and where, in the Pakistani context, the state's investments in the norms of purdah clash with its need for operational reasons, to penetrate zones of gendered privacy.

(2) Examining stigma in this zone of multiple boundaries allows us to understand what it is that stigma does. And understanding stigma's purpose helps us to apprehend similarities between settings, like Pakistan, located in the periphery, and other contexts, like the United States, located in the core. In many global settings, stigma works not just as a locally nourished mechanism of inequality but as one that is powered by both local and global, contemporary as well as historical policies and objectives.

(3) Since they occupy a unique location at the cusp of local and global forces, frontline women offer an exceptional opportunity for understanding Muslim women's agency. The recent trend in the literature on Muslim women has been to lend more and more weight to the local contexts that embed women's agency. By focusing ever more keenly on these particularistic constituents of Muslim women's agency, recent work has unwittingly revived an imperialist bifurcation in social theory. It has inadvertently produced the impression that Muslim women's agency is distinctive and unique (e.g., compliant, rather than transgressive), wholly unlike the agency of women from other settings, such as the Global North. But as I have shown in this book, as with stigma, scholarly understandings of agency can also adopt a multidimensional approach. Just as stigma, a mechanism of inequality, draws on multiple layers of structure and meaning, from micro to macro, agency also draws on multi-layered contexts of meaning and relating. Thus, the women in this book draw not only on the symbols particular to their local work settings, like veils and motherhood, but also on images and ideas that are more global, like postfeminism and cosmopolitanism. By drawing on these symbols and discourses, they sometimes seek to recruit actors within their immediate interpersonal orbit, like clients or bosses, and at other times they try in spectacular fashion to recruit more

distant allies, like journalists, social media users, or the justices of the Supreme Court.

(4) Finally, the cases of stigma on the frontlines of Pakistani public service provide useful insights into the lived experience of women workers who are the subjects of globalized gender mainstreaming policies. Pakistani frontline women are pulled into their stigmatized jobs, in part, by global agencies that make gender mainstreaming a condition for the disbursement of aid and loans. They are also inducted into these previously male-dominated public contexts of work for various operational and political imperatives of state governance. They eagerly take on these jobs, which promise them some measure of authority and dignity, and yet they are denied dignity and authority in routine ways.

(5) These cases are illustrative, therefore, of the mechanisms that a growing category of actors must grapple with around the globe. As various organizations are compelled for operational or normative reasons to induct minorities into previously homogenous workplaces, more and more people from marginalized locations are ushered into work roles that are seen as incompatible with their identities. Many of these actors will, like Pakistani frontline women, confront stigma as a primary mechanism undermining their inclusion. To better understand their experiences of partial or ostensible inclusion, this book offers scholars the framework of the stigma matrix, a schematic for understanding how stigma draws not only on its immediate surroundings but on histories of oppression as well as large-scale, even global, processes of inequality reproduction.

In what follows, I discuss some of these themes and issues in more detail, clarify the theoretical contributions of this book and then suggest how this work can be carried forward, theoretically and also in the realm of policy.

### THE POLITICAL AND ECONOMIC FUNCTIONS OF STIGMA

The stigmas experienced by frontline service workers deserve attention because stigma is not just a set of physical and symbolic marks, it is an ordering instrument employed by national and transnational elites in pursuit of various financial and political interests. In a recent book, Imogen Tyler lists some of the political and economic functions of stigma (Tyler 2020). A form of classificatory violence, stigma is employed by governments, she says, to devalue certain people, places, and things. The devaluation that stigma manufactures is productive. Low-value people are more easily ejected from public lands and more effortlessly dispossessed of public assets. The evacuation of depreciated people creates new opportunities for capital accumulation by elites, who are able to bring the cleared-out public land, wealth, and assets under their own private control. Devalued people, moreover, are more easily transformed into commodities. Their labor becomes more abundant as a result of their immiseration and cheaper through their devaluation. Thus, the policies of corporatization, commodification, and privatization, which are signal features of the neoliberal project, rely in part on the dehumanization and devaluation that stigma produces.

A similar process of capital accumulation through stigmatization may be observed in the machinations of nineteenth-century empires. The stigmatization of indigenous women's sexuality, as I argue in chapter 1, was very productive for the British colonial project in India. Drawing on Durba Mitra's book and other sources, I describe how the sexuality of local women was stigmatized under empire and how this process of stigmatization helped British colonialists to justify the necessity of colonial rule and also to develop and refine social scientific methods and theories, which aided the development of disciplines like sociology and helped to make that rule more rational and efficient (Mitra 2020).

Devalued and made more sexually accessible as a result of these stigmatizing processes, indigenous women also came to serve, as Ronald Hyam argues, as erotic motors of empire. The availability of indigenous women for sex became a motivating factor for Victorian Englishmen, who were willing to go and work in the remote reaches of empire, in part, because of the easy access these settings provided to "a range of sexual consolations" (Hyam 1986). Thus, stigma aided capital accumulation for empire in two ways. First, sexual stigma worked to devalue indigenous people (whose sexual excesses were seen as a sign of underdevelopment) and to justify their dispossession by empire as a form of necessary discipline. Second, the devaluation of indigenous women transformed their bodies into a commodity, a cheap resource white men could claim, in addition to the other forms of compensation they received, for their service to empire.

The stigmatization of women's sexuality also served political and economic functions in postcolonial Pakistan. Under General Zia-ul-Haq, sexual stigmas worked to deprive women of their rights and their capacities for participation in public life. Their devaluation worked not only as a signal of the success of Zia-ul-Haq's Islamization project but also as a form of currency, which the regime used to purchase the allegiance of religiously motivated political parties and actors.

Today, the stigma surrounding women's presence in Pakistan's public spaces continues to be reinforced by those who benefited from Zia-ul-Haq's Islamization project. Religiously oriented political actors continue to use stigmatizing rhetoric around women's sexuality as a lever for gaining visibility and relevance in politics. They tap into the general alarm and consternation produced by events like the Aurat March (Women's March) to reassert their own moral authority. Their discourse works to shore up their own visibility, but it also firms up the construction of a religiously based, collective national identity, one that is premised primarily on the regulation of women's sexuality.

Right-wing religio-political parties are not the only ones to benefit from the ongoing stigmatization of women in society. Stigma works for elites in Pakistan, as it does for elites elsewhere, as an instrument that can be used to colonize the productive capacities of particular groups of people, in this case women. Formal and informal rules surrounding women's sexuality, such as the norms that dictate when and where women can appear, operate not only to regulate women's bodies but also work to constrain women's political and economic activity. Women who are excluded from workplaces are more likely to become dependent on men at home, who benefit from their domestic labor. Discourses, such as the one about the veil and four walls, don't just contain women's sexuality; they also impede women's economic and political mobility, complicating their ability to participate in jobs, like the ones the women in this book take on, and also their capacity within these jobs to exert authority or inhabit leadership positions.

Stigma doesn't just serve elites by facilitating their capture of women's productive capacities, it works also as an explanation for the failure of various elite-led policies and programs. In Pakistan, women's purdah violations become explanations for crises, like the COVID-19 pandemic, which religious elites claimed was a consequence of society's lax morality, a laxity exemplified by the increasing presence of unveiled women in the public sphere. A similar propitiatory use of stigma is evident also in Western contexts, where migrants, especially undocumented ones, are constructed in popular discourses as responsible for unemployment and other economic conditions, which are actually a consequence of neoliberal policy (Castañeda and Shemesh 2020).

Finally, sexual stigmas are productive for the part they play in supporting the state's coercive apparatus. Stigmatized people don't just support capital accumulation; they also invite security interventions. Devalued people are not just evicted from public land; they are criminalized and transformed by discourse into threats (see Savci 2021). Or conversely, as in the case of Muslim women, stigmatized people are constructed as requiring increased protection and defense, including via armed intervention. Thus, colonialists in the nineteenth century used the trope of white men saving brown women from brown men as a justification for the violence perpetuated by empire (see Spivak 1994). And U.S. action in Afghanistan in the early part of the twenty-first century was justified, at least in part, as a response to the gendered oppressions perpetrated by the Taliban.

In short, stigma serves a number of political and economic functions. It devalues people, places, and things, freeing up land and other forms of capital for elites to accumulate. It can be used as a source of legitimacy for various disciplinary projects, such as colonization and Islamization, and it can serve as a propitiatory tool, supplying ready-made moral explanations for structural failures caused by policies, such as those associated with neoliberalism. Stigma aids in the commodification of people, who are then either offered up as compensation to empire's agents or transformed into human machinery that toils for the expansion of various capitalist projects.

This book has been concerned with documenting the experiences and the agency of this human machinery, that is to say, the women who toil on the front lines of public service at the behest of local and global economic and political projects. It has done so by employing a new framework for examining both, stigma's constitution as well as its contestation. The stigma matrix developed in this book not only illuminates the complex of factors that contribute to the organization of stigma but also draws attention to the local and global structures and signs that configure women's responses to it.

### PURDAH AND THE QUEST FOR DIGNITY

While doing polio vaccination rounds, Shagufta told me, she collapsed one day in the midst of work. "It was a very sunny day," she said, "and I felt faint and fell down somewhere on the road, totally senseless," Like many of her fellow lady health workers, Shagufta had abstained from drinking water that day because she knew there would be no bathrooms to use as she completed her door-to-door work. "The people around me raised a hue and cry," she said. "They were saying, 'She has died.'" While Shagufta was saved by the kindness of strangers, who carried her to a hospital, other women said they relied on veils and family members to manage the corporeal constraints posed by their stigmatizing service work. Constable Roshan, for instance, said that when she was assigned to provide security at a mosque under threat of terrorist attack, she took her mother and her breast-feeding baby along, so that she could feed her baby without forsaking her official duty. Her mother watched the baby, while Roshan provided security to worshippers, and then when it was time to feed the baby, Roshan would retreat to the side and do her "other duty" as she put it of breastfeeding. When I asked her where she went when she needed to feed the baby, she said, "I just go to one side, there is no private place as such, I use a *chador* for cover, and I feed my baby."

In enduring such corporeal privations, like forgoing water or attempting to breastfeed in the midst of a physically exacting workday, these Pakistani women are not unlike poor or working-class women in other contexts. The privations they suffer are reminiscent of those endured by agricultural workers in the Beed district in Maharashtra, India, for instance, who opt for hysterectomies in order to avoid having to deal with menstruation while working in the fields or the adversities borne by U.S. women, who hide in closets or retreat to their cars to pump breastmilk at work, or the women who worked in a Nabisco factory in California, who were compelled to use diapers to manage their lack of restroom breaks (Chatterjee 2019; Linder and Nygaard 1998).

The classed and gendered bodily privations working-class women must endure for their wages are not unique to the Pakistani context. But

CONCLUSION 237

for working-class Pakistani women, privacy dilemmas of this kind are expressed and solved through the various idioms of purdah, a set of symbols and techniques working-class women use in order to recuperate the privacy and respectability they lose when economic needs propel them into public spaces that are culturally understood as out of bounds for women.

Not all women abide by purdah's strictures in their pursuit of dignity at work. Some, as I have shown in this book, jettison the aesthetics of purdah and try instead to convey brutality or cosmopolitan postfeminism. Others do cling to purdah's various modalities, working in various ways to convey the delicacy, the modesty, and the maternity associated with the classed and gendered norms of purdah. Their efforts are often onerous. Abiding by the modalities of purdah sometimes requires women to forego various comforts. It requires them to abstain from drinking water because doing so would require the removal of a face veil. Or it requires them to leave a police van where others are engaging in "dirty talk." And it requires them to forego the financial rewards they could have obtained during work travel if they had been willing to share a room with their male colleagues. Those who discard purdah's modalities must endure the reputational repercussions of their transgression.

But while these various costly purdah practices, whether invoked or transgressed, do provide women with a sliver of honor in their stigmatized occupations, they also wind up reinforcing some of the cultural ideas that buttress women's marginality within their fields of work. When women mobilize the gendered signs of purdah fidelity, such as veils, whiteness creams, and motherhood, in order to convey delicacy or modesty, they wind up reinforcing the notion that women are essentially unsuited to occupy and enact public roles. Their need to care for children or to manage menstruation become explanations for their marginality within their fields of work.

When women reject the gendered signs associated with purdah, however, by embracing a male-coded swagger that suggests competence and corruptibility or by mobilizing the idioms of jihad usually associated with masculinity, their performances are hamstrung by a different set of hierarchies, those centered on class, that make college degrees, or feminine delicacy into crucial signs of respectability and honor. In short, performances that circulate around the idioms of purdah are bounded by both class and gender structures. When they use these idioms to redefine the classed meanings of their social situations, women are ensnared by gender structures. When they use purdah's idioms to redefine the gendered meanings that complicate their social status, they are hamstrung by the structures of class.

But purdah is not just a set of classed and gendered modalities that women use or discard in the course of their frontline service work. Purdah is a set of modalities enacted also by the Pakistani state. In the hands of the state, purdah serves as a modality of security—a technique that instrumentalizes gender in order to secure cover for the state in the course of its security operations. Part of the reason the state employs women as frontline service workers is because they allow the state to enter into the private, intimate arenas of homes that are protected by norms of purdah, without upending these norms. In these operations, as I outlined earlier, women serve as sheaths, shielding other women from the abrasive masculinity of the state and its global allies, and in doing so, armoring security agendas from accusations of brutalizing or offending the dignity of women during the conduct of routine security operations.

The state's purdah modalities are illustrated by the rules it crafts around women's presence during security operations. The police, for instance, are formally disallowed from conducting raids upon houses where women might be present unless their security force is escorted by women police. When they do go on raids, women are placed in the vanguard to serve as the soft edge of the state's entry into private space. When they perform this role, women are mostly not provided with weapons, bulletproof vests, or other protective equipment. "Because," as Lubna, a constable, explained, "our bosses feel that as women, we will be spared violence, no one will attack a woman." Yet, Lubna says she was shot at in the course of one such operation. Bullets were fired at Lubna during an anti-encroachment operation.

"We were told that this settlement has to be vacated," she told me. "The people had to be evicted from there." The residents, she said, "were not cooperating, they were difficult people." To get the settlement cleared, the senior officers gathered policewomen from all over Karachi—"they brought us there on a bus." To fend off the police, the people of the settlement had used copies of the Quran to construct a border. "They made like a barrier. They must have thought that the police would not be able to cross this line."

But one of the officers went around picking up the holy books and placing them respectfully in a police vehicle. "Then," Lubna said, "the officers commanded us, the ladies, to walk into the area. They thought that since we are ladies, no one will hurt us."

Lubna and the other women began walking into the settlement. "Some boys [from the village] were standing nearby," she recalled. "They looked like they were just talking, we didn't think they were a threat, so we kept going," she said. "But when we got near the settlement, they started firing, straight fire." The women were unarmed and had no protective gear. The police vehicles that had come with them fled the scene. "We were alone, we were on the road," Lubna recalled. "Some girls fell to the ground. Some took cover in nearby shrubs." The bullets whizzed past Lubna, "some went under my arm, some pierced my dupatta," she said. "One went through my veil and hit a man who was with us, it killed him on the spot." Lubna, who said she felt very bitter about this experience, concluded, "They just left us ladies there without weapons. They thought no one would shoot at ladies."

This incident, which was recounted to me not just by Lubna but a few of the other women who had witnessed it, illustrates the state's use of purdah as a modality of security. The officers in charge of the anti-encroachment operation Lubna was ordered to support sent women in the vanguard for two reasons. "They sent ladies first," Lubna explained, "because there were ladies inside [the settlement] who had to be removed. They wanted us to handle the ladies because of purdah—the ladies' purdah should not be disturbed." Second, the officers assumed, wrongly, that the squatters would not go so far as to attack or hurt women. "They must have thought these are poor people, they won't do anything to harm women," Lubna said, "but they should have realized that no one would give up their home so easily." Since they assumed that women were somehow inviolable, they used them as a kind of armor, crafting a buffer made up of women's bodies, which the state could use to penetrate a zone of domesticity. This incident depicts ways that purdah operates as a modality of security for the state. Women are thought to provide the state with cover and with permeability.

Between the state's use of its modalities and women's own uses, purdah transforms into a powerful prism, one that refracts both the structures of gender and those of class. Within the grip of these intersecting structures and forces—state, class, gender, and globalization—women are caught in a complicated paradox. Their veils and their purdah modalities are used to further various operational imperatives connected with globalization, such as securitization. And the same modalities are used also as explanations for women's marginality in their fields of work.

Since the norms and modes of purdah have a history as well as a social location, I began to see this prism as a matrix, a kind of super-prism where older as well as more recent local and global forces operate at different scales, macro to micro, to structure women's experiences of privacy and public space. A matrix that generates both stigma and destigmatization responses.

In other words, the stigma matrix, as I conceive it, is forged in the Pakistani context around the notion of purdah. Purdah refers to a set of classed and gendered signs, stereotypes, and techniques that individuals as well as empires have used to buttress various hierarchies through the mechanisms of stigma and dignity. The signs and stereotypes connected with purdah are mobilized in various ways and by various actors. The state uses these modalities in pursuit of operations, like discipline or security. Women invoke these modalities in pursuit of dignity, connection, and distinction. Their colleagues, their families, their communities, and their clients also invoke purdah, sometimes to stigmatize the women and sometimes to connect with them. Transnational agencies instrumentalize purdah's modalities in service to their own agendas and imperatives. They use frontline women to carry global missions into purdah-protected zones and to bring data out of them. Together this complex of practices and imperatives produces what I call the stigma matrix, which shapes both, women's dilemmas as well as their responses. Their destigmatization efforts are often impeded by the refractions produced within the matrix. How then can women escape its binding effects?

### REPRODUCTION AND CHANGE

The women described in this book all serve as human machinery for the advance of various local and global agendas and objectives. Their labor doesn't just provide the state and its various allies with permeability; it also enables the state's maintenance of gender boundaries. Frontline workers—cops, health workers, air hostesses—don't just carry the state into the private, intimate, female-coded arenas otherwise closed off to it, but in doing so, they also help the state to reify the gendered boundaries that make public arenas and encounters the province of men.

Yet, women's presence in these arenas, stigmatized as it may be, also creates opportunities for change. Through their sheer presence in these roles, frontline women violate gendered norms of social life in Pakistan, even as they protect these norms by acting as a bridge between the state and its women subjects. Women agents affect change also through their various destigmatization efforts. The veiled delicacy strategies women employ in the police introduce a new kind of sensibility in this otherwise brutal and masculine arena. Those who, like Sohai Ali Talpur and Sharafat Khan, perform public acts of valor unsettle stereotypes about women's vulnerability and incapacity.

Despite their inability to escape gendered hierarchies, airline women still reshape the country's public sphere, populating it with performances of a cosmopolitan style of femininity not usually associated with working-class women. They also provide working-class girls with a vision and a strategy for class mobility.

Health workers perform a caring, connective, and engaged version of the state for their poor and working-class clients. They offer them contraceptives and empathy, kindness and confidentiality, providing their poor and working-class women clients with affects and tools that can transform their lives. Their success, as they themselves note, is illustrated by the impact their program has had on the rates of maternal and child mortality in the country.

Certainly, for each of these contributions that women make, they pay a physical, emotional, and reputational price. In exchange for their transformative service, women receive heavy disbursements of gender-based stigma. The need to manage this stigma becomes one more task they must perform, in addition to the already lengthy list of chores required by their jobs. Their destigmatization performances aren't always liberatory, but they do provide women with meaning and connection, sources of a deeply deserved dignity. And when they are able to tap into some of the signs and social resources anchored within the state, when they are able to successfully recruit others to their meanings and projects, frontline women achieve a stunning "spectacular agency," one that enables women to reverse the polarity embedded within stigma. When they wield the power of spectacle, women are able to not only stem stigma but also to publicize abuse, to discipline and punish abusers, and to protest, critique, and renegotiate the subordinate status of women in society.

## THE BROADER UTILITY OF THESE CONCEPTS AND FRAMEWORKS

This book develops a number of concepts and frameworks that can aid scholars interested in understanding the mechanics and motors of inequality, especially from a global perspective. At the same time, the primary framework developed here, the stigma matrix, works to reinvigorate the notion of stigma, an important sociological concept that is due for a postcolonial reckoning. In place of the "often individualistic, ahistorical and politically anaesthetised" conceptualizations of stigma that dominate canonical versions of this concept (see Tyler 2018), the framework developed in this book provides a multifaceted, multiscalar approach that enables scholars to trace the global and historical constituents of this inequality-making mechanism, in addition to the more local and interpersonal ones. Using this framework, scholars can examine how broader global forces, such as neoliberalism and securitization, benefit from stigma, which can produce dispossession and also work to cheapen labor. And they can examine how global processes associated with capitalist expansion work to impose stigma not only on the subjects of global projects, like those involving securitization, but also compel some of the agents, such as cops, who further these projects to endure stigmatization.

In the case of Pakistan's frontline women, stigma was connected with norms of purdah. While purdah may not be a central schematic in the production of stigma in other contexts, it is nevertheless a useful concept that can help social scientists understand how structures and forces intersect at different levels and scales to help constitute stigma. Scholars interested in racial stigmas may find it useful to adapt the notion of purdah, a central symbol in the stigma matrix described in this book, by drawing on the work of W.E.B. Du Bois and Frantz Fanon who have written about a similar structure in their discussions about "the veil" (Fanon 1959; Du Bois 1903, 1920; see also Baehr 2019).

But beyond purdah, the stigma matrix framework can help scholars understand how stigma is constituted at multiple levels and scales—micro, meso, and macro, global and local. In other contexts, other varieties of the stigma matrix will also likely have a history as well as economic and political functions. Scholars wishing to employ the stigma matrix can work outward as I did. They can begin at the micro level by identifying the local structures that stigmatizing and destigmatizing interactions express. Then, in the next step, they can examine the histories behind these structures and practices. As they do so, they will begin to see what the stigma matrix produces in the case they are focused on, and for whom. And finally, they can focus on the agency of stigmatized actors who are persistent in grappling with stigma, even when their efforts misfire or produce only small impacts.

The framework can and should be used, I would argue, not only to examine instances of exclusion, eviction, and evacuation, themes that stigma studies are already focused on, but also to examine instances of ostensible inclusion and incorporation, as this book does. In recent years institutions, such as states, universities, and media conglomerates are increasingly seeking to recruit women and people of color in a stated effort to enact values of diversity, equity, and inclusion. The workers inducted through these diversity drives are pioneers, who must bear the weighty impact of shifting boundaries. As they move past old lines of exclusion, these minorities are compelled to endure the various stigmas, often already baked into their work settings. They have to contend with the stereotypes that imply that they are mismatched with their new positions. The cultural resources at their disposal—symbols of office, signs of status, and the tools necessary for dignity performances—were likely crafted for other identities and therefore may misfire in these minority hands. The symbols that indicate prestige and competence for dominant groups might create meanings for the minorities who deploy them that are less savory. In addition to the significant burdens that these marginalized people are required in their new positions to shoulder, these new inductees will also need to undertake tasks related to destigmatization. It is in such situations, where the stigma matrix is ostensibly dissolving, that its structures and its composition are best observed.

The framework described in this book can also provide useful insights about the connection between stigma and gendered inequality in other settings, such as the United States. It can be used, for instance, to better understand a gender-based form of violence that is also related with stigma—gaslighting, a social mechanism of violence wherein abusers manipulate their victims into questioning their own sanity and capacity for reason. In a recent article, Paige Sweet has described how gaslighting emerges out of a constellation of factors—stereotypes about women, tactics that instrumentalize these stereotypes, and institutions—which form the context for the exercise of such tactics (Sweet 2019). Each of these different factors, which operate at different scales, come together to mark women in specific ways—as crazy, hysterical, and unreliable—stigmas that set them up as ripe subjects for gaslighting. Thus, gaslighting succeeds because a host of micro and macro factors (interpersonal interactions and institutional arrangements) come together to stigmatize women and, in doing so, force them into a situation of surreality.

By providing a comprehensive organizing framework, the stigma matrix can help us to more easily understand Sweet's theory and also to expand it. It allows us to see stigma as a central mechanism in the production of gaslighting, a mechanism that operates like a matrix to produce a particular outcome related with power and inequality—gaslighting. In gaslighting, as in the case of the dignity assaults and authority threats outlined in this book, stigma hobbles women's agency by obstructing their ability to recruit allies in the doctor's office, in the police station, in court rooms, and in work settings. The framework of the stigma matrix also suggests that gaslighting may be shaped by another, macro layer of gender-based stigmas, a layer that warrants further investigation by scholars. This could include investigations into the ways that transnational entanglements, both past and contemporary, work to shape the stereotypes and stigmas that support gaslighting. Or it may investigate the ways that larger contemporary processes like neoliberalism, securitization, and the globalization of religious fundamentalism contribute to the stigmas that make women vulnerable to gaslighting.

Two further concepts developed in this book will likely be useful for scholars of inequality. The concept of gendered authority threats outlined in chapter 6 provides a more precise vocabulary for understanding a category of gendered challenges women face at work. These challenges are usually subsumed under the broad category of "backlash." The problem with the notion of backlash, though, is that it lacks conceptual clarity. It is used to describe too many distinct varieties of opposition to women's economic and political participation in the public sphere. On the one hand, backlash refers to sudden shifts in public opinion following policy change; on the other it is used to describe individual and social reactions ranging from arson and murder to silent disapproval or civil noncompliance (see Walsh et al. 2017). The literature on backlash tends also to focus on women politicians or those in positions of influence. The notion of gendered authority threats, in contrast, describes a specific kind of backlash, a form that involves stigma and that works to undermine women's authority in more routine activities, like frontline work.

Finally, the concept of spectacular agency provides scholars with a new vocabulary for understanding forms of action that utilize publicity in service to various liberatory objectives. Instances of this form of agency have been proliferating in the contemporary media landscape, where social media and the possibility of virality provide people with greater access to spectacular contention. Spectacular agency has been deployed by women who make #MeToo claims in places as different as the United States, Pakistan, India, Turkey, and Iran. Scholars interested in investigating such trends can draw on the notion of spectacular agency as a destigmatizing strategy and evaluate the various relational capacities this form of agency affords.

## POLICY IMPLICATIONS

The various findings reported in this book are suggestive. The experiences and struggles detailed in the preceding chapters can provide valuable insight for those tasked with crafting policy aimed at increasing women's participation in the public sphere and helping to boost their effectiveness in various arenas of the state. For such readers, these chapters suggest that to succeed, gender mainstreaming efforts must rely on measures that go beyond quotas or recruitment drives. Gender mainstreaming policies need also to create tools women can use to manage gendered authority threats and other mechanisms of exclusion that are anchored to stigma. Although the Pakistani government has in recent years passed important anti-harassment legislation that my participants were aware of, in each case that I describe in chapter 6, women relied on their own ingenuity to manage the gendered authority threats they confronted at work.

Threats, moreover, as the chapter suggests, can also work as opportunities. To safely address gendered authority threats, women require material, relational, and emotional support. They need money to fund some of their spectacular ventures; they need social support from colleagues, bystanders, and the media; and they need access to cultural resources they can use to reframe the meaning of their visibility and the terms of their repudiation.

Similarly, policy implications may be drawn also from the description of the challenges women face in accomplishing extension via recruitment. Inequality, this book has suggested, is partly reproduced because the relational wing of women's agency is hamstrung by various class and gender structures. In chapter 3, for instance, Huda and Sana's leadership is hobbled not through formal policy or law but through their inability to access the cooperation of their subordinates. This failure at recruitment, in turn, frustrates their effort to get recruited into the networks that serve as a conduit for the movement of various resources within the state. Since women's inequality in this case is structured by clandestine networks and alliances, these findings suggest that neither the law nor individual empowerment are sufficient nodes of policy intervention. Instead, since social relations and alliances are crucial vectors for the reproduction of gender inequalities encoded within the state, policy aimed at addressing these inequalities should focus on shoring up women's relational capacities and opportunities in addition to their formal skills and competencies. This could entail boosting the number of women in a particular work context, providing women workers with networking opportunities, assigning them with mentors, and working to help them foster the kind of alternate network culture that Rehmat, a senior woman police officer, expressed a desire for creating. "We are trying," she said, "to create our own, like a *Gulabo Gang* [Gang of Roses] but we don't have enough women in the force to do so." By supporting women like Rehmat to foster such alternate networks, policy makers can ensure that gender mainstreaming measures do more than simply insert more tokens into a previously male-dominated arena.

A mere eight months after she was attacked by a mob, Sharafat Khan made the headlines again. This time, the media reported that the bold officer had gone undercover to lure a jewel thief into police custody. Pretending to be a teenager, Khan called up the suspect on his phone and arranged to meet him at a local restaurant. At the restaurant she disguised herself in an abaya and engaged the man in conversation. Once he had confessed to the robbery, Khan took him into custody. A news story covering this operation was posted to YouTube. In comments on this video, various audiences praised Khan's bravery and ingenuity.

Although reports about this operation did not enjoy the virality that the mob attack story did, the coverage of Khan's intrepid undercover operation illustrates the complicated role frontline women play in the gendered landscape of Pakistani security. Yesterday's victims might show up in tomorrow's newspaper in the guise of heroes. Their veils provide them with a permeability that allows them to penetrate zones otherwise closed off to state agents. Their gender serves as an instrument with which to lure and lull the subjects of security.

As they enact these evolving scripts, frontline women gradually produce new meanings and new connections between gender, purdah, and the forces of globalization. This book has testified to their efforts to do. Pakistani women are by no means alone in their struggles to cultivate inclusion within the state. By focusing on their journeys, this book has outlined new frameworks for understanding both the obstacles and resources at their disposal.

## *Appendix:*
## *Researching Stigma in Pakistan*

In this methods appendix I discuss issues connected with studying stigma, gender, and globalization in Pakistan. I describe how data were collected and analyzed, how access was obtained, and how my questions changed through my interaction with gatekeepers as well as participants in and outside the field. And I reflect on some of the broader issues and events that framed my research project.

Although most of my data were collected during my visits to Pakistan, my interest and understanding of themes I encountered in the field were necessarily shaped also by my conversations and media exposure in the United States as well as Pakistan. I was born and raised in Pakistan but lived and studied in the United States on and off between 2007 and 2019. During this time, I returned to Pakistan frequently (once or twice a year) not only for research purposes but also to teach university courses and to connect with my family and friends. This was a turbulent time of life for me. Each time I moved back and forth, I was forced to readjust not only to different time zones and norms of presentation and interaction but also to different perspectives and ways of knowing and understanding the world and relating to it.

When I was collecting data, analyzing them, and writing about them, therefore, I was never just in one place, Pakistan or the United States—I was in both. I was reading newspaper stories about Pakistan in the United States, and I was hearing my friends' and research participants' views about America and its relation to Pakistan, while in the field.

In 2019, I moved to Canada as an immigrant and entered yet another field of information and communication about the United States, Pakistan, Islam, gender, and globalization. I discuss how some of these dislocations shaped my focus in the field and my understanding of data once I had left the field. I conclude with a reflection on the unique issues an ethnographer of Pakistani origin encounters when writing about home for a largely foreign set of audiences.

## THE DATA

Data for this project were collected between 2015 and 2017. The book draws on two forms of primary data: (1) ethnographic observation, which helped me to understand and contextualize (2) 120 formal, in-depth interviews with Pakistani frontline women workers. I conducted 40 interviews each with policewomen, lady health workers, and airline attendants. The interviews lasted between one and seven hours each, and I formally interviewed some participants multiple times. Interviews were conducted almost entirely in Urdu; I am a native Urdu speaker. Interviews were recorded on tape and transcribed and coded for analysis.

Participants were not given any financial compensation for their participation; however, I offered some of my interlocutors a package of locally manufactured Cadbury's eclair toffees at the end of each interview. When I visited women at their homes, I brought along a box of pastries. At police stations, I paid for tea and snacks, which were ordered from a nearby roadside teashop, and on a few occasions, I brought along food I had cooked at home for the policewomen. I also received hospitality from many frontline women, who made or ordered tea and snacks for me when I visited them at work or in their homes and sometimes even sent food home for my mother.

In addition to interview transcripts, this book draws on extensive fieldnotes that I wrote at the end of each of my visits to the women's workplaces, their homes, and their training centers. In addition to these notes, I also used the notes app on my cell phone to write up observations and to transcribe informal conversations while in the field. I drew on field notes to deepen discussions during interview sessions, for instance, asking participants to help me understand unfamiliar terms and to comment on incidents I had observed. And I relied on interviews to better understand my observations. At the police station, for instance, interviews helped me to understand the relational dynamics I had observed operating between bosses and subordinates.

This project also draws on two sources of secondary data: (1) formal and informal conversations with a number of actors associated with each field site—the frontline women's colleagues, supervisors, and trainers; their family members, neighbors, and friends; and journalists and aid workers who interacted regularly with the women. (2) Media, social media, and official texts related to the frontline women's professional activities and their fields of work.

### RESEARCH VISITS

I made a total of three research visits to Pakistan. I first traveled to Pakistan in the summer of 2015 for an exploratory visit. On this first trip, I visited an elite police commando training unit in Peshawar in the northwest of Pakistan as well as a special security police unit in Karachi, my hometown. In Peshawar, I spoke with a number of women trainees, their trainers, and senior police officers. I also spoke with journalists and local residents to understand how issues related to security shape social life and ideas about women and policing in this high-security setting.

In Karachi, where I eventually collected the bulk of the data that informs this book, I spent part of the summer of 2015 talking to journalists and local residents about issues related to gender, security, and policing, and I began collecting secondary data, including news media articles and publicity materials associated with policing in Pakistan. In Karachi that first summer, I also participated in an antiterrorism training workshop at the Special Security Unit (SSU), a branch of the local police department that is focused on providing security to VIPs. During this training session, I gained firsthand experience with various aspects of training, such as firing an AK-47, and I met with a number of policewomen as well as journalists who cover security and policing in Karachi. The training also provided an opportunity to observe police interactions with media professionals as well as media professionals talking among each other about the police.

After I returned to the United States in August 2015, I spent the next year communicating with the police department for permission to undertake my research. Some of these interactions took place over email and over the phone, and some involved the help of my friend Nadia Naqi, a local journalist who acted as an ambassador for my project and was instrumental in helping me gain access to the policing field sites. While I was initially able to get permission to undertake research with the police in both Karachi and Peshawar, the latter city eventually backed out of the research project because they said that their plans to continue training and recruiting women into the elite commando unit had been halted indefinitely.

In Karachi, the inspector general of police for Sindh province permitted me to carry out my research but allowed individual officers to exercise discretion over whether or not they or their staff would participate. This arrangement was ideal from an ethical perspective because it afforded each participant the freedom to choose whether or not to engage with my research. However, it also meant that the heads of various police stations or training academies had to first call up headquarters to confirm that I had permission to talk with them. Additionally, the terms of my official permission created ongoing anxieties for me, as they allowed any officer, even one who was only peripherally connected with a particular site, to refuse to allow me to continue doing research at any time. I might as well have relaxed, though, because only one officer, a woman I was very eager to speak with, refused to meet with me. Everyone else that I contacted freely and generously agreed to participate in the project. Many introduced me to other people they felt I should speak with, and all were candid in their discussions with me, although several did ask me at times to switch off my recorder.

My second trip to Karachi began in May 2016 and ended in August 2017. During this visit, I spent time at two women's police stations, a police training academy, and the High Court of Sindh. I visited policewomen at their homes, and I drove around with them in their vans. I also spent time with male police officers at their offices, spoke with them over the phone, and exchanged regular text messages with them on WhatsApp. As we became friends, policemen and -women would get in touch with me over the phone or invite me to have tea with them and meet with their families or just to gossip. I spent roughly two days a week at police sites over the next fourteen months.

My research questions and focus changed within the first month of interacting with policewomen in 2016. During my early interviews, women dismissed the questions I was asking, which were focused on issues related to the body, and instead directed my attention to stigma. They kept telling me that the key issue they faced in their work was the stigma surrounding women's involvement in policing, an occupation that they considered especially polluting of women's reputations. They said that although women's work is not usually seen in a positive light by society, there are three jobs that are seen as especially problematic—policing, health work, and air hostessing. Policewomen that I spoke with had friends and relatives who were engaged in health work and air hostessing, and they would recount stories about the harassment and stigma that their sisters, cousins, and neighbors had faced in these other fields of work. As a consequence of these early conversations, I redesigned my research project and began seeking permission to conduct research in the local health department and at PIA, a quasi-state institution. Once again, my friend Nadia was instrumental in helping me reach out to senior officers and bosses in each of these organizations and helping me obtain permission for my research.

I first met with lady health workers in August 2016. They had gathered at a medium-sized government hospital in the north of Karachi. They came to this location regularly to attend meetings with their supervisors or to drop off data and collect assignments. I visited this hospital several times a month over the next year. Once I got to know women at this hospital, they began inviting me to visit them in their districts and at their homes. I spent several months visiting one particular district located in the east of the city, which I call Shamsheer. In Shamsheer I observed health workers' experiences at a local government hospital, as well as their Health House (a room set aside in their home for health work). I also made visits to two other districts, where I observed LHWs founding informal investment groups, organizing community events, and interacting with neighbors. I also spent time at health workers' homes, drove some of the health workers to their meetings, traveled with them to meetings in rickshaws and taxis, and followed them on polio vaccination drives. Like the police, health workers also interacted with me via phone calls and WhatsApp messages to carry on conversations or keep up a relationship beyond the field visit.

At PIA, most of my observations took place at the head office, which is located in Karachi's old airport, locally referred to as the Star Gate Airport. A senior officer at PIA introduced me to Mehreen (a pseudonym), who acted as my guide and helped me to coordinate my visits to PIA. At headquarters I spent much of my time in the union office, the grooming room (a set of rooms focused on inspecting and regulating airline attendants' appearance), and in the offices of those airline attendants who also did administrative work in addition to their flight duties. I also spent time at the "briefing room," the room where airline attendants wait for their flights, at Jinnah Terminal, Karachi's main international airport, and at a training center where airline attendants go for refresher courses. I visited PIA about two days a week for ten months.

In each of these field sites, interview participants were recruited in the course of observational visits and via snowballing introductions from men and women I came to know through my fieldwork. In each site, I spoke formally and informally not only with frontline women but also their colleagues, bosses, friends, and family members.

I made a follow-up visit to Karachi in early 2018 for two months. On this visit, I spent time reconnecting with the men and women I had come to know in all three field sites and observed some of their work activities.

**Analysis:** I spent more than a year transcribing and analyzing data. Data were coded and analyzed on NVivo. The analysis followed Charmaz's prescriptions in *Constructing Grounded Theory* (2014) and was conducted in three stages. In the first, discovery stage, I undertook a line-by-line coding of field notes, interview transcripts, as well as media texts. At this initial coding stage, analysis was grounded and remained open to multiple possible theoretical directions. These initial codes were then condensed and refined based on their frequency and apparent significance into a set of focused codes, which were used to facilitate analysis in the next stage of coding.

In the second, directed coding stage, I used focused codes to sort, synthesize, organize, and integrate data across field notes and transcripts. I began thinking about how codes operated in different contexts and how they were related to other codes.

In the final, analytical stage, I wrote detailed memos to think through ways that codes might relate to each other, for instance examining how codes about veiling might relate to codes about corruption. To verify my interpretations, I discussed emerging themes and patterns with participants, with journalists, and with local academics. I also compared my research findings with those reported in the literature focused on frontline women's work in Pakistan. Finally, I presented some of this research to students and academics at a Pakistani university and relied on their questions and comments to deepen my understanding about local ways of knowing and understanding issues related to my research and my participants.

## CASE SELECTION AND THE STORY OF STIGMA

Like other ethnographies, this research project did not follow a straightforward trajectory but instead grew out of observations and interactions in the field. When I first flew to Pakistan in 2015, I wasn't thinking at all about stigma. At the time, my research was concerned primarily with questions related to policing and was focused specifically on women's corporeal experiences with commando training. I was drawn to the policing site by a set of media stories that showcased Pakistani women supporting various global initiatives, such as the war on terror, through their bold service for the state. I had seen stunning pictures of these women in the local and global press. In both they were pictured in their veils and niqabs (or face coverings), shooting rifles, running, and doing push-ups. I was transfixed by these women. Although my primary interest was theoretical—I was interested in understanding how people navigate the cultural changes precipitated by global processes and exchanges, such as those that place veiled women in risk-filled arenas usually associated with men—the case of women police was interesting for political reasons also. In many of the news stories, the women were depicted as ciphers in Pakistan's ongoing battle against extremist ideologies. The women pictured in the news stories were residents of Pakistan's northwestern province, Khyber Pakhtunkhwa, which borders

Afghanistan, and the media suggested that they were training to tackle the Taliban.

Since the U.S.-led war in Afghanistan, which had important ramifications for Pakistan also, was at least partially waged in the name of gender, the various mediated instances of women's integration into the apparatus of state security raised important questions. Was the integration of women into the arenas of security in this purportedly gender-conservative Muslim country connected with the war? Was the confrontation between the United States and the Taliban pulling Pakistan in a more gender-progressive direction? Was war paving the way to a more egalitarian future, one that allowed women also to become equal partners in that important kind of sacrifice that scholars say provides men with a heightened claim to citizenship? Or was their integration merely cosmetic, having more to do with the construction of a specific, gender-egalitarian image of the Pakistani state and its allies? These questions get at the heart of a long-running puzzle in the literature on globalization and gender. Is globalization beneficial for women?

But when I arrived in Pakistan in 2015, I found a much more complicated story. Global forces, such as the U.S. mobilization in Afghanistan, did help to pull more women into security roles in Pakistan. But the impetus was not purely egalitarian; it was also tactical. Women whet the violent capacities of the state (and of its global allies). The United States learned this lesson in the course of its engagement with Afghanistan. There, local norms of gender segregation limited the U.S. military's ability to question or scrutinize local women. A very large proportion of the population was therefore lost to intelligence efforts. To overcome this weakness, the U.S. Marine corps created Female Engagement Teams (FETs), using them not only to search women at checkpoints and interrogate them in an all-female setting but also to develop trust-based and enduring relationships with Afghan women. This initiative later spurred the development of Cultural Support Teams (CST), units that served in attachment with special operations teams and that took on a variety of missions involving different levels of violence, from the relatively benign Stability Operations to the more violent direct-action missions that involved the killing or capture of high-profile targets and required the calming and quick interrogation of women detainees (see Kareko 2019).

Women appeared to provide a similar extension to security in Pakistan too. Over and over in my field work, I heard supervisors and managers say that women are necessary to security operations, that they can do what men can't do, and, conversely, that men can do what women can't. Many of these people appeared to see women as complementing rather than matching the capacities of the men they worked alongside. Policewomen, therefore, weren't just diversifying the state's forces; they were extending these forces by enabling them to reach into the intimate gendered regions of privacy, which are fortified in Pakistan by a set of gendered norms I describe as *purdah* norms. These are norms that circumscribe women's interactions with non-kin men. Not all Pakistani women perform purdah in the same way. Some choose to ignore these norms; some engage in the modalities of purdah by wearing headscarves, lowering their gaze, and keeping interactions with non-kin men strictly business-like. But some women, such as the clients of LHWs, engage in stricter forms of purdah by keeping largely to their homes and avoiding interaction with non-kin men. By carrying the state into the homes of these purdah-practicing women, frontline workers help the state to expand its reach deep into the boundaries of privacy and purdah.

Frontline women don't just extend state operations by carrying it into zones of privacy, however; they also help to reinforce purdah norms. By helping the state enter zones of privacy without upending or violating purdah norms, frontline women both penetrate and preserve these zones. By moving across the gendered boundaries of public and private spheres of life, frontline women help to keep these boundaries stable. Their boundary maintenance, however, is contingent on their own personal violation of purdah norms, a violation that is productive of stigma.

Seeing frontline women as extenders of state operations and preservers of purdah helped me to understand how each of the research sites investigated in this book is connected not only by stigma but also by global forces. In each site, women's work is guided not only by local imperatives and policy prescriptions but also by global ones. Policewomen facilitate antiterrorism operations that are connected with global agendas around security. Health workers aid transnational agendas surrounding vaccination and contraception. Airline attendants are tasked with ensuring safety and maintaining discipline on board national and international flights.

The work they perform is not only shaped by global processes, such as neoliberalism, but also helps to further global processes like securitization. All three groups of women are pushed into the workforce by the economic policies associated with neoliberalism. All three help the state achieve security objectives. Policewomen permit the state to apprehend and address women complainants and informers; airline attendants allow the state to extend surveillance to veiled women aboard flights and monitor suspicious activity, while lady health workers allow the state to patrol the borders of disease by pushing vaccination and gathering data around outbreaks. By patrolling the borders of crime, aviation, and health, each group helps enhance state security. But what precisely is security?

In the decade after September 11, 2001, the word *security* became associated in the public imagination with a specific set of concerns and practices. When we think of security, many of us think of metal detectors and x-ray machines, delays at airports and public buildings, wiretaps, drones, and infringements on our privacy. Similarly, the agents we think of when we think about security are also connected with a post-9/11 transnational frenzy—border guards at airports and land borders tasked with detecting threats, airline attendants who notice something suspicious and report it, soldiers who travel to distant lands and police them, police officers who surveil local groups in search of radical elements. Such images and ideas reinforce what scholars call a "traditionalist" notion of security, wherein security refers to safety—the tasks a state undertakes in order to ward off attacks and guarantee freedom from fear (Goldstein 2010).

Traditionalist notions obscure many aspects of security—how old is the global preoccupation with it, what security involves, and what it accomplishes. The global preoccupation with security predates September 11, 2001; encompasses a broad range of activities; and works to produce not just safety but also inequality.

For national and transnational agencies, security is not just about managing "conventional" kinds of threats or patrolling the usual borders. States and global agencies patrol a number of frontiers in pursuit of security. They patrol the border of disease, for instance, by monitoring its outbreak and working to discipline or restrict the movement of bodies that carry it. They surveil the poor and they try to track migrants. Police officers don't just arrest criminals; they also clear up land encroachments and protect corporations in the process of acquiring public resources (e.g., the armed response to Standing Rock protesters; see Skalicky and Davey 2016). In short, security is not limited to armed responses against distant and proximate foes; it also centers on the movement of people, information, disease, and capital within and across borders.

In the course of patrolling the movement of people, information, and disease, security processes mark people. Children who have received the polio vaccine in Pakistan, for instance, are marked with black ink on the thumb. People cleared to fly at airports receive stamps on their boarding passes and passports. Those in police custody are marked by manacles and handcuffs. Protesters, like the LHWs described in this book, may be marked with batons, which leave bruises on their bodies.

Security, in short, is inflected at its very core with stigma. Using tools like stamps and registers, handcuffs and ink, the various agents of security, including cops, health workers, and aviation staff, mark certain people as dangerous, as deviant, as undesirable, or as processed and free to move. They do so in both tangible and intangible ways, by inking people's bodies or by recording details about them in official registers. Such stigmas can be formal or informal. Agents can mark people by using legal instruments, such as stamps on a passport or by employing informal ones, such as clandestine violence, foot-dragging, or corruption.

In the course of working with the three frontline occupations described in this book; however, I came to understand that security processes don't just mark the subjects of security; they mark security's agents as well. The agents of security are sometimes marked by their appearance via uniforms and badges and at others by their tools, such as guns, vaccine coolers, and rubber stamps. And in the case of Pakistan's frontline women, security agents are marked by their transgression of the norms of purdah that they also, through their boundary-violating work, help to preserve.

Security work confounds frontline women's ability to practice purdah even as it exacerbates these needs. For to perform their security duties women must sometimes visibly step out of gendered zones of privacy and inhabit public spaces. They must stand on busy streets searching and frisking citizens; they must trudge from door to door vaccinating children; or they must trek up and down plane aisles checking to ensure that seatbelts are fastened. When executing these public duties, policewomen and airline attendants are not allowed to cloak their uniforms or conceal their faces. They must declare their connection with the state in order to embody its authority and secure citizen compliance. Health workers do not wear uniforms, and many are permitted to wear *abayas* (full-body gowns) when they go out to complete their duties; however, they are forbidden from covering their faces, as doing so might frighten or alienate citizens.

In each of the frontline sites investigated in this book, therefore, women cannot veil, except in circumscribed ways. Their inability to veil is not only a threat to their modesty but can also pose a risk to their safety. What they often wish to cover is their connection with the state.

The inability to veil their connection with the state can put frontline women at risk. At least seventy polio workers have been killed in Pakistan since operation OBL (Osama bin Laden), which involved the use of polio workers for intelligence gathering. The police have been valued targets for terrorists for much longer, and several are killed in targeted attacks every year. Airline attendants face a different kind of danger. Their uniform can sometimes make them the target of sexual harassment. Such dangers were never far from my mind. The academy in Peshawar where I began my field work was hit by a terrorist attack one hour after I had left it—thankfully, no one was hurt. A police academy in Quetta was attacked by terrorists while I was working at the academy in Karachi.

The generalized fears such episodes triggered were given more concrete form each time I visited PIA or the police academy. At both sites, I was required to navigate protracted security procedures at the start of each visit. Yet, I was only a visitor and free to skip work on an especially risky day. My participants enjoyed no such luxury and were therefore much more keenly aware of the danger of their jobs. Thus, besides stigma, codes that came up frequently in all three field sites included jihad (holy war), sacrifice, and danger. All three codes were tightly connected with the code of "purdah." Women talked about purdah not just as a shield for securing their reputations; they discussed purdah as a mask for their association with the state, a slender form of protection against physical harm from those who may hold a grudge against state agents.

Lubna, a police constable, told me that she had started wearing her full-body veil only after she began training at the academy. "I wear the abaya because, who knows, someone might see my uniform when I am traveling to or from work and identify me as police," she said, explaining that "at the academy, they [the instructors] told us not to go out in police dress. They suggested that we wear an abaya." The threat was real, she argued. Someone she knew had been attacked and killed. "And actually, it happened in my neighborhood. a policewoman was traveling to work, and someone fired at her and killed her. So, we were told that the *awam* [public] are enemies of your uniform, because a lot of people don't like the police . . . so we were told to stay in our abayas and cover up our uniforms."

Men at the academy echoed Lubna's words, saying that women were fortunate to be able to cover up their uniforms with their abayas, while men had to come to work in civilian clothes and change into their uniforms at the academy or at work.

On their way to and from work, women are able to rely on various tools, like abayas, to mask their connection with the state, but when they are sent out for official duty, they cannot camouflage their identity as state agents. Indeed, it is precisely in the riskiest situations that the state requires them to carry out a signal as well as an operational function. In such situations, the uniformed bodies of state employees reassure citizens that the state is taking a hand in things. Moreover, to garner compliance, women undertaking risky tasks—doing polio work, conducting stop-and-frisk operations, or undertaking crowd control—need most urgently to display their affiliation with the state. In such situations, any easy understanding of purdah as a pursuit of dignity and privacy is turned on its head. In these instances, women's uniforms are both a source of dignity and stigma, a mask that covers their individual identity while leaving their gendered particularities unveiled. Signals of state affiliation simultaneously mark women workers as abstract, empowered agents of the state, its sexualized public servants, as well as vulnerable targets for those who bear the state a grudge.

Thus, the notion of *purdah* looks very different from the perspective of the state's working-class women employees who shield and shelter women citizens by compromising their own dignity, security, and privacy. From their perspective, purdah may be seen not just as a form of seclusion or segregation or a simple matter of veils and harems but as a painful, risky, and ultimately tenuous pursuit for privacy, dignity, and security within the gendered apparatus of the state.

### DOING FIELDWORK IN PAKISTAN

When I first considered pursuing this project, my friends and family told me I was crazy. Even if there was some way to swing official permission and gain access to these securitized field sites, they said that I would be in considerable danger when I was in them. Danger not only from terrorists, who target state facilities, but also from officials within the state itself, who may view my interest with suspicion and may react violently if they felt I was putting their reputations at risk.

If I managed to pull this study off, it is thanks primarily to the women whose experiences I document in this book, who welcomed me so warmly into their ranks. Their hospitality is all the more remarkable in light of my positionality. While the frontline women I followed in the course of this research were primarily working-class, they knew me as a middle-class, westernized, single woman who was living and studying alone in the United States and had returned to Pakistan solely for research purposes. Since I was unmarried, childless, and a student, the women were very protective of me. They appeared to see me as both an ill-defined "expert" who could provide insight into their personal problems but also as a child-like quasi-insider, who knew the language but not the mechanics of local social life.

Their perception was a boon for my research, as they saw me as both safe for confidence but also in need of patient and careful instruction into the granularity of local social processes. Thus, while many men in each of my field sites used various strategies to restrict and manage my access (i.e., subjecting me to long wait times, asking for repeated submissions of written requests for access, etc.), the women were very hospitable of my presence and my questions. In each site, I sensed that their eagerness to participate in my research was motivated by considerations of honor and recognition. At the High Court, for instance, Sana proudly introduced me to various people we met as her "sister," a researcher from the United States (see chapter 1). She was not alone in introducing me to people this way. Many women appeared proud to introduce me to their families, colleagues, and friends, as a sister or a close friend. They appeared to see my interest as evidence of the significance of their work—which it was—and appeared excited to be the subjects of research.

Many of them lectured me on what they considered to be my duties as a Pakistani writing about Pakistan for an American audience. Health workers, like Humera, said that I should work to reveal to interested outsiders how aid funds come to be misused in ways that add to the burdens of women workers. I have described her perspective in chapter 4. Airline women, like Bee, instructed me to work toward creating a more balanced portrait of Pakistani life for foreign, especially American readers, who, she thought, saw Pakistan only as the home of radical versions of Islam. For such readers, women like Bee hoped that my work would communicate the depth and complexity of Pakistani women's visions and aspirations. I took such recommendations to heart, and as I describe in the introduction, such perspectives helped me to construct my methodological approach.

Although frontline women appeared honored to be the subjects of my research, my participants also sought to control and manage my investigations in various ways. LHWs and policewomen both worked to teach me how interviews and observations should be conducted. My western modes were "too nice," they argued, and I should work to incorporate the kinds of gestures and tones they used with their clients, which they felt were more likely to elicit confidences from my respondents. As they modeled these techniques of voice and interaction for me, I came to see how intimately performance was linked in frontline work with various relational agendas. To win over subjects of research, my participants suggested, I needed to embrace specific performative styles that helped to foster intimacy and friendship. I needed to speak in soft and dulcet tones, to frequently repeat the subject's name, to touch her hand or her knee and to ask a number of questions about her children and her siblings, and to give her compliments on her beautiful management of work and home.

Women also sought to manage my research by aiding and supporting my mobility within the field. Their solicitude was shaped in part by their apparent delight in my attention. In all three of my field sites women said they were very pleased to be the focus of a foreign research project. "Thank

God, at least someone has thought of us" [*shukr hai kisse ko tau hamara khyal aya*], Shiza, a lady health worker, said.

To facilitate my research, therefore, women tried in various ways to assist my safe mobility within the field. When I traveled from one site to another, women plotted routes for me, telling me which buses to take. They also instructed me about the varying veiling codes they followed. Policewomen, for instance, wore headscarves at the academy, along with their uniforms. At the women's station, they would take the scarf off; some would wear a loose stole on their head, whereas others wore it around their shoulders. But when they ventured out in the streets, they put on a full *abaya* (a black gown worn over clothes that hides the figure), and they told me to wear one too. They also told me how to behave. I must not smile in the presence of men or joke with men. I must keep my expression "serious" and "strict." If someone sent me text messages, I was to ignore him and never reply. I was to lower my gaze when speaking to a man. I was to keep my distance, retreating into the background and not attracting attention.

Besides giving me such instruction, women also accompanied me to various research locations, such as the court or to various hospitals. If they couldn't go with me, they would call ahead and try to introduce me to other women I could rely on for help. When we visited new locations, such as a new station house, women would speak on my behalf to the men, who were the official gatekeepers in each setting. They went out of their way to help me, they said, because they wished to speed up my research so that I could go back to the safety of my home in Virginia. They therefore also worked to recruit interview participants for me and tried to instruct me in research methods with the hope that my work would go faster.

I have wondered about their remarkable solicitousness, and I am not entirely sure what brought it about. It could be my childlike appearance, as I am less than 5 feet tall and, at the time of my field work, weighed less than a hundred pounds. But I think that their solicitude was also guided by their desire to support a woman, who like them was working for a living. Many women showed similar solicitude for their clients, neighbors, siblings, and cousins. They were eager to help women rise in the world, and my relatively privileged class background didn't stand in the way of their kindness and compassion.

While the women's kindness was invaluable for my research, it also complicated my writing. It is never easy to write about Pakistan, a country that is associated so strongly with so many stereotypes in western contexts, especially when it comes to questions about gender and security. These stereotypes were never far from my mind as I wrote this book in the United States and in Canada. In the United States, when strangers I met on a train or at a bus stop learned where I was from, they would begin to ask questions that reinforced media stereotypes about Pakistan. "Do you wear a veil when you go there?" or they would ask questions about jihad and terrorism. Such stereotyped comments came not only from strangers but also from friends. One academic I knew, introduced me to her colleagues as 'the woman who studies "Jihadi women."' During ethics review, one commentator on my proposal was worried about the possibility that my participants or I would get honor-killed in the course of research. At a meeting where we discussed research findings, one researcher laughed at one of the quotes I presented, which had come from a participant. I was never sure whether the laughter signaled discomfort and surprise or was intended to mock. When I spoke about Pakistan in the U.S. classroom, students would come up to me afterwards and say they had no idea that Pakistani women went to school: 'we thought, like Malala, you would get shot for wanting an education.'

How do you write about your own country in the face of such stereotypes? How do you blithely engage in an activity that could further your own career but that may damage the interests of the people who cared for you and shared their lives with you and went out of their way to help you?

And yet, I did grow up in Pakistan and cannot pretend that women there do not face various difficulties at work, even in elite contexts, like the ones I worked in. I worked in Pakistan as a TV news producer for five years. I later went back and taught at a local university for two years. In the first job, I faced routine sexual harassment and discrimination. In the second I was treated with tremendous dignity.

But I have also faced harassment and discrimination in the United States and Canada. And I am aware that gendered bias and gender-based violence are not unique to Pakistani contexts. As a Pakistani woman, I know that it is important to draw attention to the difficulties Pakistani women face at work. But as an academic working in North America, I am aware that

Pakistani women are neither unique nor alone in facing sex and gender-based mechanisms of inequality at work or in their intimate lives.

As a sociologist, then, I had to find a position from which I could write without feeling like a traitor to either Pakistani women or my chosen profession. I had to find a way to be loyal to both my native country as well as my discipline. I had to find a way to write fairly, without obscuring difficult observations just because these might reinforce stereotypes about Pakistan but also without revealing findings in a decontextualized way that would certainly reinvigorate biases and stereotypes.

I cannot say that I have found and settled into a solution. I still write from a position that feels uneasy and uncomfortable. I still write from a place of dislocation, constantly tacking back and forth between my many homes. Writing about your native country for a foreign audience is a task that requires constant reflection and renegotiation. It is an ongoing balancing act, always requiring reevaluation and recalibration. And yet, it is precisely this difficulty that makes the task so urgent. I take solace in the hope that writing about Pakistan will become easier once many more people are doing it. When the daughters of my participants also obtain admission in the North American academy. When my Pakistani students also read and write and respond to writing about Pakistan. As writers, we seek out and follow the trails left behind by other travelers, and when there are many trails and many pathways, we are able to worry a little less about the marks that we are making as we pass, because we know that our impressions are merely joining a rich, layered, and diverse set of inscriptions left by others.

# Notes

**Chapter 1**

1. Many of my research participants, when introducing me to others, referred to me as their sister.

2. Simla, now known as Shimla, is a city in India that served as the summer capital of British India.

3. Bilateral aid refers to the direct transfer of funds or other assets from one government to another country.

4. For example, IMF loans in 1993, 1994, 1995, 1997, 2000, 2001, 2008, 2013, and 2019.

**Chapter 2**

1. Sexual assault victims are often stigmatized in Pakistan, India, and Bangladesh. Fear of humiliation can prevent reporting (see Shahid et al. 2021).

2. "Midcity" and "Heerabad" are names I gave these locations in order to protect participant privacy.

3. This last phrase means something like "or I'll eat my hat."

**Chapter 3**

1. I was told that women civil servants were forbidden from opting for police work until the Musharraf era (2001–2008).

## Chapter 4

1. LHS manage LHWs and receive marginally different salaries (about $50 more), but as they are part of the same health force, beset by similar problems, in this chapter I will describe both simply as LHWs unless the distinction is pertinent to the discussion.

## Chapter 6

1. Sabira is the attendant's actual name. Sabira was not interviewed as part of this research. The description of this case is derived from accounts provided by other attendants and from media accounts of this incident.

2. Status in state jobs is partly measured via what is known as "grade." This is a number the state assigns to distinguish official ranks across departments, e.g., police heads of a station house are usually grade 14 officers, while doctors are grade 17 and above.

## Conclusion

1. A recipient of the Order of the British Empire.

# Bibliography

Abbas, Syed Ahsan. 2020. "Police Reforms: Public Perception and Introspection." *Pakistan Journal of Criminology* 11(3):155–62.

Abu-Lughod, Lila. 2002. "Do Muslim Women Really Need Saving? Anthropological Reflections on Cultural Relativism and Its Others." *American Anthropology* 104(3):783–90.

Adams, Julia. 1996. "Principals and Agents, Colonialists and Company Men: The Decay of Colonial Control in the Dutch East Indies." *American Sociological Review* 61:12–28.

———. 2011. "1-800-How-Am-I-Driving?" *Social Science History* 35(1):1–17.

Akhtar, Aasim Sajjad. 2014. "Economic Theory 'Privatization at Gunpoint.'" *Monthly Review*, June 30. Available at www.monthlyreview.org/2005/10/01/privatization-at-gunpoint/.

Alexander, Jeffrey. 2004. "Cultural Pragmatics: Social Performance between Ritual and Strategy." *Sociological Theory* 22(4):527–73.

Ballhatchet, K. 1980. *Race, Class, and Sex under the Raj: Imperial Attitudes and Policies and Their Critics, 1793–1905*. London: Weidenfeld & Nicholson.

Bauman, Zygmunt. 1998. "On Globalization: or Globalization for Some, Localization for Others." *Thesis Eleven* 54(1):37–49.

Baumann, Gerd. 2017. "Dominant and Demotic Discourses of Culture: Their Relevance to Multi-ethnic Alliances." In *Debating Cultural Hybridity*, edited by P. Werbner and T. Modood, 209–25. London: Zed Books.

BBC. 2016. "Pakistan's Women Only Police Station." *Witness History*, BBC News World Service, February 10. Available at www.bbc.co.uk/programmes/p03hjvzr.

Bell, Vikki. 2008. "From Performativity to Ecology: On Judith Butler and Matters of Survival." *Subjectivity* 25(1):395–412. doi:10.1057/sub.2008.31.

Berger, Mark T. 1988. "Imperialism and Sexual Exploitation: A Response to Ronald Hyam's 'Empire and Sexual Opportunity.'" *Journal of Imperial and Commonwealth History* 17(1):83–89. doi:10.1080/03086538808582781.

Bhambra, Gurminder, K. 2013. "The Possibilities of, and for, Global Sociology: A Postcolonial Perspective." In *Postcolonial Sociology*, edited by Julian Go, 295–314. Bingley: Emerald.

Bourdieu, Pierre. 1984. *Distinction*. Cambridge: Harvard University Press.

Brown, Geoff. 2016. "Pakistan: Failing State or Neoliberalism in Crisis?" *International Socialism* 2:150. Available at www.marxists.org/history/etol/newspape/isj2/2016/isj2-150/brown-g.html.

Burke, Kelsey. 2012. "Women's Agency in Gender-traditional Religions: A Review of Four Approaches." *Sociology Compass* 6:122.

Burney, Samya. 1999. "Crime or Custom? Violence Against Women in Pakistan." Human Rights Watch. Available at www.hrw.org/reports/1999/pakistan/.

Butler, Judith. 1993. *Bodies That Matter*. London: Routledge.

Callon, M., and Latour, B. 1981. "Unscrewing the Big Leviathan: How Actors Macro-structure Reality and How Sociologists Help Them to Do So." In *Advances in Social Theory and Methodology: Toward an Integration of Micro- and Macro-Sociologies*, edited by Karin Knorr Cetina and A.V. Cicourel. London: Routledge.

Castañeda, Ernesto, and Amber Shemesh. 2020. "Overselling Globalization: The Misleading Conflation of Economic Globalization and Immigration, and the Subsequent Backlash" *Social Sciences* 9(5): 61. doi:10.3390/socsci9050061.

Chadbourne, Julie Dror. 1999. "Never Wear Your Shoes after Midnight: Legal Trends under the Pakistan Zina Ordinance." *Wisconsin International Law Journal* 17:179–280.

Charmaz, Kathy. 2014. *Constructing Grounded Theory*. 2nd edition. London: Sage.

Chatterjee, Patralekha. 2019. "Hysterectomies in Beed District Raise Questions for India." *Lancet* 394(10194):202.

Clegg, Stewart R. 1989. *Frameworks of Power*. London: Sage.

Closser, Svea. 2015. "Pakistan's Lady Health Worker Labor Movement and the Moral Economy of Heroism: Pakistan's Lady Health Worker Labor Movement." *Annals of Anthropological Practice* 39(1):16–28. doi:10.1111/napa.12061.

Collins, Patricia Hill. 2000. *Black Feminist Thought: Knowledge, Consciousness, and the Politics of Empowerment.* Rev. 10th anniversary ed. New York: Routledge.

Connell, Raewyn. 2007. "The Northern Theory of Globalization." *Sociological Theory* 25(4):368–85. doi:10.1111/j.1467-9558.2007.00314.x.

Critelli, F. M., and J. Willett. 2010. "Creating a Safe Haven in Pakistan." *International Social Work* 53 (3):407–22.

Dalrymple, William. 1994. *City of Djinns: A Year in Delhi.* London: Flamingo.

———. 2003. *White Mughals: Love and Betrayal in Eighteenth-Century India.* London: Viking.

Deeb, Lara. 2006. *An Enchanted Modern: Gender and Public Piety in Shi'i Lebanon.* Princeton: Princeton University Press.

Donaldson, Laura. 1992. *Decolonising Feminisms: Race, Gender, and Empire-Building.* London: Routledge.

Du Bois, W.E.B. 1903. *The Souls of Black Folk.* 2007 edition. Oxford: Oxford University Press.

———. 1920. *Darkwater: Voices from within the Veil.* 1999 ed. New York: Dover.

Fadil, N., and M. Fernando. 2015. Rediscovering the Everyday Muslim: Notes on an Anthropological Divide. *HAU: Journal of Ethnographic Theory* 5(2):59–88.

Fanon, Frantz. 1959. *A Dying Colonialism.* Translated from the French by Haakon Chevalier, with an introduction by Adolfo Gilly. 1965 ed. New York: Grove Press.

Forster, E. M. 1924. *A Passage to India.* New York: Harcourt, Brace, and Co.

Foster, William. 1921. *Early Travels in India, 1583–1619.* New York: Oxford University Press.

Gates, Bill. 2022. "Optimism and Resolve on Pakistan's Last Mile to End Polio." *GatesNotes,* May 24. Available at www.gatesnotes.com/Health/Last-mile-to-end-polio-in-Pakistan.

George, Sheba. 2000. "'Dirty Nurses' and 'Men Who Play': Gender and Class in Transnational Migration." In *Global Ethnography: Forces, Connections, and Imaginations in a Postmodern World,* edited by M. Burawoy, 144–74. Berkeley: Univ of California Press.

Ghosh, Durba. 2006. *Sex and the Family in Colonial India: The Making of Empire.* Cambridge: Cambridge University Press.

Gill, Anton. 1995. *Ruling Passions: Sex, Race, and Empire*. London: BBC Publications.

Gilmore, Aideen, et al. 2015. *Rough Roads to Equality: Women Police in South Asia*. Commonwealth Human Rights Initiative Report. Available at www.humanrightsinitiative.org/publication/rough-roads-to-equalitywomen-police-in-south-asia-august.

Go, Julian. 2016. *Postcolonial Thought and Social Theory*. New York: Oxford University Press.

Goffman, Erving. 1991. *Stigma*. New York: Simon & Schuster.

Goldstein, Daniel M. 2004. *The Spectacular City: Violence and Performance in Urban Bolivia*. Durham, NC: Duke University Press.

———. 2010. "Toward a Critical Anthropology of Security Comment." *Current Anthropology* 51(4):499–517.

Grünenfelder, Julia. 2013a. "Discourses of Gender Identities and Gender Roles in Pakistan: Women and Non-Domestic Work in Political Representations." *Women's Studies International Forum* 40: 68–77.

———. 2013b. "Negotiating Gender Relations: Muslim Women and Formal Employment in Pakistan's Rural Development Sector." *Gender, Work, and Organization* 20(6):599–615. doi:10.1111/j.1468-0432.2012. 00609.x.

Gupta, Akhil. 1995. "Blurred Boundaries: The Discourse of Corruption, the Culture of Politics, and the Imagined State." *American Ethnologist* 22(2): 375–402.

Handelman, Don. 1997. "Rituals/Spectacles." *International Social Science Journal* 49(153):387–99.

Hassan, Syeda Mahnaz. 2015. "Problems Faced by Women in Police Stations: Need for Police Reforms in Pakistan." *Pakistan Journal of Criminology* 7(1): 85–100.

Heilman, Madeline E., Aaron S. Wallen, Daniella Fuchs, and Melinda M. Tamkins. 2004. "Penalties for Success: Reactions to Women Who Succeed at Male Gender-Typed Tasks." *Journal of Applied Psychology* 89(3):416–27. doi:10.1037/0021-9010.89.3.416.

Hochschild, A. R. 1979. "Emotion Work, Feeling Rules, and Social Structure." *American Journal of Sociology* 85:551–75.

Hudson, C. 2013. *Beyond the Singapore Girl: Discourses of Gender and Nation in Singapore*. Copenhagen: NIAS Press.

Husain, Fauzia. 2020. "Halal Dating, Purdah, and Postfeminism: What the Sexual Projects of Pakistani Women Can Tell Us About Agency." *Signs: Journal of Women in Culture and Society* 45(3):629–52. doi:10.1086/706470.

———. 2022. "Dead Goat on the Runway: Disruptive Fusion, Affective Citizenship, and Gender." *Poetics* 92:101616. doi:10.1016/j.poetic.2021.101616.

Hussain, Sajjad, Basharat Hussain, Waqar Ahmed and Hamid Alam. 2016 "Problems Faced by Women Police in Pakistan." *Pakistan Journal of Criminology* 8(1):74–90.

Hyam, Ronald. 1986. "Empire and Sexual Opportunity." *Journal of Imperial and Commonwealth History* 14(2):34–90. doi:10.1080/03086538608582712.

Jafar, Afshan. 2005. "Women, Islam, and the State in Pakistan." *Gender Issues* 22(1):35–55.

Jamal, Amina. 2006. "Gender, Citizenship, and the Nation-State in Pakistan: Willful Daughters or Free Citizens?" *Signs: Journal of Women in Culture and Society* 31(2):283–304.

———. 2013. *Jamaat-e-Islami Women in Pakistan: Vanguard of a New Modernity?* Syracuse: Syracuse University Press.

Jauregui, Beatrice. 2014. "Provisional Agency in India: Jugaad and Legitimation of Corruption." *American Ethnologist* 41(1): 76–91.

Kandiyoti, Deniz. 1988. "Bargaining with Patriarchy." *Gender and Society* 2(3):274–90. doi:10.1177/089124388002003004.

Kareko, Raymond. 2019. "Female Engagement Teams." *Army University Press*, October 25. Available at www.armyupress.army.mil/Journals/NCO-Journal/Archives/2019/October/Female-Engagement-Teams/#bio.

Kayani, Nadeem, Samina Naeem Khalid, and Shamsa Kanwal. 2016. "A Study to Assess the Workload of Lady Health Workers in Khanpur UC, Pakistan by Applying WHO's WISN Method." *Athens Journal of Health* 3(1): 65–80.

Khan, Niaz Ullah, Asad Aslam Khan, and Haroon R. Awan. 2009. "Women Health Workers: Improving Eye Care in Pakistan." *Community Eye Health Journal* 22(70).

King, Anthony. 1976. *Colonial Urban Development: Culture, Social Power, and Environment*. London, Routledge.

Kolsky, Elizabeth. 2010. "'The Body Evidencing the Crime': Rape on Trial in Colonial India, 1860–1947." *Gender and History* 22(1):109–30. doi:10.1111/j.1468-0424.2009.01581.x.

Korteweg, Anna C. 2008. "The Sharia Debate in Ontario: Gender, Islam, and Representations of Muslim Women's Agency." *Gender and Society* 22(4):434–54.

Lamont, Michèle. 2018. "Addressing Recognition Gaps: Destigmatization and the Reduction of Inequality." *American Sociological Review* 83(3):419–44. doi:10.1177/0003122418773775.

Lee, Nick. 2001. *Childhood and Society: Growing Up in an Age of Uncertainty*. Philadelphia: Open University Press.

Linder, Marc, and Ingrid Nygaard. 1998. *Void Where Prohibited: Rest Breaks and the Right to Urinate on Company Time.* Ithaca: ILR Press.

Mahmood, Saba. 2005. *Politics of Piety: The Islamic Revival and the Feminist Subject.* Princeton: Princeton University Press.

Mainwaring, Cetta, and Stephanie J. Silverman. 2017. "Detention-as-Spectacle." *International Political Sociology* 11(1):21–38. doi:10.1093/ips/olw016.

Maqsood, Ammara. 2017. *The New Pakistani Middle Class.* Cambridge: Harvard University Press.

Mills, Sara. 2003. "Gender and Colonial Space." In *Feminist Postcolonial Theory: A Reader,* edited by Reina Lewis and Sara Mills, 692–719. Edinburgh: Edinburgh University Press.

Mitra, Durba. 2020. *Indian Sex Life: Sexuality and the Colonial Origins of Modern Social Thought.* Princeton: Princeton University Press.

Mumtaz, Khawar and Farida Shaheed. 1987. *Women of Pakistan: Two Steps Forward, One Step Back?* London: Zed Books.

Nair, Janaki. 1990. "Uncovering the Zenana: Visions of Indian Womanhood in Englishwomen's Writings, 1813–1940." *Journal of Women's History* 2(1):8–34.

Niazi, M. Z. 2013. "Police Women in Pakistan: A Long Way to Go." *The Frontier Post.*

Papanek, Hanna. 1973. "Purdah: Separate Worlds and Symbolic Shelter." *Comparative Studies in Society and History* 15(3):289–325.

Patel, Reena. 2010. *Working the Night Shift: Women in India's Call Center Industry.* Stanford: Stanford University Press.

Perez, Chris. 2014. "The Tough Female Police Commandos in Pakistan Who Fight Terrorism." *New York Post,* December 22. Available at https://nypost.com/2014/12/22/the-tough-female-police-commandos-in-pakistan-who-fight-terrorism/.

Phillips, Rachel, Cecilia Benoit, Helga Hallgrimsdottir, and Kate Vallance. 2012. "Courtesy Stigma: A Hidden Health Concern among Front-line Service Providers to Sex Workers." *Sociology of Health and Illness* 34(5):681–96. doi:10.1111/j.1467-9566.2011.01410.x.

ProPakistani. 2018. "How Pia Air Hostess Slipped Away in Canada?" September 28. Available at propakistani.pk/2018/09/28/how-pia-air-hostess-slipped-away-in-canada/.

Pugh, Allison J. 2014. "The Theoretical Costs of Ignoring Childhood: Rethinking Independence, Insecurity, and Inequality." *Theory and Society* 43(1):71–89.

Rai, Shirin, Nafisa Shah and Aazar Ayaz. 2007. "Achieving Gender Equality in Public Offices in Pakistan." Islamabad: United Nations Development Programme.

Raja, Masood Ashraf. 2011. "Neoliberal Dispositif and the Rise of Fundamentalism: The Case of Pakistan." *Journal of International and Global Studies* 3(1):21–31.

Rajan, Rajeswari. S. 1993. *Real and Imagined Women: Gender, Culture, and Postcolonialism*. London: Routledge.

Rajput, Faysal. 2015. "Pia All Set to Re-Style Their Ground and Cabin Crew." *Stars with FR*, March 6. Available at starswithfr.wordpress.com/2015/03/06/pia-all-set-to-re-style-their-ground-and-cabin-crew/.

Reed, Isaac A. 2011. *Interpretation and Social Knowledge: On the Use of Theory in the Human Sciences*. Chicago: University of Chicago Press.

———. 2017. "Chains of Power and Their Representation." *Sociological Theory* 35(2):87–117.

———. 2020. *Power in Modernity: Agency Relations and the Creative Destruction of the King's Two Bodies*. Chicago: University of Chicago Press.

Reeves, Philip. 2014. "Workers Brave Militant Attacks to Vaccinate for Polio." NPR, November 30. Available at www.npr.org/2014/11/30/367544506/workers-brave-militant-attacks-to-vaccinate-for-polio.

Rinaldo, Rachel. 2014. Pious and Critical: Muslim Women Activists and the Question of Agency. *Gender and Society* 28 (6): 824–46.

Rosenthal, Anton. 2000. "Spectacle, Fear, and Protest: A Guide to the History of Urban Public Space in Latin America." *Social Science History* 24(1):33–73. doi:10.1215/01455532-24-1-33.

Rouse, J. Shahnaz. 1994. "Gender Struggles: The State, Religion and Civil Society." In *Against All Odds: Essays on Women, Religion, and Development from India and Pakistan,* edited by Bhasin Kamla, R. Menon, and Nighat Said Khan, 16–34. Charlottesville: University of Virginia Press.

Rudman, L. A. 1998. "Self-Promotion as a Risk Factor for Women: The Costs and Benefits of Counterstereotypical Impression Management." *Journal of Personality and Social Psychology* 74: 629–45.

Rudman, L. A., and P. Glick. 2001. "Prescriptive Gender Stereotypes and Backlash Toward Agentic Women." *Journal of Social Issues* 57:732–76.

Salvatore, Armando, and Mark Levine, eds. 2005. *Religion, Social Practice, and Contested Hegemonies: Reconstructing the Public Sphere in Muslim Majority Societies*. New York: Palgrave Macmillan.

Savci, E. 2021. *Queer in Translation: Sexual Politics under Neoliberal Islam*; Durham: Duke University Press. doi:10.1515/9781478012856.

Sehlikoglu, Sertaç. 2018. "Revisited: Muslim Women's Agency and Feminist Anthropology of the Middle East." *Contemporary Islam* 12(1):73–92. doi:10.1007/s11562-017-0404-8.

Shabna, P., and K. Kalpana. 2022. "Re-Making the Self: Discourses of Ideal Islamic Womanhood in Kerala." *Asian Journal of Women's Studies* 28(1):24–43. doi:10.1080/12259276.2021.2010907.

Shaheed, Farida, and Khawar Mumtaz. 1990. "Islamisation and Women: The Experience of Pakistan." *New Blackfriars* 71(835):67–80.

Shahid, Rudabeh, Kaveri Sarkar, and Azeem Khan. 2021. "Understanding 'Rape Culture' in Bangladesh, India, and Pakistan." *South Asia Source*, January 26. Available at www.atlanticcouncil.org/blogs/southasiasource/understanding-rape-culture-in-bangladesh-india-pakistan/.

Shahin, S., J. Nakahara, and M. Sánchez. 2021. "Black Lives Matter Goes Global: Connective Action Meets Cultural Hybridity in Brazil, India, and Japan." *New Media and Society*. doi:10.1177/14614448211057106

Shams, Tahseen. 2020. *Here, There, and Elsewhere: The Making of Immigrant Identities in a Globalized World*. Stanford: Stanford University Press.

Sharma, Shweta. 2021. "Imran Khan on Rising Sexual Violence, Says 'Women Wearing Few Clothes Impact Men, Unless Robots.'" *The Independent*, June 21. Available at www.independent.co.uk/asia/south-asia/imran-khan-interview-womens-clothes-sexual-violence-b1869777.html.

Sharpe, J. 1993 *Allegories of Empire: The Figure of Woman in the Colonial Text*. Minneapolis: University of Minnesota Press.

Skalicky, Sue, and Monica Davey. 2016. "Tension between Police and Standing Rock Protesters Reaches Boiling Point." *New York Times*, October 28. Available at www.nytimes.com/2016/10/29/us/dakota-access-pipeline-protest.html.

Spivak, Gayatri Chakravorty. 1994. "Can the Subaltern Speak?" In *Colonial Discourse and Postcolonial Theory: A Reader*, edited by Patrick Williams and Laura Chrisman, 66–111. New York: Columbia University Press.

———. 1999. *A Critique of Postcolonial Reason*. Cambridge: Harvard University Press.

Staff Reporter. 2017. "Women Make Up Less than 2pc of Country's Police Force: Report." April 26. Available at www.dawn.com/news/1329292.

Stoler, Ann L. 1989. "Making Empire Respectable: The Politics of Race and Sexual Morality in Twentieth-Century Colonial Cultures." *American Ethnologist* 16 (4):634–60.

Swan, Jonathan. 2021. "Prime Minister Imran Khan's Complete Interview on HBO Max with Jonathan Swan." YouTube, June 21. Available at www.youtube.com/watch?v=p8sU9okIGoU.
Sweet, Paige L. 2019. "The Sociology of Gaslighting." *American Sociological Review* 84(5):851–75. doi:10.1177/0003122419874843.
Thurlow, Crispin and Giorgia Aiello. 2007. "National Pride, Global Capital: A Social Semiotic Analysis of Transnational Visual Branding in the Airline Industry." *Visual Communication* 6(3):305–44. doi:10.1177/1470357207081002.
Toor, Saadia. 2014. "The Political Economy of Moral Regulation in Pakistan." In *Routledge Handbook of Gender in South Asia*, edited by Leela Fernandes, 129–42. Abingdon: Routledge.
Tyler, Imogen. 2018. "Resituating Erving Goffman: From Stigma Power to Black Power." *Sociological Review* 66(4):744–65. doi:10.1177/0038026118777450.
———. 2020. *Stigma: The Machinery of Inequality*. London. Zed Books.
Tyler, Imogen, and Tom Slater. 2018. "Rethinking the Sociology of Stigma." *Sociological Review* 66(4):721–43. doi:10.1177/0038026118777425.
Wade, Robert. 1982. "Corruption: Where Does the Money Go?" *Economic and Political Weekly* 17(40):1606.
Walsh, Denise, et al. 2017 "Increasing the Civic and Political Participation of Women: Understanding the Risk of Strong Resistance." USAID Report.
Weiss, Anita M. 1992. *Walls within Walls: Life Histories of Working Women in the Old City of Lahore*. Oxford: Westview Press.
Wolpert, Stanley. 1984. *Jinnah of Pakistan*. New York: Oxford University Press.
Zahra, Farwa. 2018. "Suhai Aziz Talpur: Celebrated Worldwide but Mocked in Her Own Country?" *The Express Tribune*, 30 Nov. 2018, tribune.com.pk/article/74857/suhai-aziz-talpur-celebrated-worldwide-but-mocked-in-her-own-country.

# Index

Note: Page numbers in *italics* indicate a reference that appears in a figure or table.

*abayas*, 96, 147–48, 247, 260, 264, 268na.1; for masking, 261. *See also* veiling
accused woman/*mulzima*, 99, 108
affordances, 161, 164, 192, 201, 226; relational, 169, 193
Afghanistan, 46, 50, 51, 62, 136; U.S.-led war in, 182, 235, 256
Afghan-Soviet War, 50, 51
ageism, 212, 213, 218, 226
agency, 10, 16, 20–21, 24–25, 81; compliant, 84, 86–87, 90, *90*, 235, 243; costly, 225; enacting, 84, 113, 114, 122; modesty and, 85; pious, 21, 87; relational, 85, 88–90, *89*, *90*, 111, 116, 123, 184; resistant, 87; spectacular, 15, 201, 203, 205, 211–13, 225, 242, 245. *See also* symbolic agency; women's agency
aid money, 4, 6, 51, 56, 263. *See also* bilateral aid, US; USAID

All-Pakistan Lady Health Workers Association (APLHWA), 220
Aman Foundation, 12, 17, 72, 73, 74, 119
America. *See* United States
Americans, 118, 137, 163. *See also* United States
Amies, Hardy, 78
anti-harassment laws, 54, 186, 227, 246
APLHWA (All-Pakistan Lady Health Workers Association), 200
Arain, Bushra, 220
Aurat March (Woman's March), 35, 234. *See also* protests
autonomy/freedom, 82, 161, 169, 173, 176, 182, 184, 191–95, 252; of agents of security, 259; of airline women, 170, 171, 172; from fear, 258; from work, 38–40, 52

backlash, 9, 35, 212, 245
Baloch (ethnic group), 145

280 INDEX

Bangladesh, 267n2.1
bathrooms, 14, 68, 92, 118, 120, 236. *See also* toilets
Beed district, Maharashtra, India, 236
*bharam*, 67, 101, 102, 103, 105, 111. *See also* swagger
Bhutto, Asifa, 147
Bhutto, Benazir, 92, 123, 147, 221
Bhutto, Zulfikar Ali, 50, 51
bilateral aid, US, 50, 51, 228, 267n1.4. *See also* USAID
bin Laden, Osama, 260
binary logics, 21, 40, 48, 53, 84, 182, 226
biopolitics, 50
birth control, 62, 74, 127, 131, 132, 148, 155. *See also* contraceptives; family planning
Bourdieu, Pierre, 170
bravery/courage, 18, 77, 137, 146, 194, 217, 247; of frontline workers, 2; of lady health workers, 140, 148, 223; in polio work, 145, 147; spectacular agency requires, 213
Brazil, 182–83
breastfeeding, 142, 149, 214, 236. *See also* infant care; maternity; motherhood
British India, 7, 36, 39, 42–48, 228, 233, 267n1.3. *See also* colonialism; India
brutal swagger, 100, 103, 105, 113, 114. *See also* swagger
bucking norms, 83, 86, 87, *87*, 90, *90*
bureaucracy, 54, 214, 224, 228; in frontline women's work, *63*; in health work, 138, 148–52, 154–56
burka, 41, 58, 98, 144, 268na.1. *See also* veiling
Butler, Judith, 86, *87*, 88

Canada, 183, 250, 265. *See also* North America
capitalism, 49, 233, 235, 242, 259

Cardin, Pierre, 78
Carter, Jimmy, 51
caste, 45, 47, 104, 210
*chador*, 52, 57, 58, 59, 101, 236; in Islamization, 52, 53, 55; in negotiating stigma, 21. *See also* veiling
*chador aur char divaar*/veil and four walls, 52, 53, 55, 57, 234
chains of power, 89, 90, 111, 115
chaperones, 40, 160, 170; policewomen act as, 17, 22, 34, 91, 99; as sign of purdah, 14
Charmaz, Kathy, 254
child mortality, 11, 117, 133, 241
China, 18, 191
Chowdhury, Iftikhar, 224
civil lines, 42, 43
civil servants, 27, 91, 228, 267n3.1. *See also* service work
class mobility, 159, 160, 163, 198, 241
clerics, 35, 39, 40, 48; *ulama*, 50
Closser, Svea, 74, 75
clothes, 98, 264; of airline women, 192; civilian, 216, 261; colorful, 222; expensive-looking, 151; flashy, 100; frilly, 28; middle-class, 72; Pakistani, 176; skimpy, 35, 36. *See also* fashion
Collins, Patricia Hill, 5, 30
colonial binaries, 48
colonial India. *See* British India
colonial rule, 42, 44, 45, 59, 60, 182, 233
colonialism, 23, 233, 235; biases of, 19, 20; coded public space as sexually threatening, 59; policies and practices of, 31; produced racialized stereotypes, 60; sexual threat and, 45–48; sexuality, stigma, and, 36, 42–45; stigma and, 122, 230; in stigma matrix, *7, 13*
commodification, 80, 233, 235

community health, 23, 60, 72, 117, 123, 126
compassion, 124, 141, 143–44, 148–49, 156, 264
competence, 3, 237; of airline women, 182, 184, 187; interactive, 170, 178, 179; of policewomen, 71, 83, 215; purdah norms limit, 115; symbols that indicate, 243; veiled delicacy and, 114
complainants, 66, 105, 106, 109, 112, 207; policewomen chaperone, 17; women as, 258. *See also mudda'ii*
compliant agency, 84, 86–87, 90, *90*
condoms, 12, 131, 132, 155, 220. *See also* family planning
Connell, Raewyn, 19
constraint, 58, 123, 163, 164, 173
consumerism, 21, 161
consumption, 49, 78, 80, 160, 192, 193. *See also* cosmopolitan consumption
contamination, 2, 43, 93, 94. *See also* pollution/polluting
contextualization, 85, 250
contraceptives, 2, 17, 117, 131, 132, 241, 257. *See also* birth control; family planning
conversations, 99, 198, 212, 247, 249; of airline women, 175; of policewomen, 101, 102. *See also* field conversations
corruption circuit, 111, 112, 114, 115
cosmopolitan consumption, 81, 161, 162
cosmopolitanism, 14, 192–94, 231; of airline women, 161, 175; postfeminist, 81, 168–69, 170, 182–83, 184, 202
COVID-19, 1, 4, 35, 48, 182–83, 234
criminalization, 54, 235
Cultural Support Teams (CSTs), 256

dancing, 35, 48, 103, 104
danger, 259, 262; to airline women, 191, 260; to frontline women, 2; to lady health workers, 77, 122, 136, 145, 147; of native areas, 43; sexual, 32, 62, 63, 94; of white men to Indian women, 44
data analysis, 22, 254, 255
data collection, 21, 22, 249, 250, 251, 262. *See also* fieldwork
decency, 53, 94, 100, 129, 163, 164, 208; displays of, 84; gendered, 14, 81, 101; norms of, 99; signaling, 114. *See also* indecency; modesty; propriety; respectability; virtue
dehumanization, 233. *See also* devaluation
delicacy, 14, 39, 71, 101, 103, 115, 237. *See also* veiled delicacy
deregulation, 49, 51, 56, 128
destigmatization performance, 16, 123, 184, 194, 202, 203, 241
destigmatization strategies, 82, 96–103, 116, 195
devaluation, 74, 77, 138, 193, 233, 234
*dharna*/sit-ins, 221, 222, 223. *See also* protests
diseases, 121, 141, 258; sexually transmitted, 94–95. *See also* COVID-19; measles; polio eradication; tuberculosis
dislocations, 250, 266
distancing, 98, 148, 264; of airline women, 169, 179, 193; for COVID-19 prevention, 4; gendered, 3, 22, 83, 96, 100, 103; logics, 96
distinction, 198, 210, 240; of airline women, 169, 170, 173, 192, 193, 194; whites from natives, 43
door-to-door work, 2, 22, 121, 125, 131, 136, 259; in distant communities, 126; lack of bathrooms in, 236; sexual overtures in, 172
Du Bois, W. E. B., 242
*dupatta*, 55, 103, 135, 209, 228, 229, 239. *See also* veiling

economic functions, 232–36, 243
education, 130, 132, 224; of airline women, 159, 174, 177; class dependence on, 14; from experience, 173; of lady health workers, 124, 149, 152; of policewomen, 23, 70, 97, 103, 197; public programs for, 227; safety of, 265; Western, 30, 157; of working-class women, 22
Egypt, 86, 173
English (language), 16, 35, 73, 76, 77, 107, 154, 155; airline women training in, 186, 189
ethics, 252, 265
ethnography, 21, 250, 255. See also fieldwork
Europe, 19, 41, 176, 177. See also United Kingdom; Westerners
exclusion, 80; contesting, 201; cultural forms of, 8; examining, 243; gendered, 4, 9; managing, 15; mechanisms of, 9, 25, 245; from power, 84; from public sphere, 200; structure of, 93

faith, 146, 148. See also prayer
family planning, 17, 131, 221. See also birth control; condoms; contraceptives
Fanon, Frantz, 242
fashion, 134, 161, 175, 192. See also clothes; grooming; makeup; purses; shoes
Female Engagement Teams (FETs), 256
femininity, 116, 155, 156, 193; of airline women, 12; of cosmopolitan consumption, 162; cosmopolitan style of, 241; fashion and style, 192; of frontline women's work, 63; middle-class kind of, 97, 98; postfeminism involves, 161; private space connected with, 53

feminism, 10, 11; perspectives, 85; postfeminism, 21, 161, 192, 231, 237; postfeminist cosmopolitanism, 81, 168–70, 182–84, 192–94, 202, 237; scholars of, 11, 86, 87, 88
FETs (Female Engagement Teams), 256
field conversations, 19, 251, 253, 254, 255; with airline women, 187, 190, 191; with lady health workers, 134, 137; with policewomen, 66, 97, 101; reporting, 23. See also conversations
field notes, 105, 107, 250–51, 254. See also data collection
field sites, 32, 36, 181, 257, 263; code of purdah at, 260; conversations at, 251; desire for visibility in, 197; dressing for work in, 170; *majboori* of, 173; managing stigma in, 195; mediate globalization distinctly, 82; organizing structures of, 63; participant recruitment at, 254; policing, 252; safety of, 171; securitized, 262; traveling between, 264
fieldwork, 262–66; with airline women, 79, 159, 170; with airline workers, 191; in Karachi police force, 91; with lady health workers, 150, 151; male interactions during, 94; others' views of, 157; questions on women's agency, 10; regularization begins during, 224; with supervisors and managers, 257; terrorist attack during, 260. See also data collection
flag carrier airlines, 78, 80
Forster, E. M., 43
freedom/autonomy. See autonomy/freedom
frontline women's work, 49, 63, 255
fundamentalism, religious, 230, 244

gaslighting, 7, 244
Gates, Bill, 12, 17, 71, 72, 74
gender mainstreaming, 3, 67, 245; policies, 6, 56, 227, 232, 246
gender progressiveness, 18, 66, 67, 81, 256
gendered authority threats, 200–203, 227, 244, 245, 246
gendered dynamics, 128, 161, 188, 191, 198
gendered logics, 29, 53, 55, 96
gendered privacy, 19, 215, 231
gendered signs, 14, 96, 193, 237, 240
gendered stigmas, 15, 52, 59, 84
glass ceiling, 90, 112, 115
global actors, 78, 130, 135, 137, 145; cynicism about, 5; frontline women interact with, 12, 74, 81
global agencies, 5, 12, 16, 67, 74–76, 126; agendas of, 81; pursue security, 258; require gender mainstreaming, 232
global agendas, 17, 18, 60, 240, 257
global forces, 9, 24, 256, 257; effects on frontline women, 231; effects on Pakistani women, 6; purdah and, 240; stigma and, 48, 59, 122, 242; in stigma matrix, 7, 13
global imperatives, 9, 17, 19, 123
Global North, 16, 19–21, 31, 74, 182, 230–35
global policies, 5, 18
Global Polio Eradication Initiative (GPEI), 74, 76, 82, 121
global processes, 63; affect working-class women, 59; configurations of, 13; configure work contexts, 12, 258; degrade health work, 127; frontline women serve as conduits for, 17; gender relations and, 49; of inequality reproduction, 232; Pakistan's experience with, 20, 31; pose risk to modesty, 54; precipitate cultural changes, 255;

pressure women, 6; stigma and, 16, 30, 60, 122, 230, 242
Global South, 13, 16, 19, 31, 82, 226, 230
Go, Julian, 19, 20
Goffman, Erving, 28, 30
government of Pakistan. *See* Pakistani government
grooming, 166, 170, 171, 175, 254. *See also* fashion
Gulf region, 97, 268na.1

Haider, Khwaja Razi, 229
*halal*, [legitimate] 146
harem/zenana, 39, 40, 46, 262
headscarves, 176, 228, 257, 264. *See also* veiling
High Court, 22, 26, 252, 262
Hindus, 39, 47
historical forces, 7, 13
holy war. *See* jihad/holy war
holy warriors, 71, 77, 81, 82, 122, 146, 155
Hudood Ordinance, 53, 54. *See also* Islamization
humiliation, 52, 200–201, 205; of airline women, 158, 172; class and, 30; of frontline workers, 9; of lady health workers, 74, 129, 132–34, 137, 150; of policewomen, 207, 215; from sexual assault, 267n2.1; stigma and, 28
Hyam, Ronald, 45–46, 47, 233
hysterectomies, 236

identity card/NADRA card, 151–54
idioms, 138; of jihad, 14, 82, 146, 147, 237; of martial motherhood, 122, 148; of purdah, 15, 237–38
immorality, 3, 133, 163
imperial-era logics, 53
imperialism, 21, 45, 231
indecency, 35, 103, 132, 135, 163, 194. *See also* decency

India, 50, 229, 236; #MeToo in, 245; movies, 33; police violence in, 215; sexual assault in, 267n2.1. *See also* British India
Indian Civil Service, 91, 228
Indian Uprising/the Mutiny, 43
infant care, 118, 119, 140, 149, 155, 236. *See also* breastfeeding
interconnection, 20, 21, 49, 78, 230
International Monetary Fund (IMF), 31, 49, 51, 56, 127
interviewing, 22, 250–51, 253, 263. *See also* field conversations
intimidation, 2, 4, 11, 154
Iran, 51, 62, 245
Iranian Revolution, 51
Islamabad, Pakistan, 67, 191, 223, 225
Islamization, 52–54, 57; consequential for gender relations, 49–50; effect on stigma matrix, 60; middle-class women's visibility in, 56; purdah and, 6; reinforces stigma against women, 234; sexual stigmas shaped by, 230; stigma legitimizes, 235; in stigma matrix, 7, 13, 23; stigmatizes women's occupations, 59
Islam/west binaries, 21, 226

Jamaat-i-Islami (political party), 56
Jamal, Amina, 52
Jameel, Maulana Tariq, 35
jihad/holy war, 144, 155, 156, 194, 265; idioms of, 14, 82, 146, 147, 237; Islamization circulates, 52; in martial motherhood, 137, 145, 147; purdah and, 260; as signifier of Muslim identity, 50; as symbol of honor, 168. *See also* martyrdom
Jinnah, Mohammad Ali, 229
Jinnah, Ruttie, 229
Jinnah Terminal, 254

journalists, 22, 135, 229, 251, 252, 255; on airline women, 79; on policewomen, 66, 95; recruitment of, 21, 232; in staged spectacle, 212, 218
*jugaar*, 185

Kandiyoti, Deniz, 88
Karachi Electric Supply Corporation, 128
Khan, Imran, 35, 36, 48
Khan, Sharafat, 3, 5, 9, 16, 241, 247; attack on, 1, 2, 4, 199
*khidmat-e-khalq*, 63, 76
Khyber Pakhtunkhwa province, 255
kinship language, 21, 45, 113, 149, 156, 160, 169, 194
Kipling, Rudyard, 39
Kolsky, Elizabeth, 45
Kryolan TV Paint Stick, 176. *See also* makeup

lady health supervisors (LHS), 117, 120, 124, 130, 224, 268n4.1
Lahore, Pakistan, 222
Lamont, Michelle, 9
Larkana, Pakistan, 220, 221
legitimacy, 49, 50, 146, 147, 150, 195, 235
lipstick, 168, 170, 176, 192, 193, 222. *See also* makeup
logics, 53; gendered, 29, 53, 55; of gendered distancing, 3, 96; global, 60; imperial-era, 53; of maternity, 139; of purdah, 98, 99; of rule, 50
low-ranking police officers, 51, 111, 115, 267n1.1. *See also* rankers

MAC (brand), 160, 174, 175, 192. *See also* makeup
Maharashtra, India, 236
Mahmood, Saba, 20, 86, 87, 88
*majboori*, 129, 163, 173. *See also* constraint

makeup, 170, 211; in aesthetics of good conduct, 70; airline women use, 78, 81, 160, 161, 164, 174, 176; as gendered symbol, 192, 193, 194; policewomen use, 28, 69, 101, 196; required, 58; tool for navigating stigma, 11. *See also* fashion
male gaze, 37, 38, 41
marginality, 9, 84, 115, 183, 237, 240; class amplifies, 123; destigmatization and, 243; of frontline women, 232; of lady health workers, 24, 138; local trends and, 20; navigating stigma and, 10; of policewomen, 8, 83, 84, 91, 113, 115; power of spectacle and, 200; purdah reinforces, 14, 24, 156, 237, 240; stigma relies on, 15; stigmas preserve, 7
marriage, 8, 37, 38, 47, 180, 198; certificate, 54, 94, 153
martial motherhood, 123, 149, 168; in destigmatization performance, 202; as moral performance, 24, 122; provides courage, 148; quasi-mystical healing abilities and, 138, 140; used in recruitment, 156; used to manage stigma, 155
martyrdom, 52, 77, 82, 145, 146, 155. *See also* jihad/holy war
Maskatiya, Sania, 79
maternal mortality, 11, 117, 123, 133, 241
maternity, 63, 122, 125, 139, 156, 237; instincts of, 140; logic of, 139. *See also* motherhood
measles, 126, 150, 220. *See also* diseases
Medora (brand), 174–75, 192. *See also* makeup
Mengal (cleric), 35
menstruation, 14, 205, 219, 236, 237
#MeToo, 9, 245
Middle East, 41, 96, 182

Mills, Sara, 44
misogyny, 45, 164
Mitra, Durba, 47–48, 233
mobility, 6, 41; of airline women, 78, 82, 171, 195; of the chador, 53; class, 159, 160, 163, 198, 241; economic, 22; global, 80, 192; of middle-class women, 56; political, 234; upward, 84, 115; women's, 36
mobilization, 48; of culture, 115; of familial achievements, 199; of gender stereotypes, 80; of gendered logics, 53; of purdah fidelity, 14; of resources, 116; of signs, 87, 195, 213, 237, 240; signs of, 10; by spectacular agency, 203; U.S. in Afghanistan, 256
modality of security, 238, 239
modernity, 20, 80, 161, 169, 182, 192; tradition vs., 53, 78, 79, 81, 82
modernization, 20
modesty, 260; agency and, 85; of airline women, 178; corruption chains and, 115; as gendered symbol, 155; global processes pose risk to, 5; of policewomen, 98, 100, 218; policewomen aid, 17; purdah and, 14, 237; respect requires, 71; stigmatization for, 229; veiling underlines, 70. *See also* decency
moral economy, 75, 77, 82
mortality, maternal/child, 11, 117, 123, 133, 241
mortifications. *See* humiliation
motherhood, 14, 137, 139, 147, 160, 231, 237. *See also* martial motherhood; maternity
*mudda'ii*, 105–7, 109. *See also* complainants
*mulzima*/accused woman, 99, 100, 108, 159

Mumtaz, Khawar, 55, 98
Mutiny, the/Indian Uprising, 43

NADRA card/identity card, 151–54
Naqi, Nadia, 252, 253
*nasl*, 104
National Program, 119, 125, 126, 133, 134, 144, 219; beginnings of, 123
National Refinery, 128
native/white binaries, 41
neoliberal policies, 51, 56, 57, 59, 128, 235
neoliberal reform, 49
neoliberalism, 6, 258; public space and, 29, 59; sexuality, stigma, and, 48–51, 230; stigma and, 16, 235, 242, 244; in stigma matrix, 7, 13, 23, 60; transformation of women's work and, 127–30
networks, 89, 89, 115, 167, 191, 194, 246
niqabs, 228, 255. *See also* headscarves
no-go areas, 136, 147, 148
norms of purdah. *See* purdah norms
North America, 19, 41, 265, 266. *See also* Canada; United States; Westerners

Ochterlony, David, 46
officer class, 12, 91
oppression, 39, 40, 182, 213, 216, 232; challenging, 183; significance of, 46; systems of, 30; by Taliban, 235
Order of the British Empire, 228, 268nc.1
organizational arrangements, 5, 122; in stigma matrix, 13
orientalism, 19, 21, 40, 42, 46, 182–83, 230

Pakistan Telecom, 128
Pakistani government, 80, 256; employs frontline women workers, 3, 9, 117; enacts purdah, 238; neoliberalism and, 6; passes anti-harassment legislation, 245–46; polio work and, 4, 144–45; receives World Bank and IMF loans, 127; religious nationality and, 7; Supreme Court, 150, 221, 224, 232; Women's Protection Bill, 186; Zina Ordinance, 54
Pakistanis, 79, 82, 175, 176, 182, 192, 268na.1
participant recruitment, 254, 264. *See also* fieldwork
*Passage to India, A*, 43
Pathan (ethnic group), 145
patriarchal bargain, 88, 162
patriarchy, 88, 129, 162, 230
Peers Victoria Resources Society, 183
penal codes, 47, 54
perception skills, 180
permeability, 147, 148, 239, 240, 247
personhood, 161, 176, 198
Peshawar, Pakistan, 251, 252, 260
piousness, 6, 21, 50, 87, 148
police stations, 54, 93, 94, 112, 170, 244; co-ed, 11; fieldwork in, 250, 251, 252; as place of moral corruption, 71; stigma associated with, 95; women's, 22, 32, 83, 84, 85, 91, 97, 100, 113. *See also* station houses; *thana*
policing context, 85, 90–91, 93, 102, 113, 115, 161
polio eradication, 6; Benazir Bhutto and, 147; briefly halted, 145; heroism of, 18; moral economy of, 75, 77; participation in, 126; payment for, 74; women carry out, 60
polio vaccine/vaccination, 12, 22, 58, 121, 136, 172, 236, 254; conspiracy about, 2, 4, 62; marking and, 259
polio virus, 121, 145
polio work, 140; lady health workers forced to do, 125–27; motivation for, 8; need for security, 12; police accompany, 11; riskiness of, 261; as

sacred struggle, 147; stigmatized, 2, 131–34; terrorists target, 144; unwillingness to do, 129, 212, 220; used for intelligence gathering, 260. *See also* door-to-door work
political functions, 232–36, 243
political interference, 79, 164, 165, 166, 168
political parties, 165, 185, 187, 194; religiously oriented, 7, 50, 56, 234
pollution/polluting, 75, 160; of airline women's identities, 162; of lady health workers' ideas, 132; of lady health workers' identities, 122; police work seen as, 93, 253; seclusion purdah protects from, 38; signs and gestures seen as, 113; stigma by association and, 183; travel seen as, 192. *See also* contamination
postfeminism, 21, 161, 192, 231, 237
postfeminist cosmopolitanism, 81, 168–69, 170, 182–83, 184, 192–94, 202, 237
poverty, 164, 208; of complainants, 106; forces women to work, 213; of lady health workers, 62, 75, 122, 129, 140; resource, 29, 60, 92; of rural women, 57
prayer, 77, 100, 101, 107, 144, 146, 213
pregnancy, 126, 192
privatization, 6, 49, 51, 56, 57, 128, 233
ProPakistani (digital news outlet), 79
propriety, 6, 32, 33, 34, 45, 52. *See also* decency
prostitutes, 46–47, 59, 95, 159, 183. *See also* sex workers
protests, 18, 259; Aurat March (Woman's March), 34, 234; Indian Uprising, 43; of lady health workers, 150, 174, 202, 219–26; spectacular agency used in, 201, 203, 242; against Zia-ul-Haq's reforms, 55–56

publicity, 1, 2, 197, 242, 251; cost of, 225; of policewomen, 18; as spectacular agency, 15, 200, 245; used for recruitment, 195, 202
public/private binaries, 53
purdah norms, 3, 238, 257; compliance with, 6, 96; compliance with vs. violating, 14, 100, 237; enacting agency and, 113; gendered surveillance and, 42; inhibit capacity for competence, 83; limit women's competence, 115; reinforcing, 7; rooted in colonial encounter, 5; security agents transgress, 259; state investment in, 231; stigma connected with, 242; transcendental call to service vs., 138
purdah violations, 15, 105, 148, 257; blamed for crises, 234; enacting agency by, 113; reasons for, 103; stigmas associated with, 7, 24, 84
purses, 11, 81, 118, 140, 192, 205. *See also* fashion

quasi-mystical healing, 122, 138, 140, 141
Queen Elizabeth II, 78
Quetta, Pakistan, 260

race, 31, 36, 75
racism, 45
Raja, Masood Ashraf, 52
rankers, 12, 27, 91
rape. *See* sexual assault
Reed, Isaac, 89, *89*
refashioning norms, *90*
reforms, 49–50, 51, 55–56, 128
relational agency, 88–90, *89*, *90*; opportunity and, 116; of policewomen, 85, 111; postfeminist cosmopolitanism and, 184; symbolic

relational agency (*continued*)
  agency connection, 123. *See also* symbolic agency
relational agendas, 123, 138, 263
relational capacities, 10, 105, 169, 245, 246
relational dynamics, 191, 251
religion, 36, 39, 41, 50, 110
research focus, 9, 13, 250, 253, 263
research locations. *See* field sites
research observation, 22, 250, 251–52, 253, 254, 255, 263; of police training centers, 14; of stigma navigation, 10. *See also* fieldwork
research visits, 251, 252, 255
resistance/compliance binaries, 84
resistant agency, 87
respectability, 22, 37, 98, 131–32, 237; classed, 194; gendered, 114; of working-class women, 160. *See also* decency
rituals, 52, 80, 89, 200, 204, 205; of mourning, 201, 223, 224

sacrifice, 4, 260; citizenship and, 256; of lady health workers, 74, 76, 77, 81, 82, 148; language of, 149; maternal, 139; in protesting, 219; in public roles, 199
seclusion purdah, 36, 38, 262
secondary data, 23
securitization, 6, 258, 262; benefits from stigma, 242; contributes to stigma, 122, 230, 244; Islamization tied to, 50; purdah modalities further, 240; stigma and, 59; in stigma matrix, 7, 13, 23, 60
security operations, 4, 17, 238, 257
Sellon, Edward, 46
service work, 22, 27, 91, 228, 267n3.1; discretion in, 214; purdah in, 238; repudiation from, 225; stigma from, 232, 236

sex workers, 46–47, 59, 91, 95, 183. *See also* prostitutes
sexism, 212, 213, 218
sexual assault, 35, 54, 62, 94; in British India, 43, 44, 45, 48; stigmatization of, 267n2.1
sexual danger, 32, 62, 63, 94
sexual deviance, 35, 48, 59
sexual harassment, 31, 34, 58, 94, 96, 121, 260, 265. *See also* anti-harassment laws
sexual imperative, 46
sexual propriety. *See* propriety
sexual stigmas, 183, 230, 234, 235; purdah, colonialism, and, 45, 48, 60, 233
sexualization, 114, 131, 229; of airline women, 212; of airline work, 162; of public servants, 261; of women's bodies, 54
sexualization of space, 43, 44, 45, 52, 53, 92, 94; stigma and, 31–36
Shah of Iran, 51
*shaheed*, 145. *See also* martyrdom
Shaheed, Farida, 55
Shahrah-i-Faisal (thoroughfare), 157
shalwar kameez, 54. *See also* clothes
shame, 130, 131, 132, 218, 222; of airline women, 168; of the dole, 30; for human rights violations, 215; of lack of veil, 98; of police lockup, 33; spectacular agency and, 205, 225
Sharpe, Jenny, 43–44
shoes, 160, 176, 188, 192. *See also* fashion
shut-up call, 204, 205, 216, 218, 226
*sifaarshi*, 166
Simla, 43, 267n1.3
Sindh province, 91, 176, 209, 220, 228, 252
Singapore, 80
*sipahi*, 27, 267n1.1. *See also* low-ranking police officers

sit-ins, 221, 222, 223. *See also* protests
Skinner, James, 46
social media, 251; commentaries on frontline women, 23; Mengal sermon on, 35; spectacular agency and, 200, 202, 211–13, 218, 245; Twitter, 211–12; used for recruitment, 21, 226, 231–32; WhatsApp, 253, 254; YouTube, 197, 247
social norms, 5, 88, 199
Soviet-Afghan War, 50
Soviets, 50, 51
Star Gate Airport, 254
state jobs, 22, 57, 201, 226, 268n6.2
station houses, 11, 95, 99, 101, 105; co-ed, 1; fieldwork at, 107, 109, 264; gendered, 94; male, 91, 92; male-dominated, 29; as place of sexualized corruption, 33; sexualization of, 34; stigma attached with, 100; wearing headscarves in, 98. *See also* police stations; *thana*
stigma matrix framework, 5, 7, 31, 122, 230, 232, 243; macro layer stigmas in, 244
stipend/*wazifa*, 12, 74, 76, 125, 127, 146
subordinate status, 201, 226, 242
Supreme Court of Pakistan, 150, 221, 224, 232. *See also* Pakistani government
swagger, 67, 111, 112, 189, 237. *See also bharam*; brutal swagger
Sweet, Paige, 244
symbolic agency, 87–88, *87*, 90, 170; of airline women, 160, 161, 162, 168; amplifies marginal status, 123; classed obstacles and, 156; as destigmatizing strategy, 96; enacted with brutal swagger, 103; global dimension of, 10; postfeminist cosmopolitanism and, 169; purdah transgressive, 100; in toolkit for grasping women's agency, *90*; veiled delicacy as, 113. *See also* relational agency
symbolic capacity, 10
Symington Amendment, 51

Taliban, 18, 146, 235, 256
Talpur, Sohai Ali, 3, 5, 16, 66, 199, 200, 241; thwarts terrorist attack, 1–2, 18
teaching, 55, 56, 57, 97, 130, 163
terrorism, 251, 262, 265; lady health workers killed by, 62; lady health workers threatened by, 74, 122, 144, 145; policewomen combat, 12, 60, 236, 257; policewomen threatened by, 260; Sohai Ali Talpur thwarts, 1–2, 18; War on Terror, 19, 182, 255
*thana*, 26, 29, 64, 110, 196; Hirabad, 67; stigmatized, 33, 93; USAID aids, 66. *See also* police stations; station houses
toilets, 14, 35, 102. *See also* bathrooms
tradition, 36, 40, 47, 129, 209; gendered patterns of, 193; Islamic, 54; modernity vs., 78, 79, 81, 82; notion of security, 258; values, 53; weddings, 90
tuberculosis, 117, 155, 221. *See also* diseases
Turkey, 245
Twitter, 211–12. *See also* social media
Tyler, Imogen, 5, 29, 30, 232

*ulama*, 50; clerics, 35, 39, 40, 48. *See also* political parties
unions, 57, 63, 128; of airline women, 158, 165, 167, 184–87, 254; of lady health workers, 150, 220, 221, 223, 225
United Kingdom, 20, 29, 30, 205, 206, 218, 230. *See also* Westerners

United Nations, 73, 76, 77, 119, 136
United States, 27, 67, 236, 252, 262, 263; #MeToo in, 245; action in Afghanistan, 235, 256; aid, 50, 51, 228, 267n1.4; airline worker travel to, 172; culture, 64, 104; Department of the Treasury, 49; dollars, 12, 160; education, 157; media coverage of Pakistan, 249, 250; media outlet, 18; Pakistan connected with, 20, 31, 230; Pakistani views of, 2; polio in, 75; stereotypes about Pakistan, 265; stigma in, 231, 244; Symington Amendment, 51; Washington Consensus, 49, 127. *See also* Americans; North America; USAID; Westerners
Urdu, 8, 11, 35, 72, 77, 146, 228; airline women training in, 189; interviewing in, 22, 250
USAID, 12, 65, 66, 145

veil and four walls/*chador aur char divaar*, 52, 53, 55, 57, 234
veiled delicacy, 194, 202; brutal swagger vs., 103, 114; draws on gendered signs of class, 96; most frontline women use, 98; policewomen use, 24, 100, 113, 168, 241; requires styling of temporalities, 99
veiling, 3, 14, 36, 70, 71, 83, 84, 194; *abayas*, 96, 147–48, 247, 260, 261, 264, 268na.1; burka, 41, 58, 98, 144, 268na.1; *chador*, 21, 52–53, 55, 57–59, 101, 236; *dupatta*, 55, 103, 135, 209, 228, 229, 239; headscarves, 176, 228, 257, 264; niqabs, 228, 255
Victorian Englishmen, 46, 233. *See also* colonialism
VIPs, 165, 166, 168, 193, 217, 251
virtue, 52, 77, 132, 145. *See also* decency

Wafaqul Madaris, 35
Wahl, Rachel, 215
Washington Consensus, 49, 127
*wazifa*/stipend, 12, 74, 76, 125, 127, 146
weddings, 89, 90, 153, 158
Westerners, 229; aid agencies, 67; bluntness of, 180, 182; culture of, 183; hypocrisy of, 110; Islam/West dualism, 21, 87; mannerisms, 263; men, 48; polio conspiracy, 2, 4, 62; require polio drives, 75, 76; stereotyping, 265; stigma, 235; views of Muslim sexual practices, 228; women, 21, 83. *See also* Canada; Europe; United Kingdom; United States
Westernization, 53, 59, 262
WhatsApp, 253, 254. *See also* social media
whitening cream, 14, 69, 97, 237
widows, 39, 47, 130, 163
Woman's March (Aurat March), 34, 35, 234. *See also* protests
women's agency, 9–10, 20–21, 84–86, 90–91, *90*, 226, 231; of airline women, 160–62; in navigating stigma matrix, 25
Women's Protection Bill, 186
World Bank, 49, 51, 56, 127
World Health Organization (WHO), 12, 135, 136, 137, 145, 146

YouTube, 197, 247. *See also* social media

zenana/harem, 39, 40, 46, 262
Zia-ul-Haq, Muhammad, 50–53, 55–57, 59, 234
Zina Ordinance, 54

**GLOBALIZATION IN EVERYDAY LIFE**

---

*Aid and the Help: International Development and the Transnational Extraction of Care*
    Dinah Hannaford  2023

*Forbidden Intimacies: Polygamies at the Limits of Western Tolerance*
    Melanie Heath  2023

*Unruly Speech: Displacement and the Politics of Transgression*
    Saskia Witteborn  2023

*Seeking Western Men: Email-Order Brides under China's Global Rise*
    Monica Liu  2022

*Children of the Revolution: Violence, Inequality, and Hope in Nicaraguan Migration*
    Laura Enríquez  2022

*At Risk: Indian Sexual Politics and the Global AIDS Crisis*
    Gowri Vijayakumar  2021

*Here, There, and Elsewhere: The Making of Immigrant Identities in a Globalized World*
    Tahseen Shams  2020

*Beauty Diplomacy: Embodying an Emerging Nation*
    Oluwakemi M. Balogun  2020

Printed in the USA
CPSIA information can be obtained
at www.ICGtesting.com
JSHW022032211123
52297JS00001B/1